MURDER IN THE FAMILY

MURDER IN THE FAMILY

HOW THE SEARCH FOR MY
MOTHER'S KILLER LED TO MY FATHER

JEFF BLACKSTOCK

ROY MACSKIMMING
Editorial Collaborator

VIKING

VIKING

an imprint of Penguin Canada, a division of Penguin Random House Canada Limited

Canada • USA • UK • Ireland • Australia • New Zealand • India • South Africa • China

First published 2020

www.penguinrandomhouse.ca

LIBRARY AND ARCHIVES CANADA CATALOGUING IN PUBLICATION

Title: Murder in the family / Jeff Blackstock.
Names: Blackstock, Jeff, author.
Identifiers: Canadiana (print) 20200179004 | Canadiana (ebook) 20200179039 |
    ISBN 9780735236615
(softcover) | ISBN 9780735236622 (HTML)
Subjects: LCSH: Blackstock, Jeff—Family. | LCSH: Murder—Case studies. |
    LCGFT: Case studies.
Classification: LCC HV6515 .B63 2020 | DDC 364.152/3—dc23

Cover and book design by Kate Sinclair
Cover photos: courtesy of the author; (frames) alubalish / Getty Images
Interior photos: courtesy of the author

Printed and bound in Canada

10 9 8 7 6 5 4 3 2 1

Penguin
Random House
VIKING CANADA

Bad men need nothing more to compass their ends,
than that good men should look on and do nothing.

JOHN STUART MILL, 1867

To Carol Janice Gray Blackstock

CONTENTS

PROLOGUE

I THINK THAT my father murdered my mother. My sister, Julia Blackstock, and I came to that conclusion after uncovering a disturbing trail of evidence and pursuing it to the end.

Our father, the late George Blackstock, was a career diplomat in Canada's foreign service. He was never convicted of Carol Blackstock's murder. He was never even charged. Through calculated deception on his part, an apparent cover-up by the Canadian government, dereliction of duty by medical and police authorities on two continents, and sheer luck, our father literally got away with murder.

I cannot take credit for uncovering what happened to our mother. It was our maternal grandfather, Howard Gray, who first set out to find the truth and ultimately discovered the cause of his daughter's death. He offered to share his discoveries with me, but I was a teenager at the time, with conflicting loyalties between the two most important men in my life, my father and my grandfather. I was unwilling to hear the truth.

After our grandfather died, it was Julia who found his papers. They left no doubt about the shocking way our mother had died and immediately cast suspicion on our father. And yet, when he protested his innocence, I still wanted to believe him. I felt deeply reluctant to accept that Dad could have committed such a horrible crime.

But I continued to think about it. I was nagged by inconsistencies in our father's account, and by common sense. New evidence Julia and I discovered led in only one direction. Even so, it took time, and repeated testing of our father's self-proclaimed innocence, before I could move from doubt to reluctant suspicion to hard, bitter certainty. It also took the example of my sister's perseverance and courage. In the end, I realized that Julie was right: it was impossible to live in denial, and the only way forward was to know the truth.

This is a true story, and unlike a mystery novel, real life is messy. There will be no neat resolution tying up the loose ends, no smoking gun, no confession, and no ghost pointing an accusing finger. Instead, our mother's case turned on deception, deceit, and out-and-out lies, which left a messy picture indeed, like pieces of a puzzle scattered on a table. Two things were clear, however: the horror of our mother's murder, and our father's lying about it. Once we confronted those realities, there was no turning back. Our loyalty to our mother, our sense of justice, and our outrage with our father demanded it.

Telling our mother's story is a challenge. It's one thing to have lived through the emotional turmoil surrounding her death, quite another to reassemble fragments, deliberately sundered and clouded, to expose what really happened and put it down on paper, so that others can see it too. This has been a voyage of discovery—a lifelong journey ranging far beyond our mother's short lifespan—revealing how much she suffered, the pain and anguish of our grandparents, the treachery of our father and those who enabled him, the unravelling of their subterfuge, and, finally, the lasting effect on my sister, my brother, Douglas, and me. While this is Carol Blackstock's story, it's ours too.

I was eight years old when our mother died, the oldest of her three children. Though I remember her clearly, telling her story means portraying her and our father as they were before I was born and when I was too young to retain more than blurry fragments of memory. Fortunately, I've been able to turn to relatives and family friends for knowledge of our parents' childhoods, brief courtship, and early married life. Many letters that they wrote to each other and their families have survived. Letters and photographs have the power to bring our parents alive as they were in the 1950s, and I use both to tell the story. Other documents that have come into my possession—official correspondence, diplomatic cables, medical records, journals—have been invaluable in untangling and substantiating the web of events around our mother's death.

Our mother was a more prolific correspondent than our father, especially during her last year of life, when our family was living on diplomatic posting in Buenos Aires. Between raising three kids and meeting the demands of a daunting social schedule as a diplomat's wife —attending receptions and cocktail parties, hosting dinners for distinguished visitors—she frequently made time to write to her parents in Toronto. Reflecting her high spirits, intelligence, and loving nature, her letters convey the flavour of the local culture and provide clear-eyed insights into embassy politics and the demands of diplomatic life.

Reading our mother's words as she wrote them has helped me revive and relive my own memories of her. To my brother and sister and me, she was a devoted, often demanding mother who wanted the best for us and from us. Her witty and keenly observant letters, handed down to my siblings and me by our maternal grandparents, reveal her in ways I was too young to appreciate at the time: living a sometimes glamorous, often exhausting life in exotic Argentina, the only country she'd ever visited outside North America, and clearly savouring the novelty of it all. And yet this vibrant, radiant, resilient young woman didn't live to see her twenty-fifth birthday.

No doubt others in my family would tell the story differently. But they didn't know our mother as Julie and Doug and I did—or care so deeply about what happened to her. They didn't hire investigators or seek out and read all the documents that came into our possession, both before and after our father's death. They didn't track down and interview physicians, lawyers, former household staff in Argentina, relatives, family friends, and scores of others who might have knowledge of what befell our mother. They didn't question our father face to face, as we did, or witness his revealing reactions to the evidence we'd uncovered. They didn't fit pieces of the puzzle together until they formed an unmistakable pattern.

This is the story told by that evidence.

Since the story is a true one, I've used the real names of the people involved, except where otherwise indicated. In making every reasonable effort to protect those who are collateral to the main story, I have changed or omitted some names, and in some cases have changed other identifying details.

1

TO BUENOS AIRES

IT WAS MARCH 1958. I was seven years old and standing on the passenger deck of the SS *Argentina*. The enormous ship was berthed in the Hudson River, at a terminal on the west side of Manhattan, awaiting departure to Buenos Aires.

I'd never been on an ocean liner before. Everything was new to me: seagulls screaming in the chilly grey sky, the smell of sea air, the frenzied whistles and shouting on the dock below. Policemen moved people away from the dock's edge. Stevedores stood by to remove the gangplank. From the terminal's observation deck, people were calling and waving farewell to the passengers around us.

I could barely hear Mom's voice through all the noise.

"Jeff, hang on to my belt with one hand and the rail with the other. You too, Doug," she told my five-year-old brother.

She was wearing a new belted coat. In her arms she held my two-year-old sister, Julia, whom we mostly called Julie.

From what I'd heard her say to Dad, I knew she worried about letting us kids up on deck. With all the passengers jostling around us, she feared we might be pushed into the water. She too had never been on an ocean liner before. Dad just laughed and told her not to fuss.

The previous evening, Mom and Dad had left us with a babysitter in our Manhattan hotel room to go nightclubbing. This morning had been a scramble: last-minute checkout, a taxi ride to the wharf through sluggish traffic that Dad cursed under his breath, checking in at the Moore-McCormack Lines wicket. We found our cabins, one for Mom and Dad and Julie, one for Doug and me, and porters wheeled in our steamer trunks. I was glad Mom had agreed we could go up on deck, even if there was no one to wave us goodbye.

Doug and I jumped when a deafening blast erupted from the horn on the ship's funnel, like a gigantic tuba, shaking the entire ship. Mom assured us this just meant we were leaving. The ship began to move slowly away from the dock. Passengers and well-wishers ashore waved even more frantically, as if they were never going to see one another again. I watched spellbound as tugboats moved us farther into the river.

Mom was silent, lost in her own thoughts, reflecting, perhaps, on what she'd gone through to reach this point in her life. Here she was at twenty-three, with three children, sailing to Buenos Aires, where her husband would take up his first diplomatic post. She was excited about the adventure, yet wistful about leaving home. She was an only child, and her immediate family in Toronto was just her parents, now well into middle age. She worried they'd miss her too much. She felt apprehensive not knowing what lay ahead in Argentina. And what about the kids? How would they fare in this strange new life?

Leaving Ottawa, where we'd lived for the past four years, had been a blur of packing, our mother shopping for us as well as herself and Dad, sorting things out with schools, attending goodbye parties, dealing with the never-ending inventory lists required by the government from foreign service officers. A stopover in Toronto had been less work but more difficult emotionally, because of saying goodbye to her parents.

I'd overheard Mom and Dad quarrelling about where to stay in Toronto: at her parents' modest apartment or with Granny Blackstock, Dad's widowed mother, who had a six-bedroom house. I know Mom believed it was her parents themselves whom Dad wanted to avoid. That was what really bothered her, and not being able to spend as much time with her parents as she'd like before a three-year absence far from home. After all, Granny Blackstock could afford to visit us in Buenos Aires. But Mom's parents couldn't, so it only seemed fair to stay with them.

Still, the last thing Mom wanted was more fighting with Dad on the eve of departure. In the end, she'd acquiesced for the sake of family peace.

I was too swept up in the excitement of our adventure to be missing anyone. Just the day before, we'd gone all the way to the top of the Empire State Building, the tallest building in the world at 102 storeys. We'd explored Times Square and the crowded canyons of Manhattan. Big, bustling New York made Ottawa seem like a sleepy village.

As the SS *Argentina* began leaving Manhattan behind, Mom said to Doug and me, "That's the Statue of Liberty, boys. And look at that skyline!"

Dad looked over at the Statue of Liberty, then at Mom and us kids against the collage of skyscrapers. His gaze returned to the mouth of New York Harbor and the open Atlantic beyond. From my time in the foreign service much later, I can appreciate what he must have felt: a sense of pride and achievement as he embarked on his first posting. If someone had told him a few years earlier that today he'd be sailing to Buenos Aires, a freshly minted diplomat, third secretary at the Canadian embassy, with a wife and three children and enormous responsibilities at age twenty-four, he wouldn't have believed it. One thing had just led on to another, and now *this*. It was as though some invisible guiding hand had kept the out-of-control train of events on some hidden track.

We were now in the open sea, Manhattan only a few hazy bumps on the horizon. "Time to go to the cabin and get dressed for dinner," Mom said.

I was ready to go below. Julie was fast asleep bundled up in Mom's embrace, but Doug and I were shivering from the cold wind picking up on the water.

"I'll go check on our dinner seating," Dad said. "I'll meet you in the cabin."

ROUGH WEATHER AND heaving decks soon had me feeling seasick and bumping into walls in our stateroom. Mom wouldn't let us go out on deck unless she was holding on to us. She took us with her when she had her hair done in the beauty salon or went exploring the shops selling fancy watches and duty-free liquor. We all liked the lounges with picture windows, where we could watch huge white-capped rollers chasing the ship. Doug, Julie, and I had temporarily lost our appetites, but Mom and Dad enjoyed the elaborate meals served on crisp white linen in the big dining room. Our pet collie, Lassie, whom we visited every day in the ship's kennel, had never eaten so well in her life.

Even if she didn't say it, my mother would have had very mixed feelings about leaving Canada just when her own mother was going into hospital. Carol wrote her first letter home to her parents on air-mail stationery stamped with the Moore-McCormack Lines logo and "On Board S.S. *Argentina*."

March 24, 1958

Dear Mom and Dad,
You were absolutely right when you predicted the lack of sleep we'd get aboard. There is never a dull moment. . . .

> *For three days out of N.Y, the weather was the roughest they had*
> *had in years. Everyone was sick, but we (George and I) didn't miss a*
> *meal. The kids all were sick but recovered very quickly. Lassie is on the*
> *boat deck being fed steak and doing very well.*

The days warmed up, the sea calmed down, and I started really enjoying myself. Doug and I went into the pool a lot, supervised by the swim instructor. We didn't see much of Dad. He was probably in a deck chair, lost in a book by one of his favourite authors—Agatha Christie or P.G. Wodehouse, or perhaps a paperback about the Second World War. Mom told her parents that she and George were out almost every night after dinner.

> *We are well into the tropics now and it is so humid that none of our*
> *clothes will dry. Last night we had a Sadie Hawkins dance and it was*
> *a lot of fun. The food is absolutely wonderful, never had anything like*
> *it in all my life. Seven course meals all the time....*
>
> *Jeffrey is doing very well in his swimming. He can go half way*
> *down the pool. Douglas still has his tube. I was told so many times ...*
> *about what a lot of trouble I'd have with Julia's training. She has been*
> *an angel. Never puddles and eats like her Dad.*
>
> *There is dancing every night and we always have a swim before*
> *going to bed.... Tomorrow night is the masquerade party and it*
> *should be lots of fun.*

Always sociable, Carol enjoyed getting to know the passengers and crew. Observing the cast of cruise ship characters made her wish she were a writer.

> *The people at our table are very amusing. One older couple going*
> *to Rio are with Ford and look very much like Aunt Marion and*
> *Uncle Phil. Both of them. Another woman from NY reminds me of*

Aunt Teddy but she's not as nice. A girl of about thirty travelling alone for the cruise and a Southern widow who is a scream. The Chief Engineer is the officer at our table. We are always the last table to leave....

I am sure you have seen movies or read about these cruise ships. They are absolutely dead right. I wish I was a writer as I am sure I could make a fortune. There is the deck walker and the girl who missed the boat on her man and is still looking, and the rich bleached widows and the nouveau riche. They are all here. The ship's comedian and the handsome typical blond brush-cut, clean-cut American diplomat. They haven't missed a thing even to the romantic music and the soft sea breezes. I must be getting old and cynical – even the muscle-bound gym instructor doesn't impress me.

For Carol Gray, who had never travelled beyond Buffalo, just over the border from Toronto, it was—in spite of her tongue-in-cheek cynicism—like entering a fascinating new world.

CAROL TOLD HER parents that as the ship sailed south, she and George had more and more of a good time.

We had dinner at the Captain's table and made some very nice friends on board. We danced almost every night and went swimming often at three a.m. They had a wonderful nurse for the kids and I would sleep sometimes all morning. I got a chance to wear all my new dresses and enjoyed every minute of our stay.

Carol and George were such a popular couple on board that, for one of the balls, they were named honorary ship's "stewards." We had a good time too.

We took a tour of the hold and the engine room which the kids thoroughly enjoyed. . . . The dog was very well looked after and had a reasonably comfortable journey. She was right above the kids' playroom and would howl pitifully when she heard them. The nurse would lift Julie up and Lassie would give her big kisses.

When the ship put in at Rio de Janeiro for a few hours, a colleague of Dad's from the Canadian consulate met us and drove us to the top of Mount Corcovado. We viewed the giant statue of Christ the Redeemer, his arms outstretched, looking down over the city to Sugarloaf Mountain and the sea. We drove past Copacabana Beach to Ipanema for lunch. I'd never seen such huge and beautiful beaches.

The next port of call was Santos, the port for Brazil's largest city, São Paulo, situated over thirty miles inland. Dad wanted to make a quick visit to see São Paulo, but as Mom sensibly pointed out, we were in port only for the day, so he might not get back in time. Dad went anyway. On his return, he nearly missed the boat, arriving just as the gangplank was about to be pulled away. Mom was pretty upset.

The next morning, I noticed the water in the toilet was muddy. We'd entered the enormous delta of the Rio de la Plata, the gateway to Buenos Aires. A little later, stewards arrived in our cabins to carry out our steamer trunks.

"The boat trip is over and we were all very sad to leave it. We had a wonderful time," Carol wrote.

Our life in Argentina was about to begin.

2

BEGINNINGS

MY FATHER, George Edwin Bell Blackstock, married my mother, Carol Janice Gray, in Toronto on May 6, 1950. It was a Saturday in spring, the traditional season for weddings. But nothing about this one seemed traditional—least of all to the two families involved.

George and Carol had both grown up in Toronto, but their families occupied very different social strata. The Blackstocks came from what people called Old Toronto Money. The Grays had worked hard all their lives to achieve a place in the middle class, and to make a better life for their daughter. Under normal circumstances, the two families would probably never have met. They were thrust together, for good or ill, by their children.

I never heard my parents tell stories about their wedding, nor have I ever seen any photos of it. I can picture my mother, girlishly thin yet buxom, and very pretty, with lustrous dark hair and eyes, dressed smartly; and my father, a bit gangly, with pockmarks on the cheeks where his childhood acne had been, tall and handsome, nevertheless, in a suit and tie. But all I have to prove they were once married is a certificate with her name, its spelling botched, scrawled by the justice of the peace who performed the ceremony. It took place in Etobicoke, a western suburb of Toronto, far from where either family lived. Their mothers signed the certificate as witnesses. I'm sure Carol's father was there as well, but I haven't heard of anyone else attending the ceremony. George's father had died nearly five years earlier.

It must have been a very quiet affair indeed. No doubt Carol had dreamed of a big church wedding, complete with organ music, bridesmaids, beautiful bouquets, and herself stunning in a white satin gown. She must have been disappointed with an unromantic civil ceremony before a Justice of the Peace in some nondescript office.

This story begins, then, as a tale of two families.

BY 1950, THE BLACKSTOCKS had been in Canada for six generations. They were descended from pioneers who arrived from the British Isles in the 1830s. Succeeding generations of Blackstocks became wealthy from the professions and the liquor industry—ironically, since an early forebear was a circuit-riding Methodist minister who preached temperance in the backwoods.

My father's great-uncle, George Tate Blackstock, was an eminent lawyer who had a town, Blackstock, Ontario, named after him. He was counsel to the Canadian Pacific Railway and a staunch ally of Sir John A. Macdonald, Canada's first prime minister. His entry in the *Dictionary of Canadian Biography* makes George Tate Blackstock sound eerily similar to Dad: "Said to have possessed a commanding physical presence in the courtroom, he was described as 'a dark-haired, good-looking fellow, with an easy and friendly gift of conversation and an entire freedom from restraint or nervousness on social occasions.'" It seems Great-Uncle George's wife divorced him in 1896 on grounds of non-support.

Dad's grandfather, Thomas Gibbs Blackstock, married into the wealthy Gooderham family, wedding Harriet Victoria Gooderham in

1880. The Gooderhams owned Gooderham & Worts, the largest distiller of alcoholic spirits in Canada. Thomas Gibbs Blackstock went into business with his father-in-law as a partner in the Toronto Bank, a forerunner of TD Canada Trust, now the country's second-largest financial institution.

Dad's father, my grandfather George Gooderham Blackstock, was a graduate of Upper Canada College (UCC), the leading prep school in Toronto, and the Royal Military College (RMC), in Kingston, Ontario. During the First World War, he served as an officer in the Canadian Army. At twenty-four, he was promoted to lieutenant-colonel on the battlefield in France and put in command of 2,400 men. Twice mentioned in dispatches, he was awarded two of the British Commonwealth's highest honours: the Military Cross and the Order of the British Empire.

I never met my paternal grandfather, who died before I was born, but during my childhood his memory loomed large over our family. His portrait in military uniform hung in the trophy room at Toronto's Badminton and Racquet Club. He'd founded the club in 1924 with other members of the city's business elite as a recreational and dining venue for their set. He was an outstanding badminton player, winning the Canadian doubles championship three times. Dad kept a framed caricature of his father lunging to swat a shuttlecock, awarded on the occasion of one of his victories.

After the war, my grandfather married my grandmother, Bessie Bell, daughter of a socially prominent Ontario family, and went into business. He gained notoriety as a high roller on Bay Street, Toronto's financial centre, where he apparently won and lost a fortune or two and was a senior executive with various companies, including Steep Rock Mines. The 1920s were a boom time for the mining industry and the liquor trade, mainstays of the family fortune. My grandparents lived in a big rambling country house in York Mills, just north of the city, where my father grew up. He once told me there was "a lot more money around" in those days than there was in our own house a generation later.

According to family lore, my grandmother was a proper young woman, initiated into a fast-paced, high-spending lifestyle by her worldly husband. There were gin and tonics before dinner, cocktail parties, hired help at home, and badminton and tennis foursomes at the club. There were summer holidays at Longwood, the Blackstock family's country home on Lake Simcoe, north of Toronto, and skiing weekends in winter.

A couple of years after they married, my grandmother gave birth to Katherine, my Aunt Kay. It was another decade, after several miscarriages (so relatives told me), before my father came along in 1933: George Junior. There would be no more children.

During the Depression, the family's financial fortunes declined, though it remained well-to-do. George Senior became preoccupied with business pressures and had less and less time for his family. An early photo of my father shows a small boy with neatly combed hair holding a racquet and looking seriously into the camera. My grandfather, a middle-aged man with a military moustache, sits beside him, staring intently at the racquet.

When my father was ten, he was sent away to board at UCC like his father and grandfather before him. The conditions at private prep schools were spartan in contrast to the boarders' comfortable homes. Living in a dormitory with bare floors, sagging steel-frame beds, shared baths, and wake-up bells at 6:45 A.M. was thought to build "character."

Saturdays were half-holidays, with classes in the mornings. On Saturday afternoons, George sometimes made the long trip home by streetcar or, if he was lucky, in the chauffeur-driven family car. His parents usually went out on Saturday evenings. His sister, Katherine, who would later become a teacher, took an interest in his schooling and helped him advance in French. At home, he'd listen to *The Shadow* and other favourite radio serials.

The loneliness of my father's childhood is apparent from a little letter he wrote to his mother at age ten, not long after arriving at UCC. I found it in his papers after he died.

Dear Mom,
    I am writing this letter to you in the library at school. I am writing because I came home over the weekend. It was good of you to have me home instead of leaving me here. There is a parents meeting tonight I suppose you know. I hope to come home on Sunday afternoon on the streetcar. I guess I'll have to go now.
    With love
    from
    George

Sometimes, George had to spend the whole weekend at school. Sunday mornings were reserved for chapel—Anglican, of course—and occasionally he'd be invited to midday Sunday dinner at the home of his grandmother, the previously mentioned Harriet Victoria Gooderham Blackstock. Granny B., as she was known (Great-Granny B. to me), was a throwback to another era, a quintessential Victorian matriarch. Respected and feared, she was the link connecting dozens of descendants who otherwise would scarcely have known they were related.

Old family photos show Great-Granny B. surrounded by the clan in front of her red-brick-and-sandstone house. It was a cavernous place, with bathtubs resting on lions' paws and uncomfortable settees around a coal fireplace in the sitting room, the atmosphere redolent of overcooked roast beef and rigid propriety. Children were to be seen and not heard.

My father remembered all this vividly, but I was too young to experience it myself. Born in 1855, Great-Granny B. died in 1951 at ninety-six. Years later, I'd hear my aunts and uncles lamenting that her house had been demolished and converted into a parking lot by property developers, the common enemy of Old Toronto.

George's childhood ended when he was twelve. On November 9, 1945, his father died from a heart attack after delivering a speech about Remembrance Day. George learned of it the next morning in the newspaper. He never told me how he felt. All I know is that his whole life changed in an instant. Suddenly fatherless, on the brink of adolescence, he was the only remaining male in his immediate family, which must have conferred a scary kind of freedom.

George remained at UCC, his fees paid by the Blackstock family trust. It almost turned out differently. His redoubtable grandmother had cut George Sr. out of her will, apparently believing he'd already drawn too heavily on his inheritance to finance his business ventures. In the process, she'd also disinherited George Jr. and his mother and sister, who were now without the means to live as they were accustomed. (It was out of the question for his mother to go to work.) After protests from George's mother's side of the family, the trust was amended to provide for her financial needs.

My father was a natural athlete. He played on UCC football, hockey, and cricket teams and excelled at squash and tennis. His studies came easily to him, and he was advanced a grade. He was drum sergeant-major of the UCC band and one of the school prefects, senior students who were the top dogs in British-style prep schools.

By all accounts, George's mother had difficulty coping with him. I find that easy to believe—at times, she had trouble coping with life. She seemed to come down with a headache whenever demands were made on her. When I stayed at her home, she'd lie in bed on Sunday mornings, listening to the church service on the radio rather than attending in person. Friends would arrive to take her for outings, and she'd send me to the door to say she wasn't feeling well. On the day of the funeral of Mrs. Pike, her faithful housekeeper of many decades, my grandmother asked me to phone the Pike family to express her regrets: she was indisposed. In retrospect, I think she must have suffered from depression after losing her husband so early in life.

George's mother never kept him close, even during the holidays. He spent a month each summer at Camp Temagami, north of Toronto, where he learned to swim, sail, and canoe. He spent the rest of the summers at a farm run by some older cousins near Port Hope, on Lake Ontario, helping bring in the hay and sleeping in a converted chicken coop.

I remember my father reminiscing with his cousins about the good old times they'd shared at Longwood, the summer estate on Lake Simcoe. They played badminton on the lawn, swam in the bracing waters off the rocky shore, and surreptitiously smoked cigarettes in the ice house. On rainy days, they played board games, and in the evenings they read boys' adventure stories from the well-stocked library.

According to relatives, my father was sixteen and working at the farm when he had a serious brush with the law. A local girl was maimed in an accident involving him at the wheel of a vehicle. The details are hazy, but apparently, after the intervention of family lawyers and members of the local establishment, the problem disappeared.

Despite that stain, with a family background like his it was naturally assumed George Blackstock had a golden future ahead of him.

MY MOTHER'S FAMILY too was shaped by the upheavals of the First World War, the dynamism of the Roaring Twenties, the troubles of the Dirty Thirties. But economically and socially, the Grays lived in a different world. My mother's dad, Howard Gray—Grandpa to me—grew up in a working-class Toronto neighbourhood with a father he described as an "irresponsible son of a bitch"—strong language from one of the kindest people I ever knew. Grandpa didn't say much about his mother, except that she died when he was ten. Later, he had a stepmother and stepsisters.

Enlisting at seventeen, Grandpa fought in France with a Canadian artillery regiment during the last three years of the war. Listening to his war stories is one of my most vivid childhood memories of him: a chum dropping dead without a word after being hit by a stray bullet, shady quartermasters selling the men's bacon to local stores, ladies of the night in London practically tackling young soldiers on leave from the killing fields. Grandpa confided in me as a man would, as a father would.

Back in Toronto, Grandpa worked hard to get ahead, taking a low-paying day job and studying at night to become a chartered public accountant. His family's reputation was important to him. When his father died, he struggled to pay off the old man's financial obligations. Grandpa considered them "debts of honour."

Meanwhile, he was courting Gladys Austin, my future grand-mother. At first, she and Grandpa couldn't afford to marry because of the debt repayments, but finally they'd waited long enough, and in 1928 they married. No sooner had Grandpa discharged the debts than the Depression struck, and the only work he could find was sell-ing shoes in a department store.

Carol, my mother, was born in 1934. Grandma was quite petite; she had a difficult pregnancy and was in labour nearly a week. Grandma and Grandpa decided to take their doctor's advice to "make this your family," so Carol grew up an adored only child.

When Grandpa obtained an accounting position with Provincial Paper, a major Canadian company, it marked a turning point in the family's fortunes. They were able to buy a small house in middle-class North Toronto. They enrolled Carol in a private girls' day school, Moulton College, on Bloor Street near Yonge Street.

Grandpa and Grandma Gray held liberal values for their time and place. The stain of anti-Semitism was common in society—all too prevalent, as I can attest, among Old Toronto families—but the Grays occasionally attended synagogue with Jewish friends, and Grandma used to say she found the Hebrew service beautiful. Dad's mother, on the other hand, once told me she hoped there were no Jewish boys at my boarding school, since "they wouldn't feel welcome."

With the end of the Second World War, when Carol was eleven, the family began enjoying some well-earned pleasures. They bought a small sailboat, which they took for Sunday outings in Toronto Harbour. They rented a cottage on Lake Erie. My mother's parents played their Benny Goodman and Guy Lombardo records when friends and neighbours dropped over. Grandma was proud of her cooking, and her kitchen was often filled with the delicious aromas of homemade soups, simmering stews, and cookies baking in the oven.

Carol was a keen reader and borrowed mystery stories and Victorian novels from the public library. Her girlfriends were always welcome in her home. One of her closest friends, Joan Clark, who was three years older, later told me she and Carol grew close despite the age difference because they shared the same interests in books and life, suggesting Carol was mature for her age. Later, Joan would become godmother to my sister, Julie.

Like many only children, Carol was both precocious and spoiled. Her parents bought her gifts even when it wasn't Christmas or her birthday: a new dress, books, a necklace, a bracelet. But just as she entered her teens, the Grays had to sell their house because, once again, Grandpa was sacrificing to help out relatives. The only bread-winner in the family, he assisted his stepmother and stepsisters with their financial problems. Grandpa and Grandma rented a midtown apartment near Avenue Road and Eglinton Avenue and took Carol out of Moulton College after ninth grade, enrolling her in a public high school, North Toronto Collegiate.

Carol was popular at school. A newspaper photograph taken around this time shows her standing between two bagpipers at a convention at the Royal York Hotel, where she'd been performing Highland dances. In the photo, she radiates a beautiful smile and, with her abundant wavy black hair and dark eyes, appears poised and confident.

Though my mother was extremely bright, she was evidently an average student—and sometimes worse than average. A tenth-grade report card from North Toronto Collegiate shows she was failing in all subjects except physical education and home economics. Joan Clark told me Carol had started dating George by then and was "pretty gone" on him, and obviously her school work suffered. The only reason she didn't fail was that she dropped out to get married— and to give birth to me.

MY PARENTS NEVER talked about how they met. It would only have drawn attention to their short courtship and my mother's pregnancy before they got married.

Still, I can't help speculating about how they started dating. It's surprising that George, a grade thirteen student (equivalent to a college freshman in the United States), felt comfortable dating a tenth-grade girl. I wonder if Carol told him a little white lie about her age. It's possible she was something of a wild child. Being advanced for her age, perhaps she felt bored with the boys in tenth grade. She was best friends with Joan Clark, so it's possible she ran with an older crowd through her.

Then there was the difference in social background. Typically, Upper Canada College boys mixed with girls from other Toronto private schools. From Carol's viewpoint, a UCC boy may have seemed a desirable prospect—not to mention the excitement of dating a handsome, older, more experienced young man who drove his own car.

Grandma Gray later said their dating aroused Grandpa's suspicions. When Grandpa objected to George's taking Carol out in his car, George retorted, "Why, do you think I'm a wolf?" It took Grandpa aback to hear such impertinence.

The circumstances of my conception remain uncertain. According to Grandma, the two teenagers were left alone at George's house when his mother retired early. Nature took its course.

I'm sure Grandpa believed his daughter's honour was at stake. He wasn't going to let her be exposed to humiliation, and he made it very clear to the Blackstocks that he'd accept nothing less than marriage. According to Grandma, George's mother was furious with him when she learned Carol was pregnant and told him to marry the girl. No doubt Granny Blackstock was also made painfully aware by the family lawyers of the potential consequences of Grandpa's displeasure on learning his daughter was carrying George's child.

It was, as one of my father's cousins told me years later, "a shotgun wedding." George's entire vision of his future must have changed overnight—just as it had when his father died so suddenly.

I can't say for sure if an abortion was ever proposed, though I've been told Carol didn't want one. In 1950, abortion was not only illegal but dangerous, generally practised by backstreet operators using crude methods. For most people, it just wasn't an option. My grandparents weren't going to break the law and risk getting their daughter involved with the police.

Not surprisingly, I've always been glad Mom made the choice to keep her baby. Still, there's little doubt the marriage didn't begin as a match made in heaven. George, on the verge of graduating from UCC, had just turned seventeen. Carol, eight weeks pregnant, was fifteen.

And so George and Carol were wed. I imagine Grandma giving her daughter a lingering goodbye hug, tears welling in her eyes.

Carol belonged to the Blackstocks now.

3

FAMILY YEARS

CAROL AND GEORGE spent the summer of 1950 living in a make-shift flat above Granny Blackstock's garage, away from the public eye. It must have been an isolated existence and a strange beginning to married life.

George's favourite cousin later told me most of the Blackstock clan considered the marriage a family scandal. Such things were supposed to happen on the other side of the tracks and were best kept out of sight.

That cousin, whom I'll call Sandra, felt sorry for Carol and George. Alone among his extended family, she paid them a visit, bringing with her a little wedding gift. Carol's friend Joan Clark also visited. From what Joan told me, it wasn't easy to contact Carol, and it was a trek to get there. Joan wasn't made very welcome in the main house, but Carol was delighted to see her. When I was thirteen, Joan told me I was "a love baby."

The wedding had taken place over a month before the end of the UCC term, but somehow George finished up his school year. His abrupt departure from UCC was noted in the summer 1950 edition

of the *College Times*, the school yearbook, under a photo of him with
the other prefects of Wedd's House.

> *Unfortunately, the original writer of Wedd's report found it necessary*
> *to leave the city immediately at the close of school. Since he could not*
> *be contacted, the report was hastily written by Ken H.... Many*
> *thanks, Ken, for helping us in this emergency.*
>
> *The Editors*

This can only have been a reference to George, who was on the
College Times staff as an editorial board member from Wedd's.

At the end of the summer, Carol and George moved to Guelph, a
small city about an hour's drive west of Toronto, where Dad had
enrolled at the Ontario Agricultural College (OAC). Initially, he told
me, he had notions of becoming a farmer. I can't imagine Dad, who
would live in seven countries, almost always in big cities, speak four
languages, drive expensive cars, and enjoy opera, helicopter skiing,
and vintage wines, ever being happy as a farmer in rural Ontario. I
think it's more likely the family chose OAC for him; at that time, it
was the most distant outpost of the University of Toronto, where the
family had a long history.

I was born on December 10, 1950, at the Wellesley Hospital in
downtown Toronto. By then, Carol had turned sixteen. George was
still seventeen.

At OAC, George became enthralled with economics and political science. He once told his mother he wished he could spend his
whole life immersed in books and ideas. He was by nature an intellectual person and a thinker.

My earliest memories begin in Guelph: our small rented house at
the edge of town; Mom yelling at a neighbour who had thrown me
off her property; waking in the morning to the first snowfall of winter
covering the farmer's field across the road; Dad curled up with a

book in his study under a circle of lamplight, looking up in resigna-
tion when I timidly told him I'd wet the bed.

Our living expenses were covered by the Blackstock family
trust. Granny's brother, Uncle Brooke Bell, a big-time Bay Street
lawyer, was designated to keep a stern, watchful eye on us. On
January 20, 1953, Uncle Brooke wrote my parents a letter on his law
firm's letterhead.

> *Dear George and Carol:*
>
> *I have been considering your various problems and have come to
> the following conclusions.*
>
> *As Carol feels she cannot be left alone for long periods as hap-
> pened last year, I do not believe George can continue his work with
> the Downham nurseries [where he had taken a summer job] unless
> that firm would allow him to cover territory which can be easily
> reached in day trips from Guelph. This means that George should
> immediately review the situation with Downham and if no arrange-
> ments can be made with that firm, a new [summer] job should be
> found as soon as possible.*

The trust had never been intended to provide for this type of situation, and there's no doubt Uncle Brooke expected George to contrib-
ute to our family income. To judge from the letter, the young couple
entertained grandiose expectations about their budget.

> *With regard to living quarters . . . I do not believe I can approve of
> buying property in Guelph unless you intend to live there perma-
> nently. To buy property there for your use for a year or so would be
> unwise and I am sure the Trust Company would not approve.*

The trust was already being squeezed by the special arrangements
made—at Uncle Brooke's intervention—to provide for Granny,

George, and his sister, Katherine. Uncle Brooke was there to lay down the law: there would be no reckless spending.

Apparently, relations with Carol and George's respective in-laws were not good.

> *I am very concerned about the continual friction between you and your parents. My advice to you both last year was to stay away from your respective "in-laws." You told me that you are happy together while in Guelph and from my observation you are unhappy when you come to Toronto. Therefore, I think it is in your best interest to stay in Guelph as much as possible. If Carol feels she must visit with her parents, let her do so without George. Your trips to Toronto are expensive and invariably result in unpleasantness of one kind or another. Judging by events in the Christmas holidays, Carol's parents are in a state of tension and I can easily see that George's mother is too.*

Uncle Brooke didn't come right out and say the Blackstocks and the Grays disliked each other, but I think that's pretty much how it was. George was offended by what he considered the Grays' lower social status, and he didn't bother to hide it from them: "Don't talk down to us like your dad does," my grandfather told me in later years.

Grandma and Grandpa's visits to see Carol were few (I don't remember even one). And although Carol was beautiful, well-spoken, and charming, I doubt George would have felt comfortable taking her to the Badminton and Racquet Club. As the son of the principal founder, he'd expect club members to raise their eyebrows and gossip.

There would be dire consequences, Uncle Brooke predicted darkly, if the young couple didn't heed his advice.

> *It is my belief that unless we avoid upsetting George's mother, her nerves will give way and the result will be that she will have to go to a Sanatorium.*

He drove his point home by putting it in language George would understand.

> *This would be exceedingly expensive and would probably use up all the income of the estate, leaving nothing for George and his sister.*

Uncle Brooke wanted them to avoid Toronto altogether.

> *Make friends there in Guelph and forget about Toronto for the time being. There will be lots of time for parties after George's education is complete and when he is earning regularly.*

Isolated in Guelph and shunned by George's family, my parents must have been living a pretty tame existence and missing the parties back home in Toronto. I expect it was galling for George when he saw his fellow students out dating, partying, and doing what young adults do. Meanwhile, Carol was looking after me and keeping house. She was a high-school dropout—maybe not someone with whom George's new college friends would feel comfortable, given the age gap between high-school and university students.

Uncle Brooke ended on a high note, offering some invaluable advice about George's car.

> *In the meantime, if the tires on your car are worn out, I think you should buy four new ones.*

> *Sincerely,*
> *Brooke Bell*

So how *did* they feel at that moment?

It must have been a lonely life, especially for Carol. She was stuck at home, far away from her parents, friends, and familiar surroundings, living with a husband she'd barely known before marrying him.

Meanwhile, he was away attending classes all day and studying and writing papers every night. She had to cope with motherhood mostly on her own, caring for a baby while doing the cleaning, cooking, shopping, ironing. And she did all this as a teenager.

George too had his hands full, but he had classmates and friends, and the intellectual and social stimulation of the college environment. He once told me he directed a play at college and won a drama prize. I don't know how much Carol shared those experiences with him. In the summers, he had the escape of his job, driving around the countryside selling nursery stock to farmers.

At the time of Uncle Brooke's letter, Carol was pregnant again. My brother, Doug, was born on April 15, 1953, in Toronto. There was some criticism on the Blackstock side about Carol having another baby so soon, with George still in university. But perhaps, like other young couples, they were just trying to create a family.

GRADUATING WITH A bachelor of arts degree, George quickly landed a job with the Canadian government as a personnel selection officer at the Public Service Commission. We moved from Guelph to Ottawa, where his world opened up even more. And at last he was earning his own income.

In the mid-1950s, we moved into a modest two-bedroom house in the Ottawa suburb of Manor Park. I remember racing across the green front lawns of Kilbarry Crescent on summer mornings to play with the other kids; Mom giving me a talking-to because I didn't come straight home as instructed; Mom gasping when I presented her with a wriggling frog I'd found in the garden and, when I insisted on keeping it, her telling me I'd have to feed it, then showing me the dead frog a few days later; Mom helping me struggle into my snowsuit, which took forever to unzip at school; Mom apologizing to

Mrs. Ferguson next door when Doug dug up her flower bed. Between the two of us, Doug and I were a handful.

One day, probably in spring 1955, Mom left Dad a note tucked inside an envelope addressed "George."

> *Darling.*
>
> *I have decided to go to Toronto for a couple of days. I will be back Thursday afternoon.*
>
> *Things have just got to a point where a couple of days change would make a whole lot of difference to me. I haven't been feeling well and the kids have been getting me down. This morning was just the straw that broke the camel's back. Waking up to water all over the house and cake mix spread about and that's not all. Doug screams and fights all day and Jeff whines and cries. This 2 days will be a god-send. I know you are angry about this morning and with me in general. I'm sorry and I'll try to do better. I am not going off in a huff so please don't think that. Sorry about tomorrow night but try to understand. I hope this makes sense cause I [am] upset right now. Good luck on the play, dear.*
>
> *Your loving wife*
>
> *Carol*

By going to Toronto, where no doubt she stayed with her parents, Mom would miss a play, perhaps a play that Dad was acting in or directing. But she seemed to feel so defeated that she was forced to retreat, acknowledging that he was angry with her "in general." She didn't say why, but seemed to think it was her fault. The note held great significance for Dad: he wrote on the envelope "Important—note from Carol" and kept it until the day he died.

I often overheard my parents arguing, a pattern that would continue for the rest of their marriage, but I'm not aware how they resolved that particular episode. I only know Mom came back from Toronto, and life went on.

On February 15, 1956, my sister, Julie, was born in Ottawa. I remember marvelling at her tiny fingers and feeling happy the day our parents brought her home from the hospital.

Carol wrote to her mother that George was thrilled she'd had a girl: "George is really quite batty about her and would hold her in his lap all night if I let him." Julie was nursing well and hardly ever cried. And yet three years later, in Buenos Aires, Carol's doctors would write in medical reports that she'd had "a nervous breakdown" after her third pregnancy, following a long and painful labour. According to her Argentine medical records, the breakdown entailed "tiredness, lack of interest in her surroundings and her family and came at a time when she was subjected to several other emotional stresses in the family."

I attended Manor Park Public School and didn't do very well academically at first. Because my birthday comes at the end of the year, I was a few months to a year younger than many of the other kids in my class. I received only average marks on my report cards, but Mom told me that was fine as long as I did my best.

Dad wasn't around at home much, and when he was, it wasn't always a happy experience. One day, he came back from work and asked where my tricycle was; he couldn't find it. He told me to go look for it, and if I couldn't find it I'd get a spanking. I searched all over the neighbourhood, asking people if they'd seen my tricycle. No luck. Mom asked him to give me one more day to find it. Still no trike. Dad took me upstairs to the bedroom I shared with Doug, pulled my pants down, and spanked me. I cried. Afterwards, Mom came up and put talcum powder on my bum. Since I didn't mean to lose my tricycle, I didn't understand why I got spanked, but it taught me a lesson: to fear my father. Because of that spanking, I never hit my own kids.

Sometimes, Dad had a "wrassle" with Doug and me on the bed in our room—we liked that kind of horseplay—or played a game with us, pretending he and I were sick and needed to "send for Doctor Dougie." He was great at magic tricks too, making coins disappear from his hand, then finding them in Doug's ear or my pocket. Doug and I enjoyed those times.

At work, George was making a good impression. One of his older colleagues at the Public Service Commission later told me George's superiors were astonished by the amount of responsibility he handled at twenty-three. In a letter of recommendation, they expressed their admiration for his intelligence and problem-solving skills.

He was promoted to a more senior job within the Public Service Commission, requiring him to travel across the country to recruit professionals for the government. In a letter he wrote to Carol on one of his trips, he revealed something of how he was feeling.

Calgary
Wednesday [March 6, 1957]

My Darling Carol;

How I am missing you. I always do when I'm away you know. How are you, and how are our babies?

So far we have been to Winnipeg, Regina, Vancouver and Calgary. . . . The weather in Vancouver was lovely – so mild I walked around with no overcoat.

We had the most beautiful flight from Vancouver to Calgary today you could possibly imagine – sitting in the super comfortable seats looking out large pressurized windows at the sun pouring down on the Rockies while eating roast lamb with all the trimmings – it was absolutely breathtaking (even the roast lamb – it was the best meal I've had since I left home).

I don't seem to have much really exciting news to pass on as yet.
The main thing is again how much I miss you and the loving care you
always take of me. I wish you were here now.

During the same trip, he wrote again, starting on a plaintive note.

The Macdonald [Hotel]
Edmonton, Alberta
[undated]

Darling;
The longer I am away from you and the closer the time for arriv-
ing home gets, the more I think about how badly I have been missing
you. Have you been getting all my notes and postcards? I have not
heard from you for about ten days. I hope there is a letter on the way
now. I look for them every day.

He sounded perplexed, even worried, that she hadn't replied. We
know she'd received his letters and cards, since he kept them in his
papers until his death. She must have heard his plea for attention too.

As a young child, I didn't see any outward signs of this apparently passionate side of Dad's nature—no hand-holding with Mom,
no embraces or kisses—though when I was older, I certainly wit-
nessed his displays of physical affection in another marriage. One
conclusion seems clear, however: having Mom's attention was very
important to Dad, and it bothered him deeply when he didn't receive
it. I'm not sure my mother always felt the same way toward him.
Their relationship was evolving, as all relationships do. Like any
parent, I know how difficult it can be to maintain the romantic side
of marriage with young children, household responsibilities, and a
busy career in the mix.

ONE MORNING IN MAY, as I was getting ready for school, I could hear Dad talking to Mom while he was shaving.

"Is today a special day?" he asked.

"It's Wednesday," she replied.

"Yes, but is it a special day in our family?"

Mom thought for a minute.

"Oh my God! It's your birthday! Boys, we need to go shop for your father's birthday present. Oh my God!"

Mom and Dad were now able to return to Toronto from time to time. Mom's parents helped them out with gifts of kitchen and household items, little cheques in the regular exchange of letters with their daughter, lots of baby things, and babysitting when we went to visit.

I was always excited about going to Toronto. My eyes widened as soon as the city's bright lights started appearing and the old two-lane highway expanded to become a freeway. There were lots of toys waiting for us in Grandma and Grandpa's apartment, and kid-friendly stores in their neighbourhood. The only bad thing was that every time we went to Toronto, Mom and Dad fought over where to stay.

George's distaste for Carol's parents was deep-seated and visceral. Their middle-class origins and manners were an affront to his patrician sensibilities. He didn't like the cooking smells that so enchanted us kids in their walk-up apartment, nor their aging 1946 Ford parked in the back. Living at close quarters in their three-bedroom flat was a constant source of irritation to him, leading to squabbles with Carol.

George's mother had moved from York Mills into a huge six-bedroom house on Clarendon Avenue, just south of the tony enclave of Forest Hill; clearly, she had more space to accommodate a family with three kids. But Granny always found it difficult to cope with all the noise and disruption we brought along. Her house was cold and rather shabby, since little had been done to update it. Of course,

Granny had her housekeeper, Mrs. Pike, who had been with her since anyone could remember and did all the cooking, cleaning, and laundry. In the end, Carol and George compromised by staying at one parental home and then the other.

Despite Granny's fastidiousness, we kids loved her dearly, and so did Mom, who had worked hard to win over her mother-in-law. She wrote to her regularly with news about us and about Dad, who wasn't a frequent letter-writer. Mom played the piano for Granny while my brother and sister and I wandered about the faded, rambling Edwardian property, exploring its mysterious attic and basement spaces and creeping about the wildly overgrown greenery in the grounds. There seemed to be an unspoken understanding between the two women—perhaps because they recognized that both had endured difficulties in their lives.

Ironically, Mom's parents in their own way lent a certain respectability to our young family with their unconditional acceptance of Mom and Dad's situation. After all, if these salt-of-the-earth grandparents were okay with it, then others could darn well accept it too— and bit by bit, they did.

George's sister, Katherine, embraced her role as Aunt Kay, even though Doug once peed on her new boyfriend's lap. And sometimes we saw Carol's old girlfriends, who became godmothers or special aunts to us. They'd stuck with Carol through the last few difficult years, and she was determined to spend time with them, with or without George.

As an indication of a (probably grudging) acceptance by the Blackstocks, my parents now received occasional invitations to join the extended clan at Sunday midday dinners. Family members ranged from crusty establishment types to bona fide eccentrics to smart young professionals. Carol and George also went out to nightclubs with George's well-heeled, squash-playing UCC buddies and their girlfriends, who were won over, I was told, by Carol's warmth and liveliness. George was "one of them," and popular, but somewhat cold and wooden compared to Carol.

AROUND THIS TIME, George wrote the Canadian foreign service exam. After the interview process, he was offered a place in the foreign service along with eight other candidates out of thousands of applicants. Joining the Department of Trade and Commerce in August 1957, he was on his way to a career in the diplomatic service and an overseas posting.

On August 1, 1957, Carol wrote to her parents:

Well at midnight last night George ceased to be a personnel selection officer and became a foreign service officer. He started his first day today and so far I have heard nothing from him. He seemed quite calm, cool and collected this morning as he strode out of the house without his pants.

Though Carol had a sense of humour about it, George's new responsibilities only made her busy life busier. In another letter home, two months later, she told her parents about enlisting babysitting from a neighbourhood friend, while she did all the extra running around: getting passport photos, chauffeuring George to appointments, joining him for lunch with new colleagues, and, before collapsing, "pooped out," at home, doing some family shopping.

I got Julia a nylon pale blue dress with lace and seed pearls and a belt.... I got Doug a dark green and navy plaid blazer and my, he does look sharp in it.

How typical of Mom, dressing us up to look well groomed in blazers and bow ties, primping our hair and wiping our faces with her hankie before taking us to church on Sundays. She bought something for herself too, despite her awareness of Dad's penny-pinching.

> *I went on my own merry spree and bought myself a red viyella flannel dressing gown. [George] says it costs too much and besides he doesn't like red in the morning. We'll see.*

George wanted to have a party for his new colleagues. Carol liked the idea, but wasn't sure they could manage it in our tiny house. Meanwhile, she told her parents, she waited with anticipation for news about our first posting.

> *On Oct 7 the Deputy Minister comes back and we should find out then where we are going and when. Rumours are that it is Copenhagen, Denmark. We did find out the nine places that we [the nine new foreign service officers and families] are going to. There will be some-one going to each of these, Copenhagen, Beirut, Lebanon, Tokyo, Japan, Singapore, Manila, Guatemala City, Bogota, Sao Paulo, and Buenos Aires, Argentina. One chap has just left for Tokyo and any of those places would be fine with me.*

George and the other inductees went on a cross-Canada tour to learn more about the economy of the country they'd be representing abroad. There were special training courses, orientation sessions, and a thousand things to prepare for the upcoming posting.

Shortly afterwards, Carol and George learned our destination would be Buenos Aires. Carol was thrilled at the prospect, but at the same time she worried about the disruption to the family, being away from her parents and friends, and completing all the preparations for which she was responsible. George assured her that her family and friends would come down to visit us; the kids would adapt, and he, of course, would give her all the help she needed. I became quite familiar with that speech over the years. The reality was that, while he was off travelling and staying in hotels, Mom was completing inventory lists for the move, taking us to get our shots, and making all the necessary arrangements with schools.

Soon, she must have felt, the years of struggle and drudgery would be behind them.

4

ARGENTINA: A WHOLE NEW WORLD

MY FIRST IMPRESSIONS of Buenos Aires—the Paris of South America, gateway to the pampas, home of the tango, military juntas, raging inflation, and the Nazi émigré—were those of a seven-year-old on the upper deck of the SS *Argentina*. It was now early April 1958. Hours earlier, the seawater below our bows had turned from dark blue to the muddy brown of the enormous Rio de la Plata estuary. We could make out the Argentine shore to the south but couldn't see Uruguay, which Dad told us was on the opposite shore. Screeching seagulls winged overhead, signalling our arrival.

As we approached the harbour of Buenos Aires, I grasped the middle bar of the railing, eyes fixed on the crew hurling thick tow lines to tugboats below. The tugs manoeuvred us carefully around the rock seawall and into port. When we neared the dock, the tugs cast off. The day was warm, almost hot. When we'd left Ottawa, it had been well below freezing.

Amid the mob of disembarking passengers, Dwight Fulford and his wife, Barbara, met us coming off the gangplank. Mr. Fulford was one of Dad's new colleagues at the Canadian embassy. He was tall like Dad, but looked older. Mrs. Fulford had the big belly of a woman about to have a baby. Carol wrote to her parents that, with her hair in disarray, Barbara "looked like she just crawled out of bed."

Mr. Fulford took our passports and whisked us through Argentine customs and immigration. As a diplomatic family on government service, we could bypass the other passengers queuing up in rows. An embassy translator said something in Spanish to a uniformed official, who quickly stamped our passports.

While an embassy driver delivered our suitcases and steamer trunks to our hotel, along with Lassie in her cage, we all climbed into the Fulfords' car for a tour of downtown Buenos Aires. Mrs. Fulford looked uncomfortable squeezed between her husband at the wheel and Dad in the passenger seat. Mom sat with us in the back.

We drove down a broad tree-lined avenue. Most of the other cars looked old-fashioned. We passed a park with palms and other exotic-looking trees and a big statue of a man on a rearing horse.

"That's the Plaza General San Martín," Mr. Fulford said.

"Look, Jeffrey, that's José de San Martín," Mom said excitedly, pointing to the bronze figure in Napoleonic military dress. "He's Argentina's national hero!" Mom had been reading up on local history.

Dad had more practical matters in mind. "How long do you think it will take for our car to get here?" he asked Mr. Fulford.

"A while, I'm afraid. The duties on foreign cars are sky-high, and the paperwork is staggering."

We turned onto a huge boulevard lined with trees and apartment buildings, divided by medians and a succession of grand monuments. I'd never seen an avenue that wide, not even in New York. "This is the Avenida 9 de Julio," Mr. Fulford said. "And up ahead is the Teatro Colón. It's the second-largest opera house after La Scala, in Milan."

"Have you been there?" Mom asked. She sounded impressed. I didn't understand the fuss over an opera house.

"Many times. It's a magnificent place. It has some of the best opera in the world."

Mr. Fulford gestured toward a white domed building with a row of columns in front and winged chariots on the roof. "This is El Congreso, the national parliament."

"How's the political situation with Frondizi?" Dad asked. President Arturo Frondizi had been elected just before our arrival.

"Okay so far. There's still corruption everywhere, of course, and you can never tell when there might be another coup. But at least they got rid of that crook Perón. The violence seems to have settled down."

"What's a coup, Mom?"

"It's when the government gets overthrown, Jeffrey." She leaned forward. "It all seems very European," she said to the other adults.

"It *is* very European," Mrs. Fulford replied. "That's part of the charm of living here."

Most of the foreign community shared the view of the Argentine upper class: former President Juan Perón, who had been thrown out by a military coup three years earlier, was basically a thief who'd left the country in the middle of the night with suitcases full of money. Later, I'd learn that most working-class Argentines saw him very differently, as a sort of Robin Hood figure.

"It's *so* nice to see some new Canadian faces," Mrs. Fulford said. Canadians were a rarity in Argentina, she explained. So were Americans, although a small community of American business people represented corporations such as Coca-Cola, Ford, and some New York banks. "There are big Italian and English and German communities here too," she added.

Germans, we'd discover, were the country's third-largest ethnic group. Most of them had come as a result of persecution in Europe, but after the Second World War, Perón had actively encouraged the immigration of Nazis seeking to escape prosecution by the Allies.

Doug and Julie were starting to squirm, Julie seated on Mom's lap.

"George, we need to get to the hotel," Mom said urgently.

"And I should get home to rest up," Mrs. Fulford added.

"How is the pregnancy going, Barbara?" Mom asked.

"Just fine, thank you, Carol. But I do get a little tired."

AFTER SCOUTING THE downtown area around our apartment hotel, walking Lassie in nearby parks with Mom, eating in the hotel restaurant, and playing in our suite without any friends, life in Buenos Aires got pretty boring. We couldn't go out on our own, because of the traffic screaming along the avenues. It's always the same with kids on a diplomatic posting; the initial stage of hotel living grows tedious very quickly.

Dad was away at the embassy every day. Mom was busy trying to deal with the hotel staff, her Spanish dictionary in hand. Hardly anyone spoke English. She had difficulties working the strange kitchen appliances with their weird plugs, while keeping a constant eye on Julie, who got into everything, and answering a thousand questions from Doug and me.

"What's that bowl in the bathroom, Mom? Is it for washing feet?"

"No, Jeffrey. It's called a bidet. I'll tell you what it's for another time."

Mom found the kitchen practically useless, so we took our main meals in the hotel restaurant, which served a steady diet of Argentine beef. "Believe me," she wrote to her parents, "you do get tired of steak, steak, and more steak."

Mom persuaded the chefs to make some new dishes for us. The hotel kitchen wouldn't pass a health inspection, she told her parents, but you had to adjust your expectations. She was popular with the hotel staff. They were "very, very nice" to us, she wrote.

The waiters are very sweet and just love the kids. We have a red-headed Italian, who speaks only Spanish and is Argentine by birth, who brings us lunch and tea. He always spends a few minutes playing with the kids and Julie always has a big kiss for him.

Mom got some relief from constant child care when Doug started attending an American nursery school and I entered St. John's, an Anglo-Argentine boarding school in the affluent suburb of Acassuso. I stayed there all during the school week and returned to the hotel on weekends. Babysitters helped out with Julie so that Mom had some time for herself, and she made some new friends. She enjoyed the company of a young woman who played the piano at a local restaurant she and George frequented, where she had already taught the bartender to make pink lady cocktails. The two women liked to sit and chat over tea. Local business hours kept Dad at the office until nine or ten at night, after which he and Carol had dinner together in the restaurant until ten or eleven—a big change from life in Canada.

Carol began making the social rounds expected of a diplomatic wife. She started with a call on Madame Picard, wife of the Canadian ambassador, who had the biggest apartment in the biggest hotel in Buenos Aires, as well as the biggest diamond Carol had ever seen: eight carats. Wearing her black suit for the occasion, she spent an hour with Madame Picard and found her a very charming and very busy woman.

Next, she called on Mrs. Bissett, the wife of George's immediate boss, the senior commercial attaché at the embassy. Carol found that she and Mrs. Bissett had several things in common, she told her parents: They were both wives of foreign service officers in Buenos Aires. They both had dogs. And they both had two arms and two legs. Their entire conversation revolved around the Bissetts' dog, Biff. Carol still hadn't met Mr. B., but George said he'd been generally boorish, always sneering at departmental HQ back in Ottawa.

Carol arranged for some household help from maids who came to the hotel and were paid by the hour. "I have become quite lazy," she told her parents. "I never wash a dish or make a bed or prepare a meal. It can become quite depressing, believe it or not." Yet the demands on her time and energy resulting from George's social obligations were relentless. A dinner party at the home of his opposite number at the British embassy lasted until 3 A.M. Carol wrote that she'd changed her hairstyle, wearing it "down on one side and pulled back on the other. . . . Lots of compliments."

Before long, Carol and George were drawn into the official social whirl around the inauguration of newly elected President Frondizi. They attended a reception for four thousand guests at the presidential palace, replete with fancy evening dress, numerous bigwigs, and exotic local specialties. "We ate the blood sausages with a smile, sheep entrails with a grin, and the sheep's eyeballs I couldn't even work up a leer for," Carol wrote.

At a full-dress soirée at the Plaza Hotel, Carol met US Vice-President and Mrs. Richard Nixon. "Your girl has ARRIVED," she told her parents. She suggested to the vice-president and Mrs. Nixon that in Paraguay, the next stop on the vice-president's Latin American tour, perhaps they'd meet the American friends she and George had made on the ship, a colonel and his wife, as though they ran in the same circles. When Carol related this bit of naïveté to George, she reported, he nearly broke up laughing on the spot.

Later in the evening, George was introduced to President Frondizi, but Carol "couldn't work up enough nerve for that!" Following the reception, she and George went out for dinner and dancing until the wee hours of the morning.

Our car was finally released from the tangle of Argentine red tape. It was a brand new 1958 Pontiac convertible, white with a black top, a real beauty. Carol no sooner got behind the wheel than she was hit by a horse cart that wasn't following the rules of the road. In practice, there really *were* no rules. Her description of the accident in a letter to Toronto is both amused and frightened.

> *I sat in the middle of this damned intersection with cars whizzing all around and just pulled over to the side of the road, turned off the key and closed my eyes. When I opened them, there was a mob and I mean a mob of people 6 deep . . . all around the car jabbering in Spanish. . . . I made motions for them to go away and they just laughed. I said Policez Polize [sic] and they just laughed all the harder.*

Carol wrote jokingly that George almost wished it was she who'd got hit, instead of the car: "cheaper to replace wife than windshield for 58 Pontiac." Yet George wasn't angry with her, she said. Instead, he cursed "the whole damn place," claiming there were only two traffic lights in the entire country.

She told her parents that she wouldn't hear a word of reproach from George until the day she died.

I WAS MUCH too young to be at boarding school, Mom told Grandma and Grandpa. But St. John's was just too far from the hotel (twelve miles) for me to commute every day.

My boarding house at St. John's, a rambling Victorian building that could have been a mansion once, was situated several blocks from the classroom building. It had a large sitting room where I and twenty other boys watched *The Cisco Kid* on an old television set as a Friday night treat. Most of the boarders were Argentine-born but of European heritage: English, Spanish, German, or Italian. Many came from other parts of the country, where few comparable schools were to be found, and none providing an English-language education, as St. John's did—considered a ticket to the privileged class in Argentina.

St. John's had a rigid daily routine. Breakfast at the boarding house was buns, jam, and tea with lots of hot milk. Morning classes were all in English. We learned how Sir Francis Drake defeated the Spanish Armada after a game of bowls. We learned arithmetic using pounds, shillings, and pence, in a country that used pesos and the decimal system. A hot dinner was served at midday in the classroom building, featuring a stew of stringy overcooked beef, turnip, and potatoes, with a flavourless flan or pastry for dessert. The smell in the dining room was mildly nauseating. Afternoon classes were all in Spanish, so at first I had no idea what was going on. While getting through my school year turned out not to be an issue, nevertheless, being unable to understand a word was a powerful incentive to learn Spanish.

After school, I made the long walk back to the boarding house, passing villas behind tall hedges and eight-foot white fences, and keeping a wary eye out for horse dung where vendors' carts had stopped. Later, while the other boys played soccer in the yard, I leaned against the wall in the hallway and wept from homesickness. The cleaning ladies noticed and whispered to one another.

When I gratefully returned to the hotel for the weekend, Mom said I seemed much more grown up, thanks to St. John's. I was making my own bed, shining my own shoes, tying my own tie. I didn't tell her what it was really like: getting beaten up under the blankets by my dormitory mates because I had a teddy bear, sitting in class all afternoon with little comprehension of what the teacher was saying, sobbing from loneliness. I didn't tell my parents, because I didn't want to complain.

AS I NOW realize from her letters home, Carol was homesick too. George was on the road to Mar del Plata, the first of many trips he'd take during his posting, and Carol wrote to her parents that she was bored and lonely. She felt we were "drops in the bucket . . . thousands of miles away" from the people who cared about us. With the servants running the household, she had nothing to do and felt a lack of purpose, which she found "terrible." She'd never be a successful "Mrs. Rich Bitch."

Before going on your first posting in the foreign service, they tell you that you'll go through a honeymoon period when everything is new and charming. Then you'll feel lonely, and possibly depressed, and will hate everything in the new country. But gradually you'll adapt to your environment, and things will start looking up. For Carol, sure enough, life suddenly took a turn for the better.

She and George had been unable to find a suitable home to rent within the Canadian government's budget for foreign service officers. But now they received an increase in their housing allowance and, with George back from his trip, they resumed house hunting in earnest. Life became busy again. Carol joined the American Women's Club, only to hear a presentation from a parapsychologist who was nothing but a "good fortune teller with a new twist . . . in other words, a quack!"

The economic realities of this third-world country, as it was considered then, kept intruding. A sugar strike in Tucumán province meant there was no sugar to be bought at any price. The toilet paper was "terrible when you can get it and worse when you can't." Nevertheless, Carol continued to make friends both with expatriates and Argentines. She seemed able to connect with everyone— almost everyone.

Around that time, she and Dad had a huge fight. From the bedroom I shared with Doug, I could hear them arguing in the kitchen. Mom was complaining about being cooped up in the apartment suite and Dad never being around to help out or spend time with the family. They'd had arguments like that before from time to time, but this one was a real blow-up. Mom wasn't the least bit timid about talking back to Dad. The argument quickly escalated into a shouting match.

I didn't like it when they yelled at each other. But from experience, I knew what to do. Waiting for a lull in the storm, I peeked into the kitchen and asked if I could take Doug, teddy bear in hand, to visit the apartment of some friendly childless neighbours down the corridor. Dad turned to me and said that was a good idea. We beat our retreat, and the maid took Julie out for a walk to get her away from the fighting.

Later, before Mom and Dad went out for the evening, she told the maid to serve me some tomato soup, my favourite. Mom knew I never got it at boarding school. She always found some way of making things better.

ON JUNE 21, 1958—winter in Argentina—Carol and George finally found a house to rent. Its owner was a famous local figure, Jorge Antonio, Juan Perón's business partner. According to Carol's letter home, Antonio was "crook number 2" after "crook number 1," Perón himself. It seemed Antonio had left the country in such a hurry, he took only one suitcase. The amnesty for Peronistas after the military coup did not extend to either Perón or Antonio. In his submission to headquarters seeking approval of the very reasonable rent, George's boss, Mr. Bissett, described the situation more delicately: "I think the main reason it [the house] came to the market at this [low] figure was that the owner was absent from Argentina for political reasons and may think it inadvisable to return at the present time."

In plain English, the embassy would be renting from a fugitive from justice. Later, soon after we left Buenos Aires, the house would be confiscated by the Argentine government among other illicit property held by Jorge Antonio.

The house came fully furnished. The embassy leased it for two years, with an option for another eighteen months. One problem was that it didn't come with a cook. While the maid who had worked for the Antonios was available, Carol wrote, "She does not cook and I really need a cook."

Ambassador Picard threw a huge cocktail party for George and Carol, welcoming them into the embassy "family." There were more parties around Dominion Day, our national holiday, now renamed Canada Day.

In a letter to her parents, Carol was ecstatic about our new home, describing it as "everything I could want." Located in Acassuso, the same suburb as my school, it was a white stucco two-storey villa with a huge garden for flowers and vegetables, bordered by nine big pine trees. It had a living room that was "spacious, gracious and above all cozy," with a fireplace "of dark walnut and dark green marble" (Buenos Aires gets chilly in the winter) and a big picture window looking onto the garden. The dining room was panelled in dark walnut. The kitchen was so modern that it was "a seven-day wonder for this part of the world." There were four bedrooms in the main house, a two-car garage, and a *casita*, a separate building in the back, serving as living quarters for household staff, including our new cook, Alejandra.

"I love [our new house] so much that I hate to go out," Carol wrote. "It was worth every wearisome day in the hotel."

The family moved in while I was still boarding at St. John's. By chance one day, while walking from the school to my boarding house, I was surprised to come across our Pontiac convertible parked outside the house. I ran inside to look for Mom and Dad, but found only our maid and some workmen moving furniture. The family was out walking Lassie. I was so excited that I waited eagerly until they returned half an hour later, forgetting all about tea at St. John's.

"Jeff, what are you doing here?" Dad asked.

"I was so happy, I wanted to see you."

"Well, we are happy to see you too, but shouldn't you be at school?"

"I guess so."

Mom got me a jar of peanut butter to take with me, kissed me, and sent me on my way. Mr. Legge, the headmaster, was looking at his watch when I arrived at the boarding house. Tea had started.

Before long, I was living at home and attending St. John's as a day boy. I felt as thrilled to be away from that boarding house as a prisoner released from a gulag.

It didn't take long before we all began to feel settled. Carol's letter to her parents in July 1958 describing a typical day must have amazed and amused them.

At eight o'clock Alexandra comes tripping gaily upstairs loaded with our tray of goodies for breakfast. Fresh fruit and porridge (for George, ugh), bacon or eggs (for George, ugh) and toast and coffee and tea (for me, yum). Then George gets up, takes his bath, gets dressed, reads the paper, has another cup of coffee. Then in troop the little darlings all breakfasted, washed and dressed. They stay a few minutes and then go down with Daddy to say goodbye, open the gates for him, and watch him speed off in a cloud of dust. Meanwhile, back in the bed room, the cook has come up to consult with me about the day's menu. Actually (and don't let this get about) what she does is try to tell me what we are going to eat that day in Spanish. My replies are invariably "Si, si." Then I get up and start seeing to the day's activities. Believe me there is still plenty for me to do. Why I actually made my own bed today. Then before you know it my lunch is brought in on a tray to the living room and then it is time for my siesta. When I get up I have my bath, go down and see how the children's tea is coming along and go out for a walk in the garden. Our kids are so good. Why you know, they just never cry. That is a phrase I seem to have heard somewhere else, now I know why. The children have their tea and then their bath and wait for Daddy to come home, sitting demurely in front of the fire with their dressing gowns and slippers on. (If the truth were known, tonight Dougie was dropping marbles on [the maid] Mary's

*head from upstairs, while she was trying to phone downstairs. Julia
was pushing her doll carriage around the dining room table tripping
up Alex as she came in with a load of glass and silver. Jeff was fiddling
with the TV and driving us all cuckoo and I was drying up the water
I had just spilt on the carpet. George was honking at the gates to get
in and we all dashed at once. Well, that's the Blackstock family for
you and if it wasn't that way we wouldn't be we. SO THERE.)*

Carol concluded, "Daddy, this should reach you just in time for your
birthday. I do hope you have an especially good one this year. We are
all sorry we can't be there to help you blow out the candles."

George practically never wrote to his mother. So in August, Mom
wrote to Granny with family news, including Doug's tall tale of how
Lassie had eaten the missing bananas, for which Dad gave Doug a
spanking, and Julie getting into Mom's nail polish. She mentioned
losing our housemaid, but didn't say she'd had a run-in with her
when we came home one evening and dinner wasn't prepared. The
maid quit in a huff.

My mother tapped into the expat network for a replacement and
found María, who turned out to be a treasure. María not only became
our housemaid but also devotedly looked after us children, and Mom
too. In time, she'd come to mean even more than that to us.

María was fortyish and heavy-set, with dark skin, black hair tied
back, and a round, kind face. She moved into the *casita* at the back of
the property with her husband, Martín, a six-foot-two stonemason,
and Cristina, their thirteen-year-old daughter.

I don't know where Mom found the new cook, Alejandra, who
moved into the top floor of the *casita*. Alejandra (Mom called her
Alexandra or Alex) was a shapely, tan-skinned woman in early middle
age. Other people also worked at the house—gardeners, seam-
stresses, cleaners, and painters—but didn't live in.

In a letter to Joan Clark, Carol said that with so much help around the house, she was living the "life of Riley." She and George were constantly out at parties and also entertained a great deal, as expected of diplomatic couples. On one occasion, they hosted a cocktail party for 110 guests at our home. I watched from an upstairs window as white-clad servers in the garden below wended their way among elegant strangers in evening dress conversing in various languages, cocktail glasses in hand.

MY PARENTS HIRED a private tutor, Mrs. Toppie, to help Doug and me with our homework. Mrs. Toppie was from Hungary and spoke perfect English and Spanish. She reviewed all the work we brought home from school, pencilling check marks and X marks in the margins. Then she gave us her own homework on top of the school work, which we really didn't enjoy.

I acquired a strong English accent from St. John's, Doug an American one from his nursery school, and Julie a Spanish one from the household staff. Mom told her parents that Dad had thrown up his hands about it. I soon got to know the neighbourhood kids, from the fifteen-year-old gardener across the street, to the Americans whose father worked for General Electric, to the Swedish-American family whose father worked for Caterpillar. I became friendly with the street vendors selling ice cream, gardening services, sacks of potatoes, and other offerings.

On Sundays, María, Martín, and Cristina took Doug, Julie, and me to the house Martín was building for them in Boulogne, a working-class area of dirt lots on the outskirts of Buenos Aires. I imagine Mom and Dad, with their hectic social life, were happy to have María take us off their hands for a day, and María was probably happy for the extra babysitting money. She, Martín, and Cristina always treated us as part of their family. Some of my warmest boyhood memories are those Sunday visits with them.

Back then, Boulogne was a neighbourhood in the making. A couple of hundred yards away, earth ramparts and bulldozers marked the construction of the Pan-American Highway. Someday, it would connect the neighbourhood to New York, Martín told me. He showed me how he mixed cement mortar using sand, lime, and water, then laid the bricks for the house, cutting some to make them fit. He had a charcoal pit with screening for a grill, on which he threw huge slabs of beef for our *asado*. In the outdoor kitchen—consisting of a wash pan and makeshift counters—María and Cristina would prepare a big salad.

When our *filetes de lomo* were ready, we ate them outside on a table made from a wooden door resting on sawhorses. With the steak still red and juicy inside, we had the salad and lots of crusty bread. Martín brought out *vino tinto* and gave me a bit mixed with lots of water. He said it added a little colour to kids' complexions. Afterwards, we drank *café con leche* [coffee with milk].

After lunch, I played with the neighbourhood kids. We played soccer in the dirt, putting down rocks for goalposts. We set off firecrackers that you lit like a match—no fuses. One blew up in my fingers, and I spent the rest of the day dunking my hand in a pail of water to relieve the burning sensation.

One Sunday, I asked Dad to lend me his Canadian football. I wanted to take it to María's for playing soccer with the other boys. They didn't own a real soccer ball and used anything they could find—cast-off rubber balls or tennis balls. Dad sat me down and told me how long he'd owned that football, how important it was to him, how it was the only one he had. He made me promise not to leave it where it might be stolen, or to lose or damage it.

I took the ball to María's, and it made for a strange soccer game. The oval football bounced crazily all over the place, but the other boys enjoyed it anyway. Afterwards, I guarded the ball carefully and that evening proudly returned it to Dad safe and sound. He seemed happy.

GEORGE'S BOSS UP the line at headquarters in Ottawa, Assistant Deputy Minister H. Leslie Brown, of the Department of Trade and Commerce, paid a visit to Buenos Aires. Brown knew Argentina well, having been posted to Buenos Aires from 1947 to 1950. While there, he'd proven adept at working his way around the Argentine authorities. In his autobiography, Brown recounted arranging a meeting for Mrs. Tillie Ralston, a successful provincial politician from Vancouver, with Eva Perón. She, of course, was the immensely popular and powerful wife of Juan Perón, president at the time. After Mrs. Ralston returned to Buenos Aires from a side trip to Santiago, Chile, and told Brown she'd met the Chilean president, he'd proudly replied, "Guess what? Tomorrow you meet with Evita!"

News of the meeting between the two women appeared in the Argentine tabloids. Nevertheless, Mrs. Ralston found herself in need of a special police card for her subsequent departure from Buenos Aires by boat. With only an hour to spare, Brown convinced a local official to bend the rules and issue the document, pointedly mentioning the meeting with Evita Perón. Apparently, Mrs. Ralston was so impressed by his adroitness that this story became a favourite of hers.

Since George's superiors were all away, he invited Mr. Brown to our house for dinner. Despite Brown's seniority as the man in charge of her husband and all his trade colleagues around the world, Carol found him very approachable and friendly. She described his visit in a letter home.

> It was just the three of us and really it turned out very well. He is a wonderful man and very easy to talk to. He was or seemed to be very interested in George and the job he was doing, how we were liking it

down here, how the children were getting along, whether or not we
attended church and he did it all so painlessly that it wasn't until later
did I realize just how much the man had learned about us.

As enchanting as he was, Brown wasn't afraid to say what he thought. "He was charming," Carol noted, "and at times shockingly frank and I think he will probably be a very good if not excellent Director."

The following evening, Carol and George threw a cocktail party for a hundred guests at our place in Brown's honour. The ambassadors of Japan and Finland were invited, along with several other VIPs. The whole affair was catered by the American Club, "which makes it very easy for us."

Carol wore a special new dress, "a plain sheath with one shoulder strap of a beige brocade with pale green fleurs de lis." When Brown saw her, he said, "Wow." He was "not at all stuffy," and even though dinner wasn't served until 11 P.M. and the party carried on until the wee hours, Brown stayed "until the last dog was hanged." I didn't know that's what they did at cocktail parties. Carol was clearly impressed with him, and he genuinely seemed to like her and George. She'd never know the role Leslie Brown would later play in her story.

CAROL MET MORE people who would become an important part of her life when she and George attended a fashion show held by the Ola bathing suit company. She told her parents that "the fashions down here are always ahead of those at home and in the States." It was, she added, "a rather chilly evening and we all felt rather sorry for the girls. I am sure some of the men would have been quite willing to help the girls, but there was a sign saying, 'Please Do Not Handle the Goods.'" The company was owned by Peter and Bibi Fischer, who became friends with my parents.

Another couple with whom Carol became friendly were Louise and Rolf Krapf. Louise was a Canadian from Ottawa whose grandfather had been Sir Joseph Pope, an important public servant going all the way back to Sir John A. Macdonald's day. Her husband, Rolf, was a businessman. Carol visited Louise and wrote amusingly about her "poodle crowd." Louise turned into a good friend as well, better than Carol would ever know.

Two-year-old Julie was developing by leaps and bounds. She would stay over at María and Martín's house while Mom and Dad attended a polo match or a lunch, and Cristina played with Julie to spell off her mother. Alejandra, the cook, sometimes took Julie along with her on her days off. The driver who took Julie to nursery school called her his *pequeña amor* (little love). People spoke to her in Spanish, and "she seems to understand every word," Carol wrote. She had a "fantastic memory" and recognized Grandma from a photo right away.

Despite her busy social life, Mom made time for us when we needed her. I came home from school one afternoon with a bad stomach ache. Mom was having tea with the local Anglican minister in his clerical collar. (The British community in Buenos Aires was large enough that it had its own churches, schools, hospitals, even stores. Harrods of London had a huge department store downtown.) Mom immediately told the minister they'd have to have tea another time, because her boy needed her.

For my eighth birthday, on December 10, 1958, Mom organized a big party and invited a dozen kids over to the house. We all played in the garden, while the mothers had tea inside. My main present was a bicycle, which I'd really been hoping for—I'd been spending a lot of time riding other boys' bikes around the school yard.

After the party, Mom took me upstairs to my parents' bathroom. I was surprised by this, since they'd always told Doug and me we weren't supposed to go in there. Dad was having a bath, lying back in the tub with his big penis and hairy crotch in full view. It was a shock to me. Mom said she'd brought me in so Dad could wish me happy birthday, but to me it felt like I was supposed to see his genitals. I didn't understand why. I doubt it was Mom's idea of a birthday present. Whatever the reason, it left me with a very uncomfortable feeling.

Soon it was the end of the Argentine school year, coinciding with the arrival of summer. Carol wrote her parents that I'd passed "by the skin of my teeth." At least I was starting to understand what was going on in the classes taught in Spanish. Even though Mrs. Toppie, our tutor, wasn't my favourite person, she'd helped me a lot. Having maids who spoke only Spanish helped too, since I had to speak to them in their own language.

The school was tolerant enough to understand that, while I still wasn't quite up to snuff in Spanish, it was because I'd spoken no Spanish at all when we'd arrived eight months earlier. My teachers recognized that I was improving and would probably catch up eventually, which I did—making friends, enjoying sports, and feeling very at home in the new culture.

IN JANUARY 1959, Carol planned our separate summer holidays. For her and George, this meant a five-thousand-mile road trip to Patagonia, Argentina's southernmost tip, just as the country was beset with more strikes. It was an opportunity to combine business with pleasure. George would be making professional calls along the way, visiting agricultural businesses, his specialty, such as sheep and cattle operations, and looking out for export opportunities for Canadian equipment and breeding stock. Carol would keep a diary of the trip in which she recorded their expenses, so George knew how much he could claim from the government. I don't know whether it was his idea or Carol's that she join him for the trip. Before they left, Mom prepared us kids for travelling to the Sierras de Córdoba, in the interior, with María and Cristina, who would look after us while our parents were away.

During their journey to Patagonia, Carol wrote in her diary about driving on rough dirt roads, visiting sheep farms, fishing in mountain streams, getting stuck in mudholes, riding on horseback, and being invited to dine by almost everyone they met. She described the countryside as "the real Argentina," where "people are so kind . . . that you just can't get any time to yourself." On January 21, 1959, she sent a postcard to Joan Clark from Ushuaia, "the most southern town in the world," showing the fishing port and the snow-covered peaks of the Andes beyond.

Carol and George went to the Carnival dance in Rio Grande, where she danced with "the [wool] shearers, everyone." The next day, she went out riding with a new companion named Jaime, who got thrown by his horse. It's not clear who Jaime was, or how they'd met, but Carol and he ended up on a picnic blanket together eating lunch and drinking beer.

Where was Dad? Perhaps he was busy with work, or simply not interested in dancing or riding. Maybe he was taking in the spectacular landscape of Tierra del Fuego. Mom didn't say, either in her diary or her letters.

I'm sure her little adventures on the trip were innocent enough. Yet looking back at her diary notes, I'm surprised by their frankness. I doubt she ever imagined that I, or anyone else, would read them one day. If Dad ever read them, I think that he'd have been upset, even angry, about her keeping company with men.

Meanwhile, we three were in Córdoba for ten days with María. Córdoba was her home, and she was happy to be visiting her family. María's daughter, Cristina, came along to help look after us. We all stayed at a little hotel, but ate our meals at María's mother's place. It had a dirt backyard with chickens running around. In the evenings, there was much laughter and singing, much *vino tinto*, and the best grilled beef in the world.

María and her family loved to laugh and tell stories. They talked about Juan Fangio, the international racing car champion from Argentina who, according to María, had been given a prize car made of solid silver. They gossiped about Frank Sinatra. As good Catholics, they discussed what kind of fish they'd eat on Friday, and how they'd obtain some holy water from a fountain where a saint had performed a miracle. They complained about the *Yanquis* (Yankees) and made fun of them. I imitated my father's heavy North American accent in Spanish, which made everyone laugh. Doug made faces. As I was eating a sandwich, one of the chickens snatched it away. More laughter. I asked for another sandwich.

NO SOONER HAD we all returned home from our travels than Bob and Jenny Borden arrived for a visit. The couple used to pal around with Carol and George in Toronto before we moved to Argentina. Bob had been a classmate of Dad's at UCC. His father was Henry Borden, president of Brazilian Traction, Light and Power, a Canadian multinational corporation that later became the conglomerate Brascan. His great-uncle was Sir Robert Borden, Canada's prime minister during the First World War. Bob was named after his famous forebear and had a framed Canadian hundred-dollar bill bearing Sir Robert's image hanging on his wall. According to one of Carol's letters, Jenny Borden had achieved some success as a competitive swimmer.

There was now a new Canadian ambassador in Buenos Aires, Richard Plant Bower. Fifty-three at the time, Bower, who was born in Kansas City, Missouri, must have been something of a child prodigy, since he graduated from the University of Manitoba at nineteen in 1924. He joined the Canadian diplomatic service at twenty-one, serving in various postings in Europe, Asia, Australia, and New Zealand, before being appointed ambassador to Venezuela in 1956.

The arrival of a new ambassador is a huge event for an embassy, making a big impact on the personnel and their families. (In our case, this would turn out to be an understatement.) But Carol took it all in stride—no wonder, since she'd already won over, apparently, Assistant Deputy Minister Brown, the ambassador's boss. She wrote that, after taking Bob and Jenny Borden shopping,

> *we drove home and got ready for the dinner party with the Ambassador. Louise and Rolfe [sic] Krapf were also coming and all in all it was a very nice evening. Mr. and Mrs. Bauer [sic] are very very nice. He is a very open, straightforward type and very sharp and on the ball. They have 3 children in Canada. After dinner we played Bridge. The only unfortunate note to the evening was the heat. It was dreadful.*

Carol was not cowed by anybody, no matter how important, whether Vice-President Nixon or Ambassador Bower. She also had a keen eye for character.

Carol didn't mention George in her description of the dinner party, which is surprising. For a foreign service officer, an ambassador has tremendous influence, not only on the officer's current posting but also their future career. George would have wanted to make a good impression at what was, apparently, his first social occasion with Mr. Bower. Perhaps Carol was simply enjoying the evening and the company. Years later, Louise Krapf would share with me her memory of Dad as rather stiff socially, whereas Mom was the real crowd-pleaser.

Carol, George, and the Bordens travelled to the Llao Llao Hotel, in Bariloche, a resort in the Parque Nacional Nahuel Huapi, at the foot of the Andes, for golf, fishing, and horseback riding. Carol wrote to her parents that she and Aunt Jenny, as we called her, gave George and Bob such a "hiding" at bridge that they kept playing until 5:30 A.M. to give the laggard males a chance to catch up.

George's mother also arrived at Bariloche with her friend and travelling companion Marge Van Allen and joined the party. Jenny Borden came down with "traveller's trots," so Carol went riding alone, even learning to ride bareback. She went fishing with George and Bob, and caught "the biggest brown trout that the guide said he had ever seen in that river, 6½–7 pounds," a real prize. Granny got sick, but was so taken with her doctor, Carol wrote, that "I do believe she won't get better, just so he will come again."

After several days, the party broke up. Bob and Jenny continued on their travels. George left for Buenos Aires to return to work. Carol, Granny, and Marge stayed on at Bariloche. "We liked it so well," Carol told her parents, "that we kept sending George telegrams to say we would stay just a few more days." Granny and Marge played golf and went for long walks, while Carol went off riding all day.

> I would go out at ten and not come home till about eight. I had a saddle roll and in it would be my bathing suit, towel, book and cigarettes. It was really fun. . . . I got to know many people in the district and was invited to lunch or to asados.

Carol danced every night in the hotel bar, where there was "a very good four-piece band." One evening, there was a special dance for hotel personnel. Carol "had five invitations, but had to say no," she told her parents. She continued,

> BUT, that didn't stop me from going to the dance. I had a ball, never sat down all evening. It went on until five thirty in the morning. I was dancing with an Italian boy and we won the Brazilian Samba contest. Rather a riot, eh. Four countries involved.

Carol found it amusing that all of a sudden more guests took up riding. One chap asked her, "Aren't you afraid you will get lost in the woods? Wouldn't you like me to accompany you?" She replied, "No thank you. I may get lost, but you can be sure Lucero [her horse] won't."

Carol vividly recounted all this in a letter to her parents on March 25, 1959. Apparently, she didn't feel at all abashed about going on her adventures—an unusual show of independence for a married woman in those days. No doubt, she told Granny and Marge about the fun too, since they were there. I don't know whether one of them, or even Mom herself, shared with Dad any details of the good times she was having while he was back at work. But it seems likely he'd have heard one way or another. I imagine he'd have felt none too pleased about it.

By the end of March, Carol, Granny, and Marge were back in Buenos Aires, and our home life resumed. I was now joined at St. John's by both Doug and Julie. Mom told Grandma and Grandpa that when she saw Doug and me off every morning, we looked "so smart dressed alike" in our school uniforms. Julie, now three, was picked up by a big red school bus. Carrying "a school bag which is almost as big as herself," she sat on a small seat beside the driver and was delighted to be going to nursery school.

Carol was soon riding every morning at the Club Hípico.

I have a lovely, small, pure black gelding called Kotan. He has a beautiful gait and is quite quiet. Perfect for the kids and I but too small for George. . . . We have an invitation to cross the Andes, by horseback, to the Pacific next summer and I want George to learn to ride first. I am going to get him to join the club too. It is something we can do together on weekends and will be great fun. I am anxious to have the children learn to ride properly and Jeff is just the right age to start his jumping.

On March 31, 1959, Carol wrote home to say Granny and Marge had left on a week-long excursion to the scenic city of Alta Gracia, in Córdoba province. Doug and I attended a birthday party at the home of our best friends, Michael and Danny McKenney, from the States. We thought the magician at the party was terrific.

Our family life was busy and good. Soon, it would all come crashing down.

5

CAROL'S STRANGE SICKNESS

SHORTLY BEFORE MY father's twenty-sixth birthday, on May 1, 1959, Carol started getting sick. She was twenty-four.

Even with the help of household staff, her existence was hectic—nothing like the "life of Riley" she described when we'd first settled in. It was more like a job, albeit an unpaid one, since she was contributing to Canada's presence in Argentina, as well as supporting George's career. Of course, she received little recognition for it—foreign service spouses rarely do. Cocktail parties, she wrote, were now just another chore. No wonder she'd revelled in her adventures in Patagonia and the carefree fun of Bariloche.

In addition, she had her mother-in-law visiting for two whole months. And yet she was genuinely cheerful about having Granny with us and seemed to enjoy her company, despite all the effort required.

It was while Carol was organizing social events for Granny that things began falling apart. In a letter to her parents dated May 10, 1959, she described how it all began.

I was having one of these bridge bun fights for [George's] mother and sure enough the morning of the do, María brought Julia in and said "Señora, I'm afraid Julia has chickenpox." I had to phone everyone up and tell them [that the bridge party was off]. . . . Douglas was also in bed with a cold and Jeff came home from school with a fever and a cough. It was really the most hellish day I can remember.

And yet organizing Granny's social life continued, even as Carol too started to feel ill.

I felt as if I was coming down with a cold, but sort of said to myself "Oh, I'll just work it off, I've too much to do." Never will I say that again in B.A. . . . Well we had dinner parties and dos for Mother and I just wouldn't go to bed.

By George's birthday, she was really sick: "May 1st [Friday] is a holiday here and also G.E.B.'s [George's] birthday, but I was feeling terrible so I went to bed, hoping I would be well enough to go to Uruguay next day."

My parents had planned to take Granny across the river, the Uruguayan border, for a brief visit to Montevideo. This was to help Granny avoid an Argentine surcharge on her return passage for overstaying her sixty-day visa. But since Carol was now feeling "much worse," she stayed at home, and George and Granny took the ferry to Uruguay on Saturday, May 2.

The doctor called and diagnosed Carol's symptoms as asthmatic bronchitis. María, despite having her own liver trouble, nursed her, just as she nursed everyone else in the family. María's nursing included things you didn't forget, like warm enemas and thermometers held under your armpit for long periods of time. She also made sure we had our lessons ready for our tutor, kept us in clean clothes, put us to bed on time, and did a hundred and one other things for our family.

Carol felt especially grateful to María, she told her parents.

> *Mom if I can't have you when I'm sick, María is the best substitute I could ever have. She had Martín off looking for drugs the doctor had ordered on a Sunday when they are closed and Tina off looking for a nurse to come and give injections. We got the injections but no nurse (it's always that way down here).*

A professional nurse did come to the house on Monday, but the cure may have been worse than the disease: "She came with a needle ten feet long and just about killed me," wrote Carol.

The next day, she still wasn't feeling better.

> *Tuesday I was sick at my tum all day and by then I hadn't had a thing to eat except a baked potato on Sunday, since Saturday. Well something was not agreeing with me and Doc took me off all medicine by mouth and I got it at t'other end.*

When it became clear she wasn't getting any better at home, the doctor put her into hospital, on Wednesday, May 6.

The clinical record of my mother's extensive medical treatment in Buenos Aires is dated July 17, 1959. It was compiled and signed by Dr. G.F. Mercer, an Anglo-Argentine physician who was Carol's main doctor at the hospital where she was treated—actually a clinic, La Pequeña Compañía de María (the Little Company of Mary). Dr. Mercer's report provides an important—but not the only— source for this account of my mother's sickness. Julie and I came into its possession some twenty years later, when Grandma Gray gave us our grandfather's papers after he died.

Dr. Mercer's report began:

SUMMARY OF THE CLINICAL RECORD OF MRS CAROL BLACKSTOCK

THIS 24 YEAR OLD WHITE MOTHER OF THREE WAS FIRST SEEN IN
MAY, 1959, BECAUSE OF COUGH, WHEEZING, ORTHOPNEA AND VOMIT-
ING. SUBSEQUENTLY, HER CHIEF COMPLAINT BECAME THAT OF WEAK-
NESS AND NUMBNESS OF LOWER EXTREMITIES.

    . . . IT APPEARED TO BE A CASE OF ASTHMATIC BRONCHI-
TIS. . . . SHE DEVELOPED PERSISTENT VOMITING WHICH WAS NOT
CONTROLLED BY PROMAZINE BY MOUTH OR CHLORPROMAZINE [DRUGS
TO TREAT, AMONG OTHER THINGS, NAUSEA AND VOMITING]. . . .
VOMITING FINALLY REQUIRED ADMISSION.

    <u>FIRST HOSPITAL ADMISSION</u>: THE PATIENT WAS A YOUNG, WELL
DEVELOPED, THIN WOMAN APPEARING ACUTELY ILL . . . RETCHING
CONTINUALLY. SAVE FOR THE PROLONGED EXPIRATION AND SCANT
WHEEZES, THE PHYSICAL EXAMINATION WAS ENTIRELY UNREMARKABLE.

I'm not a doctor, but I've been assured it's well known that the symptoms of asthmatic bronchitis—shortness of breath, wheezing, coughing, tightness in the chest, and excess mucus production—do not typically include "retching continually" or "weakness and numbness of lower extremities." With the benefit of hindsight, Dr. Mercer would have done well to consider those particular symptoms in arriving at his diagnosis.

To her parents, Carol described her stay in the clinic with a pinch of humour.

> I am still not really all better as I lost about eight pounds and have to get my strength back but I think I'll live now. There was a period when I was afraid I wouldn't and then another when I was afraid I would.

Dr. Mercer reported that after three days of treatment, she was well enough to go home, which she did on Saturday, May 9.

It's unclear how long George stayed in Uruguay with Granny during Carol's illness. In her letter to her parents about this first episode, Carol didn't mention his presence at all, saying only, "George and Mother had quite a nice time in Uruguay and all that, which she will tell you about."

She ended her letter with words that now seem prophetic: "Again I'm sorry to have been so long in writing but things, as I've said, have not been quite right."

BACK AT HOME, according to Dr. Mercer's report, Carol remained "asymptomatic" for six weeks, except for two days at first of vomiting and a chronic cough.

Granny sailed for New York on May 18. Carol explained to her parents that she couldn't send much in the way of presents home to Canada with her mother-in-law: her luggage was already stuffed with a fur coat she'd bought for Aunt Katherine. I guess the family trust was in pretty good shape after all.

Later, Carol wrote to Granny about what happened after we saw her off on the boat.

> You know you just about broke Dougie's heart when you left. He has never quite gotten over the fact that you left _him_. We drove the car out to the last pier and watched you sail away. Poor Doug started to cry and then came the heart-breaking wail, "She's gone." Next thing we knew we were all crying. That old saying "It hurts the ones you leave behind most," is so true.

Contrary to Dr. Mercer's statement that she was "asymptomatic," Carol experienced some new complications at the end of May. She wrote to her parents about the remedies the doctor prescribed.

About a tonic for me. The doctor gave me several different types of drugs and I got all sick and funny. My face swelled, then my tummy, then my feet. So I stopped taking everything. I am still not better. My feet are sort of numb and tingling and I wheeze. I spent four days in bed last week. I get so tired of it. It is sort of depressing to be sick.

Along with the wheezing, there was now the troubling numbness in her feet. Whatever medications the doctor was prescribing, they weren't alleviating those symptoms, so Carol stopped taking all drugs. It isn't clear whether this was the doctor's decision or Carol's own—if the latter, it would indicate limited confidence in her doctor.

Carol wouldn't report any further trouble until mid-June. In the meantime, life resumed at full pace. Despite having been sick the previous week, she mustered the strength to rejoin the social whirl and even enjoyed herself.

Last Monday we went to the Colon. Full dress. 25 of May. Big Day. I wore my pink dress, pearls, long white gloves, new bag you gave me for Xmas. María did my hair (as usual). She put it up at the back like a pony tail only the tail was five thick ringlets. I wore a very big black velvet bow on top. Of course I have to change my facial expression to match my hairdo. Sweet and niave [sic] or smart and sofistacated [sic].... It is fun when you have long hair. You can do so much with it. María is always fiddling around with new ways. She is very much like you. "Get your slippers on, button up your coat." "Have you got everything?" "Oh here's your perfume, dab a little on later." "No, you look just fine, I like [it] like that, I don't care what the Señor says..." We have a very good box with the Krapfs and the Crockers. It was the National Anthem and a short ballet by Bizet and then a long ballet by Ravel. It was excellent and such fun to see everyone in their finest

gowns and jewels. We had coffee and cognac at intermission and saw
all our friends. Afterwards we went to a French restaurant and had
dinner. This was at one o'clock in the morning.

Carol clearly enjoyed expressing her feminine side and being admired
for her beauty and flair for fashion.

A week ago Mr. and Mrs. Beaulne [of the Canadian embassy] had a
formal dinner for the Irish Minister and his wife who are leaving. It
was a lovely party. I wore my white lace and María did my hair in
ringlets and I made that piece of red velvet you gave me years ago into
a bow. . . . I made quite a sensation. (Don't read this out loud to
anyone. It wouldn't sound very nice. But you know what I mean).

George was busier than ever, as Carol wrote to her parents on June 1.

You have faint hope of hearing from George. If his Mom hears from
him every two months she's lucky. I will work on him though. He is
terribly busy at the office. And we go out so much. This week we will
be out every night.

Carol even felt well enough to spend a weekend 185 miles south of
Buenos Aires at the estancia (cattle ranch) of Peter (Pedro) and Bibi
Fischer, owners of the Ola bathing suit company, whose fashion show
they'd attended. The Fischers were a handsome thirty-something
couple with lots of money, and George and Carol had hit it off with
them. Peter and his brother Chico (some expats took local nick-
names) were German—"pre-war German," as Carol was careful to
note in a letter to her parents. It was still the post-war era, after all, and
this was Argentina. Bibi was Danish, tall, and svelte. She and Peter
both spoke perfect English.

They have a lovely 1959 four seater MacCaulay [sic]. I flew for most of the way. It is great fun and very easy.... I really can't explain it very well, but I have the most wonderful feeling of freedom in the country and for the first two or three days after I get back to the city I feel so frustrated and hemmed in.... We rode all afternoon and then went in when the sun went down and had dinner. George and Pedro played chess and the rest of us played bridge.... We had breakfast [the next morning] and then went off to the other estancia (they have 2) to see the cows.

Carol had clearly recovered somewhat.

As usual, she remembered to mention us kids in her letter home.

Julia ... is so cute and sweet and María just adores her. She always takes her with her on her day off.... The boys are getting along very well in school, but they have a terrific amount of homework. They have a tutor who comes three times a week for two hours.

Life in general was busy again. Carol wrote on June 10, wishing Grandpa a happy Father's Day.

We do hope you have a lovely day and I wish I could be with you. I love you very much.

Things are hopping around here as usual. We are terribly busy at this time of year. Last Saturday we went to a very nice dance at the Club. There are only two other English couples in the Club. The rest are German or Argentine.

This was the Club Hípico. It was in San Isidro, an upscale suburb just west of Acassuso, and only a ten-minute drive from our house. I have a letter from the club accepting Carol's application for membership, dated April 13, 1959, and written in the flowery Spanish prevalent at the time. I also have the club's activity booklet from 1959, complete with local advertising, including an ad for Ola bathing suits, the Fischers' company. Mom loved to ride so much that she wanted us kids to learn; she took us on Sundays for lessons. She loved wearing her riding breeches with the brown stripes on the sides and her dark-brown leather riding boots.

My own memories of Club Hípico are mixed, largely because of an accident I had there. On a visit in April 1959, I fell, fracturing my arm. Mom took me to the British Hospital of Buenos Aires, where the arm was set in a cast. A few months later, I was taken to the same hospital for some tests, and the following year I went there a third time, to have my tonsils removed. The British Hospital was a sizable and highly regarded institution, founded more than a century earlier. It would also play a part in my family's story.

MOM STARTED VOMITING again around June 12. She spent most days in her bedroom with the door closed, and we didn't see her very much. Sometimes, I could hear her retching in the bathroom. This was upsetting for us, so María kept us away from Mom most of the time.

I had no idea what was happening. I just felt bewildered. I worried vaguely, but had no real conception of what mortal illness was, or how serious her condition might be. I still had a child's faith that everything would turn out all right. María's job was to keep us distracted, which she did very well. She didn't try to explain what was wrong with Mom—she didn't know herself. I'm sure Mom simply didn't want us to worry, didn't want us to see her in that condition. I can understand her desire to protect us.

Then she got even sicker. Her vomiting went on for almost a week. Dr. Mercer recorded the circumstances in his clinical record.

IN MID-JUNE THE PATIENT AGAIN DEVELOPED VOMITING. SEEN AT
HOME, NO CAUSE COULD BE FOUND FOR THE DISTURBANCE. . . .
TREATMENT WAS ATTEMPTED AT HOME ON THE BASIS OF THE PREVI-
OUS EXPERIENCE AND IT WAS THOUGHT THAT THERE WAS PROBABLY
A VERY LARGE PSYCHO-NEUROTIC COMPONENT TO THE PICTURE. . . .
RE-ADMISSION WAS THEN REQUESTED THOUGH RESISTED BY THE PATIENT.

It's not clear who requested Carol's readmission to the clinic, and Dr. Mercer's account doesn't say why she resisted going back there. Perhaps she lacked confidence in him and wanted to be treated elsewhere. Although he failed to record the exact date of Carol's readmission, or even the name of the hospital, her letter home said it was June 17 when she was "again taken to Little Co. of Mary."

La Pequeña Compañía de María, a small hospital founded only six years earlier, in 1953, already had a very interesting history. In 1955, Adolf Eichmann, the infamous Nazi war criminal who found refuge in Argentina after the war, and his wife, Veronika (Vera) Liebl, had their son delivered at the clinic. The story is recounted in *Eichmann before Jerusalem: The Unexamined Life of a Mass Murderer,* by German philosopher and historian Bettina Stangneth.

> *Vera Liebl gave birth to her son in November 1955, in the Pequeña Compañía Maria [sic], a Catholic hospital in Buenos Aires. "I was not officially allowed to claim my son as my own, as I was not officially married to my wife," Eichmann explained later, as if it were not clear to everyone that the missing marriage certificate could never have been the reason. Astonishingly, the nurses referred to the child quite openly as "Baby Eichmann," but it would still have been careless to register the birth under this well-known name. Eichmann's son was registered as Vera Liebl's illegitimate child and was given his father's pseudonym [Ricardo Klement], plus a middle name that was a tribute to the priest in Genoa who made this "triumph" possible: Ricardo Francisco.*

It's apparent that the clinic was war-criminal-friendly and had a flexible attitude toward record keeping. This was in a nation that, under Juan Perón and his cronies, had encouraged and protected Nazi escape pipelines and support groups in collaboration with the Roman Catholic Church. In 1975, the clinic would be taken over by a German order of nuns, Las Hermanas de María de Schoenstatt, and given a new name, Mater Dei (Mother of God). With a former client like Adolf Eichmann, what clinic wouldn't want to change its name?

It's distinctly odd that my mother was sent back there for treatment of a serious and baffling condition—especially when a larger, more established, and reputable institution, the British Hospital, was available. Since I'd been sent there previously, the British Hospital was well known to our family, as it was throughout the expatriate community in Buenos Aires. And since Dr. Mercer's treatment of Carol at the clinic had been conspicuously unsuccessful, it would have made a lot of sense to send her to a different doctor. Who, then, sent her back to Dr. Mercer—evidently against her will? There seems little doubt it was George: in those circumstances, and in that time and place, husbands were generally considered to have authority over their wives' health care.

On first reading Dr. Mercer's report, I assumed Carol simply hadn't wanted to return to hospital. Now, having read her descriptions of the doctor's ineffective treatment, I believe she didn't want to return to *that* hospital. If it was the clinic that had delivered "Baby Eichmann" and registered the birth under a false name, who could blame her? Carol may or may not have known about Baby Eichmann, but she could easily have heard the story. According to Stangneth's book, the nurses and doctors at the clinic knew all about the baby's parentage, and Carol got to know the nurses very well. She also got to know members of the well-heeled German community of Buenos Aires, where the Eichmanns and their fellow Nazi fugitives, such as the notorious Auschwitz doctor Josef Mengele, moved freely under false identities.

It's now well documented that the Eichmanns' presence was known to scores of people, including Western intelligence agencies. Eichmann, alias Klement, even worked for the German automaker Mercedes-Benz in Buenos Aires, where he rose to become a department head. A year after Carol's treatment at La Pequeña Compañía de María, Eichmann was abducted by Mossad agents on a Buenos Aires street and spirited away to Israel, where he was put on trial, convicted of numerous crimes against humanity, and executed.

Dr. Mercer described Carol's second hospital admission: "Physical examination this time revealed an acutely ill young woman with dry, parched mucosae, dry skin, somnolent and complaining of thirst." After recording her vital signs, Mercer focused on her personal life.

AT THIS TIME A PAST HISTORY AND FAMILY HISTORY WAS OBTAINED WHICH REVEALED THAT THE PATIENT WAS BORN IN CANADA, AN ONLY CHILD, DEVELOPED NORMALLY, MARRIED AND LEFT HOME AT 15, FIRST PREGNANCY AT 17. THIRD PREGNANCY LED TO LONG AND PAINFUL LABOUR AFTER WHICH SHE HAD A "NERVOUS BREAKDOWN." THIS CONSISTED OF TIREDNESS, LACK OF INTEREST IN HER SURROUNDINGS AND HER FAMILY AND CAME AT A TIME WHEN SHE WAS SUBJECTED TO SEVERAL OTHER EMOTIONAL STRESSES IN THE FAMILY.

It is possible that Carol fibbed about her age at the time of her first pregnancy, which was fifteen, not seventeen, because she felt embarrassed about it, as anyone might understand. On the other hand, maybe it wasn't Carol who told this story. Dr. Mercer didn't say who gave him the information. It was commonplace in those days, especially in Latin countries, for doctors to consult privately with the husband about his wife's medical case, and indeed Dr. Mercer did just that, as he wrote later in his report. I don't know how Dr. Mercer interpreted Carol's "nervous breakdown" (his quotation marks) after her third pregnancy, but as his clinical record shows, he was now firmly focused on a psychosomatic explanation for her illness.

Dr. Mercer touched on Carol's relevant symptomatic history and potential causes of her sickness, only to dismiss them in the same breath.

NEVER DURING PREGNANCIES OR OTHER MILD ILLNESSES HAD SHE
REACTED BY VOMITING. SHE WAS IN THE HABIT OF DRINKING ONE
ALCOHOLIC DRINK DAILY OR LESS, NO DRUG INTAKE OR EXPOSURE TO
TOXINS. OTHERWISE THE PAST HISTORY WAS UNREMARKABLE. SYSTEM
REVIEW WAS UNREMARKABLE AND UP TO THE TIME OF HER ASTHMATIC
BRONCHITIS SHE WAS WELL.

Evidently, Dr. Mercer had raised the possibility with Carol that she'd been exposed to toxic substances—that is, poisons. But his report referred to it in cursory fashion, apparently accepting at face value her or someone else's statement that she'd had no exposure. Having thus eliminated that diagnostic possibility, he didn't bother testing for the presence of toxins in her system. But what if the patient were unaware of what she'd been ingesting?

Dr. Mercer reported that Carol's earlier physical symptoms kept reappearing.

HOSPITAL COURSE: ON THE FIRST DAY THE PATIENT . . . COM-
PLAINED OF . . . PARASTHESIAE [ABNORMAL PRICKLING OR TIN-
GLING] OF TOES OF BOTH FEET. ON THE THIRD DAY, PARASTHESIAS
AND NUMBNESS OF BOTH LEGS. . . . ON THE FOURTH DAY, SHE
COMPLAINED OF WEAKNESS OF LEGS BUT MUSCLE EXAM OF ALL GROUPS
GAVE 5 + STRENGTH. SENSORY EXAMINATION WAS VERY DIFFICULT TO
EVALUATE. THERE SEEMED TO BE A NEUROTIC ELEMENT WHICH CON-
FUSED THE EXAMINATION.

This examination was indeed confused, as the final outcome would show. Though Dr. Mercer persisted in interpreting Carol's symptoms as neurotic, it would soon become clear that neurosis had little or nothing to do with it.

ON THE SEVENTH DAY, SHE COMPLAINED OF BEING UNABLE TO WALK, BUT DID SO WITH SHUFFLING GAIT DRAGGING BOTH FEET FLAT ON THE FLOOR. THE NEXT DAY SHE COMPLAINED OF LOW ABDOMINAL PAIN, CRAMP-LIKE AND COMPARED TO LABOUR PAINS. . . . ON THE NINTH DAY, THE ABDOMINAL PAIN INCREASED AND PREVENTED SLEEP AND NO MEDICATION SEEMED TO PROVIDE RELIEF INCLUDING OPI- ATES, THOUGH IT WAS NOTICED THAT THE PATIENT FELT WORSE WHEN LEFT ALONE. . . . ON SUBSEQUENT DAYS THE PAIN WAS REFERRED TO THE UPPER ABDOMEN AND THE PATIENT WAS CONCERNED BECAUSE THE PAINS WERE PROGRESSING "UP" AND THAT THE SENSORY LEG CHANGES WERE PROGRESSING PROXIMALLY [NEARER TO THE PAIN'S POINT OF ORIGIN].

The cramps, resembling labour pains, became so severe that Carol required opiates, yet Dr. Mercer continued to focus on her personal history.

ONE NIGHT AFTER A LONG CONVERSATION WITH THE PATIENT WE WERE ABLE TO DISCOVER A STRONG DEPENDENCY ON MOTHER AND LOCAL NURSEMAID WITH A GUILT COMPLEX TOWARDS HER PARENTS. THAT NIGHT THE PAIN IMPROVED REMARKABLY AND REQUIRED NO MEDICATION.

It shouldn't have been surprising that Carol had feelings of depen- dency toward her mother and María—especially at a time when she was seriously ill and her doctor couldn't tell her why. Dr. Mercer, nevertheless, seemed to be fixated on this observation, whether it came from Carol or George, and so pursued his line of inquiry.

WHEN THE STRONG HYSTERICAL COMPONENT SUGGESTED THAT A NEURO-
PSCHYATRIST [SIC] SHOULD BE CONSULTED, THE HUSBAND REQUESTED
A CONSULTATION WITH ANOTHER INTERNIST AND THE PATIENT WAS
SEEN BY DR. RAUL KELLY, WHO . . . SUGGESTED AMONGST OTHER
THINGS THE POSSIBILITY OF COLLAGEN DISEASE.

Although George at first resisted the doctor's recommendation of consulting a psychiatrist, eventually Dr. Mercer had his way.

FINALLY NEURO-PSCHYATRIC [SIC] CONSULTATION WAS REQUESTED
AND DR. INSUA FELT THERE WAS A HYSTERICAL HYPER-REACTION TO
THE SYMPTOMS.

Although he had difficulty spelling *psychiatrist* and *psychiatric*, Dr. Mercer's preoccupation with neurosis as an underlying condition was remarkable, especially since he wasn't a psychiatrist himself. In 1959, the stereotype of the "hysterical woman" exhibiting neurotic psychosomatic behaviour was very much alive. In Carol's treatment, it created a pernicious distraction from a serious investigation of her physical symptoms and their causes—an omission that would turn out to be fatal.

More recently, I've received a professional medical opinion that the progression of my mother's neurological symptoms, together with her persistent vomiting, should have indicated the true cause of her illness—a diagnosis that was sidetracked by the preoccupation with hysteria. That opinion is disturbing enough. An alternative possibility, that Dr. Mercer actually knew what he was doing and deliberately created a distraction from the truth, would be even more disturbing, but there is no evidence of that. A third possibility, and my personal view, is that Dr. Mercer, however misguided, tried to do his best, however inadequately, with a case totally unfamiliar to him.

Carol wrote a much more down-to-earth account of her hospital treatment in a letter to Granny dated Monday, June 21, 1959. First, she apologized to her mother-in-law for her handwriting: "I can see how bad my writing is and I do hope you will forgive me. I have been sick but I am getting better." Her handwriting, which by the last page of the letter started to resemble a childlike scrawl, would soon get even worse.

> *Last Saturday I started that terrible vomiting again. That went on steadily until Thursday night when I was again taken to Little Co of Mary.... I have been getting mass doses of iron, penicillin (which causes my face to swell) and blood transfusions along with injections for stopping the vomiting. All in all I am a bit of a mess. But I am on the way up now at least. I don't know how long I will have to stay in the hospital. The doctor won't commit himself.*

Almost none of this detail was mentioned in Dr. Mercer's clinical record. At least Carol herself didn't pull any punches when describing what was happening to her. Evidently, she wasn't worried about upsetting Granny with the truth, as she had been a year earlier after her accident with the horse cart.

She ended the letter by writing, as usual, about others rather than herself.

> *George took Jeffrey to the ... concert last Wednesday. It was Beethoven's 2nd and 6th symphonies.... It didn't start until ten and I thought he would fall asleep. But no he enjoyed it thoroughly. He was telling me all about it and he blushed and said, "You know Mummy, Mr. and Mrs. Krapf invited us out to eat after." I asked him what he had had. "I ordered tomato soup and ice cream." Isn't that Jeff for you, tomato soup. It is a wonder he hasn't got it coming out of his ears.*

With Mom in hospital, Dad had an extra ticket to the concerts at the Teatro Colón, so he took me along. It was arranged that Doug and I would go to bed, as usual; then Doug would fall asleep, I would get up and dress in a jacket and tie, and Dad and I would go off to the concert. Like most cultural and social events in Argentina, it began and ended late. The after-concert dinner started around one o'clock in the morning. I don't know how I managed to stay awake through school the next day, but I did.

Carol finished her letter to Granny by saying George had to put it in the mail: "Well, George is going to mail this now, so good bye. All my love, Carol."

She also wrote to her parents from her hospital bed that same day, June 21. She thanked them for a parcel they'd sent to the house, which George had brought to the hospital after work: "It was so much fun opening it up."

Carol's handwriting looked more than ever like a child's: "My writing is so bad cause I can barely move my fingers and I am holding onto the pen like grim death."

Once again, she made the brave declaration "I have been sick but I am getting better now."

> I was sick every day (all day) for six days and I was so worn out and dehydrated that here I am [in the clinic], back again.... At first they thought I had virus pneumonia, but when they got all through the tests they found it was a rare case of fungi (yes I know, now you can call me Moldy Milly) of the lungs. It produces the spasms of the pylorax [she was referring to the pylorus, a valve in the stomach] and also is [a]ffecting the nerves in my feet and legs and my hands.

Strangely enough, next to nothing of this diagnosis of lung trouble was mentioned in Dr. Mercer's clinical record. It seems, however, that the medical staff were trying everything on Carol, no matter how painful. She didn't spare her parents the graphic details.

> I have been getting up to five injections a day in the hips, intraveno[u]s blood transfusions, pills and I really feel as if I had the book thrown at me. My backside looks like a sieve. It's so bad that the nurses spend ten minutes just looking for an unjabbed space. Not only that but the weather's lousy too....
>
> ... Well now you know. I won't say "It's not serious" (said with a high pitched voice) because I wouldn't be wearing the skin off my fanny in the hospital if it were a common cold. I have lost 10 lbs and do I look like the perennial bean pole.

She insisted that she was, nevertheless, on the mend.

> I have one of the best doctors (Anglo Argentine, studied at J. Hopkins for 3 yrs) and I am in the best private hospital in the country. I am responding well to treatment and although it is going to be an uphill march for some time, I am well on my way to recovery.

She closed with a reassuring dash of humour.

> Please please, do not get upset or worry, because I'm not. In fact when you think of it I feel fairly smart to have sumpin rare-like. You always said "Now don't be common." Does this meet with parental approval.
>   All my dearest love, Carol

Despite her natural inclination not to worry her parents, Carol was quite open about her condition. Later, George would claim she'd wanted to spare her parents the knowledge of what was happening to her—but if her letters are any guide, that was untrue.

CAROL'S LETTERS HOME sometimes went by embassy pouch, by far the fastest method, and sometimes by regular post, which in those days meant surface mail, unless marked "airmail." From the hospital, she'd told George's mother that George was mailing her letter for her. Grandma and Grandpa received her June 21 letter two weeks later, on July 5, 1959. Why did it take two weeks to reach Toronto instead of one, as it normally did, when the subject matter was so urgent? From the envelope with stamps but no airmail label I can see George must have put the letter in the slower regular mail, probably because he didn't want Grandma and Grandpa to become immediately disturbed and involved in Carol's sickness, which he knew would be the result of her letter. His solution, short of not sending the letter at all, was to delay its delivery.

Naturally, Grandma *was* upset by Carol's news. The day they got her letter, Grandma sent both an overnight cable and a letter, clearly by airmail, because Carol received it on July 8, three days after it was mailed from Toronto. While Grandma tried to be as upbeat as possible, she didn't disguise her alarm: "We were shocked to hear you were back in hospital, after being there before. . . . We are both so distressed with the second bout of illness."

What parents wouldn't be shocked? And what parents wouldn't want to take action immediately? Grandma prepared a passport application and had a passport photo taken, stamped on the back "July 21, 1959." She began looking into reserving a plane ticket to Argentina. They couldn't really afford the trip, but they were too disturbed by Carol's condition to worry about the expense.

Grandma and Grandpa took another step, one that would turn out to be highly consequential: they contacted George's employer, the Department of Trade and Commerce, in Ottawa. They wanted to alert his superiors to what was happening to their daughter, and ask them to ensure that everything possible be done to help her.

In Carol's reply, on July 8, the same day she received Grandma's letter, she asked about the inquiry her parents had made to the department.

> *I would be interested to know if it was you that informed Ottawa of my being sick. We got a long telegram demanding to know what exactly I had. This upset Mr. Bissett no end because he was about the only person we knew that hadn't bothered to inquire about me. . . . The fact that I was sick wasn't what bothered the B. But he had to go to the trouble of asking George and letting Ottawa know. That was work and believe me that guy never does any more than the absolute minimum in that line.*

From my experience in the foreign service, I'm certain it wasn't just the work involved that bothered George's boss. My grandparents had expressed their worries to the department in no uncertain terms. Apparently, the department had passed those concerns along to the embassy in "a long telegram." Bissett was upset that headquarters had caught him unaware of an important personnel matter in his own shop. He was expected to know about an illness as serious as Carol Blackstock's and to inform Ambassador Bower and his bosses in Ottawa so that, among other things, they wouldn't be blindsided by a complaint from the public. What's more, the telegram from HQ would have come to Bissett through the ambassador, who would not have been pleased with his subordinate.

No doubt the telegram from Ottawa jolted Ambassador Bower into realizing just how serious Carol's condition was, creating a real concern about her. Carol was popular with George's colleagues, and they would have wanted to know how ill she was. Embassies are, or certainly used to be, close-knit communities. In a workplace setting in Canada, Carol's illness might have been considered a private matter, but in the context of the embassy "family," it was everyone's concern.

George would not have been happy either. In all likelihood, he was annoyed that his parents-in-law had gone behind his back to his superiors, causing a disturbance at the embassy and embarrassing him and his boss.

So why hadn't George let Bissett know about his wife's illness? It was naturally the kind of thing you told your boss about, if only to explain why your mind might be on things other than work.

Carol was still in the hospital when she replied to her parents on July 8. This was the last of her letters that we could find. Unlike her other recent correspondence, it was typewritten, suggesting that the nerve trouble in her hands was making writing by hand difficult. Her spelling had deteriorated as well, as evident in the excerpts below. But she was definitely feeling more upbeat and hopeful.

> I am making excellent progress and the doctor says that I can come out of the hospital in a very few days. You will also be pleased to hear that my behind is looking much less like a pin cushion as I only get one injection a day. They have done just about everything they could think of and have samples of everything I could offer up. The only thing they haven't done is [s]queeze my head to see if my brains will come out my ears.

Her description of all the action in Room 219 shows she was back in her element, attracting people and making friends.

> I never realized just how many friends I had until I found myself stuck in here. Never has a day passed that I haven't had at least two or three friends come and vosit me. They have loaded me up woth flowers and candies and generally made life as pleasant as possible. The Sisters and the nurses here are all without exception very kind and sweet. There is always laughter in 219 to the point that other patients have inquired as to where the party is. The young ones phone there

[sic] boyfriends from my room and the night girls borrow my maga-
zines and books. I even have a nurse who can sneak in a game of
canasta between bells.

She was now able to get around in the clinic, albeit in a wheelchair, unlike a fellow patient confined to bed, who aroused her sympathy.

There is an American chap down the hall . . . here with Hepatitis and
is yellow all over. . . . He is a good head and we console each other by
trading books and jokes. He has two or three weeks more flat on his
back. Boy that would really be tough. At least I am mobile, even if it
is on wheels.

María was doing a lot to support Carol and help her recover.

María has been her usual wonderful, loving self. She is spoiling me so
terribly that it will take me years to get back to normal. She comes
every morning, does my hair, fixes my nails, jokes and tells me all the
news. . . . The nurses all tease me about how spoiled I am, but María
just laughs and calls me her baby. The doctor says she is twice as good
for me as any medicine he could recommend. You know in one way we
lead a very funny artificial life and although I have lots of very good
friends, María is really my only confidante.

María was taking care of us at home: "Today the kids started a three-week winter vacation. María has all kinds of plans for them. The zoo and the circus, riding and movies." She also went to the hospital every day to see Mom, leaving Cristina to mind Julie, so she was happy to let Doug and me visit playmates.

I had grown more independent. My Spanish had become pretty fluent. I taught some English to the fifteen-year-old gardener's helper at the enormous estate across the street. He in turn shared his racy stories about chasing girls in Buenos Aires. Doug, too young to have a bicycle yet, couldn't come with me on excursions around the neighbourhood, but he did come along when I went to visit our American friends Michael and Danny McKenney down the street. We played baseball in their front yard.

Sometimes, we went to Freddy Brander's house, only a block away. Freddy's dad was Swedish and worked for Caterpillar; his mom was from California. They had a big tiled in-ground pool, but during the time Mom was in the clinic it was too chilly to swim, so we played in the yard instead. We were just happy to get out of the house—it wasn't fun being at home when Mom wasn't there because she was so sick.

On July 9, Carol added several paragraphs to her July 8 letter, beginning with the fact that it was Argentina's national holiday: "George is taking everyone downtown to see the big parade and then they are going to come and visit me afterwards."

It strikes me as strange that while she was sick, this was one of the very few times Carol mentioned George in her letters—apart from his taking me to the opera and bringing her a parcel at the hospital. She never described him helping to look after her during her illness while she was in the clinic.

After nearly two single-spaced pages, she responded to her parents' concerns about her health. Even here, she sounded upbeat, to the point of having an eye for the young consulting doctors who examined her.

You wanted to know if this lung trouble was caused by my kidneys. . . .
Four consulting doctors have been called in (three quite young and
handsome) and they have all agreed on what I have. I had a fungi
grow on the lung which has now been cleared up. My blood count is
up to normal and all that is needed now is time. Time to get my
strength back. The muscles of my legs and hands are very weak. I am

very thin. BUT, I am better and there is not the slightest doubt in
anyone's mind that I will not be back to normal in a few weeks time.
There is not a thing to worry about.

She was heartened that the young doctors all agreed on her diagnosis—even if it was the wrong one.

We can assume that Carol's use of the double negative in her
second-last sentence above was unintentional. The truth was, however, her condition was getting worse. Reading this letter must have
left my grandparents with many more questions, but they would
remain unanswered. The lively chatter of correspondence between
daughter and parents fell abruptly silent.

AT LAST, AROUND July 12, 1959, as closely as I can tell (the clinical
record provides no date), Dr. Mercer decided Carol had recovered
enough to be discharged from the clinic: "As the patient was left with
the weakness as the only symptom and all other conditions had
cleared it was decided to send her to continue rehabilitation at home."

So Carol went home again.

But the disturbingly familiar conditions of her sickness quickly
reappeared. In Dr. Mercer's final observation in the clinical record,
which he signed on July 17, he notes that "at home," less than a week
after she left the clinic, "Mrs. Blackstock has shown slight progression of the polyneuritis."

"Polyneuritis" was the doctor's last diagnostic word before he
went on to summarize Carol's physical condition in terms of her
medical test results. Polyneuritis is synonymous with polyneuropathy, a condition characterized by damage to multiple peripheral
nerves that run throughout the body. Symptoms of polyneuropathy
include tingling or burning feelings on the skin and ascending weakness, numbness, and paralysis, starting in the feet, legs, and hands,

causing difficulty walking. Causes can include, among other things, autoimmune disorders, cancer, certain pharmaceuticals, and toxins.

My mother was a slim woman to begin with. I reckon (the clinical record doesn't say) that her normal weight was 110 to 115 pounds. By the time she went home, as Dr. Mercer noted near the end of his report, she'd lost twenty-five pounds. This would have put her at about ninety pounds. No wonder she looked like just skin and bones. Then Mercer added an ominous detail: "Today she has again started vomiting."

Years later, Julie and I learned—from Dad himself—that Dwight Fulford, his closest embassy colleague, had implored him to call in another physician on Mom's case. "For God's sake, George," he'd said, "it's your wife's life we're talking about!" But Dad resisted the idea, saying that Mercer had threatened to drop the case if he consulted another doctor. This raises an unavoidable question: Since it was clear to anyone, even outside the family, that Mercer had been completely unsuccessful treating Mom, why didn't Dad seek an independent second opinion, perhaps at the British Hospital?

Dr. Mercer's diagnosis survives to this day. I recently had a search done of the records of La Pequeña Compañía de María. The local consultant conducting the search was turned away many times, but after persisting with the plea that, since the Eichmann records had been found, there must be documents for Carol, she was finally allowed to see a handwritten registry book kept by the nuns who had worked at the clinic. There was the name "Carol Blackstock," inscribed as having been admitted on June 18, 1959. (I cannot reconcile the one-day discrepancy between this date and Carol's account that she was admitted on June 17.) Her parents' names were recorded, but not her husband's. The stated reason for admission was "neurosis histerica" (hysterical neurosis).

With Carol's relapse, Dr. Mercer himself finally admitted failure. He decided to hand off the case. In his clinical record, he made his final recommendation: "Under these conditions it is considered advisable to refer her to Canada and particularly to a neurological or medical service in a university hospital for rehabilitation and/or further diagnostic work-up."

No more psychological theories. There was little choice but to return her to Canada.

I realize now that, for my mother, the house where we lived in Buenos Aires was a death trap.

6

THE LAST GOODBYE

I REMEMBER THE morning we saw Mom in her bedroom. It was July 21, 1959. By then, seeing her at all had become a rare event. For weeks, she'd either been in hospital, away on trips with Dad, or sick in her bed at home. When she was in her bedroom, the door was closed nearly all the time. She only came out to go to the bathroom, where we would hear her vomiting.

Occasionally, we'd catch a glimpse of her as doctors, nurses, and maids scurried in and out of the bedroom. It was winter in Argentina, so we were at school for most of the day. On weekends, María and Martín would take us to their house, still under construction, in Boulogne, or on excursions elsewhere.

Mom was sleeping a lot, and when she wasn't I imagine she didn't want us to see her looking so sick. Beyond that, we really didn't know what was happening. Dad never took us aside to explain what Mom was going through. And probably that was her intention: to mini- mize disruption and worry for us. María was obviously part of the plan, helping out by keeping us occupied away from the house. So when she took Doug and me to see Mom in her bedroom that day, it felt like a visit to the queen.

It was a Tuesday, and María had wakened us a little earlier than normal. Doug and I got ready for school as usual. We put on our uniforms, then went downstairs to the kitchen for breakfast, toast with *dulce de leche*, a popular sweet spread we liked. María, who was keeping her eye on the clock, told us to hurry up, so we could see Mom before we went to school. I thought this was odd. Lately, we'd been leaving in the morning without seeing her.

María motioned to us to go upstairs, leaving Julie in the kitchen with Cristina, who was preparing her breakfast. María would take Julie up later to give Mom a kiss before putting her on the bus for school.

Upstairs, María had us wait in the hall while she entered Mom's bedroom, knocking first. Doug and I looked at each other. We wondered what was going on but said nothing. Maybe Mom was upset with us; she could be quite strict. She didn't put up with a lot of nonsense, and if we misbehaved seriously, she sometimes gave us a spanking. Maybe we'd done something wrong. Or maybe Mrs. Toppie had told Mom that I'd said "*Ya viene la vieja*" ("Here comes the old lady") to Doug when I saw her approaching the house. Doug, the little troublemaker, had repeated it to her, eliciting a scolding for me from our tutor.

María came out to usher us into the room. We entered timidly. There was Mom, sitting up in the enormous bed, propped up on pillows. I was shocked by how wretched she looked. She'd become severely emaciated with all the vomiting. She was so skinny in her nightgown, it was scary to look at her. Mom had always been a beautiful woman, with rich, wavy, shoulder-length black hair and perfect features; now her skin was sallow and her eyes bloodshot, with dark, deep-set rings under them. Her twenty-four-year-old face was lined from all the pain and exhaustion she'd suffered. There was something else in her expression too—a look of shell shock.

I noticed the pill bottles that had sat on her dressing table for weeks had been replaced by the mysterious coloured cut-glass vials of perfume we always used to see. Mom wanted to put the best possible face on this.

"Hi, boys," she said, in as cheerful a voice as she could muster. "Come sit here with Mummy."

She beckoned to us with one hand. Doug and I stood silently, as though nailed to the floor. We looked at each other, then moved haltingly toward the bedside, guided by María, who helped us up onto the high bed beside Mom.

"I've been looking at some of the homework you've been doing with Mrs. Toppie," she said, flipping through our copybooks.

I began to think my fears about Mrs. Toppie were coming true. As a topic of conversation, she was a strange choice for Mom to open a cheerful chat with us. She knew we didn't like Mrs. Toppie.

"Did *you* do this, Douglas?" Mom asked, in a surprised but pleased tone, pointing at some sums he'd done in his copybook.

"Yes, Mummy," Doug replied with a dumbfounded expression.

"And did *you* do this, Jeffrey? That's wonderful."

"Yes, Mummy. Thank you." I wondered why the rote conjugation of some Spanish irregular verbs was so wonderful.

It was all very strange. We'd seen so little of Mom in the last while, and now all this fuss over our homework with Mrs. Toppie.

Mom coughed a little, clearing her throat. "Mummy and Daddy have to go on a trip to Canada for a little while. We want you boys to look after your sister and do what María says while we're away."

So this was the reason for the fuss about homework, I thought: to get us onside with an appeal for good behaviour in our parents' absence.

"Why are you going away, Mummy?" I asked. "When will you be back?"

We'd already been through some big upheavals during and after the move to Buenos Aires. We needed and wanted our parents to be around, and this trip back to Canada sounded worrisome.

"Daddy is taking Mummy to Canada to get her sickness looked after by the doctors. We'll be back soon."

"What's wrong with you? Why are you sick?"

"Well, we don't know exactly. That's why we have to go to Canada."

"When are you leaving and when are you coming back?" Doug said.

"We have to leave tonight."

"Tonight!"

"We'll be back as soon as we can. Come on, now—you need to leave for school. Give me a big hug before you go."

I imagine Mom, after we left her, looking up at María and sobbing quietly.

It was the last time I saw my mother.

7

DEATH IN MONTREAL

NINE DAYS HAD elapsed between Carol's release from the clinic and our sad goodbye at her bedside.

During that time, a frenzy of activity had taken place over what to do next. Dr. Mercer had recommended sending Carol home to Canada for treatment; George at last began keeping Ambassador Richard Bower informed about her condition; and Ambassador Bower, clearly seized by the urgency of the crisis, exchanged a flurry of anxious cables with Assistant Deputy Minister Leslie Brown in Ottawa.

At the time, I knew nothing of this, but the events can be reconstructed from George's notes and from correspondence, official documents, and medical reports, even though our father never told us his version of what happened.

In addition, I knew many of the principal actors well—my parents, grandparents, and other family members—and later became acquainted with others involved in Carol's story. I lived through some of the relevant circumstances during that time, particularly my mother's illness. I'm also familiar with the travel involved, the locations where my mother and father found themselves, and the government and foreign service culture in which George operated.

We know that a consensus had been reached that Carol's illness was extremely serious and it was imperative to return her to Canada. It isn't clear exactly who made the final decision. Embassy cables show that Carol's doctors, Ambassador Bower, and George all agreed that the long journey home was necessary. Meanwhile, in Ottawa, the Department of Trade and Commerce was feeling the pressure from Carol's parents to take action. Whether Carol herself was a part of the decision, the record doesn't show.

The trail of official correspondence begins with Ambassador Bower sending this cable to Ottawa on July 16, 1959.

MRS. BLACKSTOCK WHO IS SUFFERING FROM POLYRIDICULO NEURITIS OF UNDETERMINED CAUSE AND INVOLVING SEMI PARALYSIS OF HER EXTREMITIES IS MAKING NO APPARENT PROGRESS. LOCAL DOCTORS AFTER EXHAUSTING TREATMENT AND TESTS CAN THINK OF NOTHING FURTHER TO DO. I FEEL THAT THE DANGER OF PERMANENT IMPAIR-MENT IS SUFFICIENTLY GREAT THAT SHE SHOULD BE SENT TO CANADA IMMEDIATELY FOR TREATMENT. AS SHE CANNOT POSSIBLY TRAVEL UNATTENDED I HOPE DEPARTMENT WILL PAY AIR FARES FOR BLACK-STOCK AND WIFE TO MONTREAL AND RETURN. BLACKSTOCK ANXIOUS TO SEE HIS TERM OUT IN BA AND WOULD RETURN AFTER MAKING NECES-SARY ARRANGEMENTS FOR HIS WIFE IN CANADA. PLEASE ADVISE BY SOONEST CABLE.

BOWER DOMCAN

The cable called Mom's affliction "polyridiculo neuritis" instead of polyneuritis, the term used by Dr. Mercer. At first it appeared that somebody simply hadn't proofread the text properly—perhaps an indication of a frantic state of affairs at the embassy. The inclusion of "ridiculo" would not have been helpful in obtaining departmental approval for financial assistance, which was the cable's objective. Closer examination, however, reveals more than a spelling issue.

"Polyridiculo neuritis" is a misspelling of polyradiculoneuritis, a recognized disease commonly associated with Guillain-Barré syndrome. Apparently, someone had come up with this new diagnosis, although Carol's medical records never mention it. It's unlikely that someone was the ambassador, who signed off on the cable. Polyradiculoneuritis is defined in the *Miller-Keane Encyclopedia & Dictionary of Medicine, Nursing, & Allied Health,* Seventh Edition (2003), as "acute infectious polyneuritis that involves the peripheral nerves, the spinal nerve roots and the spinal cord." Such a diagnosis would have served the purposes of someone who wanted a serious, recognized diseased on the record, in case Carol never made it to Canada alive, a disease above suspicion, which could explain why she'd died. Moreover, if she really had an infectious disease, such as polyradiculoneuritis, Carol would not have been permitted to board the plane home.

There was also the peculiar assurance that "Blackstock anxious to see his term out in BA and would return after making necessary arrangements for his wife in Canada." This was evidently intended to support the appeal to the department to cover travel expenses. But if Carol was in great "danger of permanent impairment," why was it so important to George to see his term out? The reference to his returning to Buenos Aires after making arrangements for Carol suggested that he might simply leave her in Canada. This seems highly inappropriate, albeit with the benefit of hindsight.

Of course, we don't know who actually drafted the cable. It was authorized and signed by Ambassador Bower, but heads-of-post rarely drafted their own cables. It might have been written by George himself. Among his papers, we found his drafting notes for another cable that the ambassador sent a few days later.

Ambassador Bower received a reply from Brown the same day.

FOR RP BAUER [SIC] FROM LESLIE BROWN DISTURBED HERE MRS
BLACKSTOCK'S CONTINUED ILLNESS. WE CANNOT AUTHORIZE PAYMENT
OF TRAVELING EXPENSES IN ADVANCE BUT MUST SUBSEQUENTLY PROVE
HARDSHIP AND NEED FOR FINANCIAL ASSISTANCE BY DEPARTMENT.
BLACKSTOCK SHOULD THEREFORE USE HIS BEST JUDGEMENT AND IF HE
DECIDES [TO] UNDERTAKE JOURNEY WE WILL DO BEST IN SUPPORT OF
APPLICATION FOR FINANCIAL ASSISTANCE

                                                      COMCO

Ambassador Bower replied to Brown the next day in a personal letter, undoubtedly sent by diplomatic pouch.

> *Bartolomé Mitre 478,*
> *Buenos Aires, Argentina,*
> *July 17th, 1959.*
>
> *Personal*
>
> *Dear Les,*
> *Your prompt reply to my telegram about George Blackstock almost brought tears to my eyes as a reminder of Trade and Commerce effi-ciency. I am grateful to you and Johnny for the sympathy which I took from your reply.*

It's unclear why the reply should have almost brought tears to Bower's eyes when Brown's message was that the department wouldn't autho-rize the travel expenses in advance. Brown had expressed his sympa-thy, but mere sympathy wasn't much practical help right then. Canadian foreign service alumni will know that "Johnny" was John

English, then deputy minister of the Department of Trade and Commerce, and Brown's immediate superior.

Ambassador Bower's letter stated the rationale for taking Carol back to Canada.

> *George's problem is a difficult one but his decision to go to Canada with his wife is exactly what I would have done had I been in his position. I think you would have done the same. His wife is obviously very ill. The consensus here is that unless there is a change for the better soon she may not recover.*

I think anyone would interpret Bower's avowal that "she may not recover" as meaning she might die. He went on to argue why George needed to take Carol to Montreal specifically.

> *George must do everything within his power to ensure his wife's recovery and he would never be satisfied that he left no stone unturned if he did not give her the benefit of the experience that is available in Montreal at the Neurological Institute and with Dr. Selye in these matters.*

The reference to Dr. Selye is especially puzzling. Dr. Hans Selye was a rising Montreal-based research scientist, an endocrinologist and author of pioneering studies of the effects of stress on the body and mind. Selye had published *The Stress of Life* in 1956, the first of his bestselling books that established him as a world-renowned expert on stress. Although trained as a medical doctor, he didn't treat patients; he was a researcher, and associated more closely with the Institute of Experimental Medicine and Surgery at the Université de Montréal than with the Montreal Neurological Institute. Carol Blackstock was a woman close to death, suffering from incessant vomiting and neurological collapse, yet it was proposed to send her 5,600 miles away to see a stress researcher. Who came up with that idea?

If not because of Dr. Selye, why *was* Montreal chosen as the place to take her? There were many excellent hospitals in Toronto and a family support network there. Not only that, Carol and George would have to stop in Toronto on the way to Montreal. That added a one-hour layover, as well as a change of aircraft and another hour and forty minutes of flying time, to an already long journey—brutally long for anyone in Carol's fragile condition. The unavoidable conclusion from the way things subsequently turned out is that Montreal was chosen primarily because it was *not* Toronto.

In his letter to Brown, Ambassador Bower addressed the question of financial assistance.

> *George does not have enough money for return passage to Canada and back for himself and his wife and I have no hesitation in providing him with the $2,000 for this purpose. I expect sooner or later I will get my money back but this is not my consideration. If the government should finally agree to reimburse him for the trip, I will probably be repaid quicker than would otherwise be the case. If not, I have complete confidence in George's ultimate settlement.*

This too was very strange—George borrowing money from his boss to pay for the airfares. His mother, who could afford a cruise, a two-month holiday in South America, and an expensive fur coat for her daughter, certainly had the means to give him the money. What's more, she had come to adore Carol and would have gladly paid for her emergency travel to obtain treatment. Two thousand dollars was a significant amount of money, worth around seventeen thousand dollars today. You can almost hear Bower, kindly and well-intentioned as he was, gulping as he told Brown about lending George such a large sum, while hoping the government would approve the expense so that he might recover it more quickly—even though he professed "complete confidence" that George would pay it back.

Bower may not have known that Granny could have advanced the money, but George certainly did. He could have phoned his mother in less time than it took Bower and Brown to exchange cables. Throughout his life, George never had difficulty asking Granny for money. Another unavoidable conclusion is that he didn't want to contact her, fearing she would alert Carol's parents, who would naturally want to be involved in their daughter's care. Maybe it was really Ambassador Bower who was anxious to leave "no stone unturned," and George who, by insisting on Montreal, was merely creating unnecessary hurdles by saying he didn't have the money for the airfare.

Apparently, little or none of this behind-the-scenes activity involved Carol herself. I can find no record of her expressing, or being asked about, her own wishes concerning these big decisions affecting her very survival. It must have been difficult for her to watch her life being taken over by other people.

According to the cable traffic between Buenos Aires and Ottawa, a nurse was needed "on doctor's orders" to accompany Carol and George on the trip to Canada. Ambulances needed to be booked. Admission to the hospital in Canada, the Montreal Neurological Institute, needed to be arranged. Canadian Pacific Airlines (CPA) needed a certificate from Carol's doctor stating that her affliction was not contagious.

As the departure approached, the cables became more specific about details. Ambassador Bower cabled Brown (the documentation shows George as the "originator," with approval from Bower) on July 20, the day before departure.

BLACKSTOCKS DUE TO ARRIVE MONTREAL CPA FLIGHT 501 JULY 22 MONTREAL TIME 23.30 HOURS STOP LOCAL DOCTOR ADVISES ADMISSION TO MONTREAL NEUROLOGICAL INSTITUTE FOR QUOTE AN ACTIVE

```
ASCENDING POLYNEURITIS ALL EXTREMITIES WITH DIFFUSE PARALY-
SIS UNQUOTE PLEASE ARRANGE FOR APPROPRIATE MEDICAL ATTENTION
HOSPITAL RESERVATION AND FOR AMBULANCE TO MEET PLANE STOP
PLEASE CONFIRM THIS EMBASSY STOP
```

When I first read this, I found it highly peculiar that the embassy—that is, George—was asking the department in Ottawa to reserve Carol's hospital bed just one day before departure for Montreal. It was already four days since Ambassador Bower's cable indicating the possibility of her "permanent impairment" and three days since his letter to Brown saying that "she may not recover."

In fact, George obtained the required quote for the airfares—first class for himself and the nurse, a lower berth for Mom, who would be on a stretcher—only on Monday, July 20, the day before departure. It was Julie who observed that, on the same page as his notes about the flight times, doctor's certificates, medications, and other urgent last-minute details for the imminent airlift of his seriously ill wife, George left this jotting: "Spring and mattress delivered. . . . Mon. Stn. wgn—late eve . . . Bradley will call."

In the midst of this emergency, George was thinking about a delivery, late on the night before their departure, of a "spring and mattress" in a station wagon. If it came with a box spring, it was certainly not a travel mattress. Why would a man desperately trying to save his wife concern himself with delivery of a mattress—especially when he was about to depart the country so urgently—unless he was worried what a later forensic investigation might find in the mattress it was replacing?

Bower's cable ended with an odd request.

```
BLACKSTOCKS FAMILY IN CANADA UNAWARE THESE PLANS AND SHOULD
NOT BE INFORMED AT THIS TIME.
                                          BOWER DOMCAN
```

Surely George's superiors must have found this directive questionable, even troubling. Carol was deathly ill, and senior government
officials were supposed to keep her parents in the dark about it?
By insisting on this, George was putting Ambassador Bower and
Brown in a very awkward and vulnerable position. Failing to notify
Carol's parents about the decision to return her to Canada, not
long after the Grays themselves had sent urgent inquiries to the
department, would look terrible. George would have known this,
and he'd have known how difficult it would be for his bosses to deal
with the Grays if their daughter were to die. Evidently, he didn't
care. And yet he had the presence of mind to ask the department to
cover his expenses.

In addition to the cable to Ottawa, George, as originator in
Bower's name (his hand-printed draft was among his papers), sent
cables to the Canadian embassies in cities where the CPA aircraft
would be stopping on short layovers: Santiago de Chile, Lima, and
Mexico City. These cables stated that Carol was "seriously ill" and
requested that embassy personnel meet her plane on arrival and provide any assistance required. It wasn't clear what sort of assistance
they could have given, short of sending an ambulance or a hearse.

ON JULY 21, after a tearful goodbye with María, Carol was taken
by ambulance to Ezeiza Airport in Buenos Aires. Canadian Pacific
Airlines flight 501 departed at 1:30 P.M. The journey to Montreal
would take thirty-five hours—nearly a day and a half. It was going to
be an extremely arduous trip.

The Argentine Red Cross nurse accompanying my parents
aboard the flight was, as far as I know, a complete stranger to Carol.
There hadn't been time for the nurse to obtain a passport, so headquarters in Ottawa was forced to pull strings and improvise arrangements for her admission to Canada, and to ask the Argentine

consulate in Montreal to provide her with special papers for her return trip.

In July, the middle of Argentine winter, the afternoon sun illuminates the full majesty of the snow-capped Andes. But to Carol in her misery, lying on a stretcher in the cramped fuselage of the droning DC-6, the sight—if she'd been able to see it at all—would have seemed cold and barren. She must have felt very frightened—not only in her state of physical pain and suffering, but also in her anxiety, knowing her condition was considered so grave that the only hope was to send her back to Canada. Was she going to make it in time? Would she ever see her kids again? Would she ever see her parents again?

It was only sixteen months since we'd all left New York for Buenos Aires with excitement and hope in our hearts. A mere three months ago, before she got sick, life had been good. Now it was sheer terror.

Carol was still vomiting and in extreme discomfort during the journey. With the semi-paralysis of her limbs, hands, and feet, she would have needed the nurse's assistance to go to the bathroom. The nurse's job would have been to keep her as comfortable as possible, yet she couldn't have provided the emotional comfort María had given her.

After the three-hour flight from Buenos Aires to Santiago, the layover was only thirty minutes. No time to get off the plane, even if she'd been able to. A couple of hours after takeoff from Santiago, night fell over the Pacific. If Carol managed to get any sleep, it would have been interrupted three hours later when they landed in Lima.

On the eight-hour overnight flight from Lima to Mexico City, perhaps Carol slept fitfully through the clatter and smells of the dinner service, the glare of reading lamps, the muttering of passengers' conversations, the constant vibration of the aircraft high over the black Pacific. I can imagine her worrying about us kids left behind without her, about friends to whom she hadn't said goodbye. Perhaps the nurse slipped an air-sickness bag under her chin when she needed it as the plane pitched and rolled over the equator.

They landed in Mexico City at 7 A.M. Even in the Mexican mid-summer, the early morning air would have been chilly when the flight crew swung open the cabin door. Perhaps the nurse draped an extra blanket over Carol's emaciated body.

After two and a half hours, they took off on the homeward leg. Carol would have to endure ten more hours in the aluminum tube droning over the Gulf of Mexico, the Southern and Midwestern United States and the eastern Great Lakes. Finally, they set down in Toronto at 8:50 P.M.

By that point, Carol would have been totally exhausted. She was in Toronto, for which she'd felt homesick on first arriving in Argentina and in the depths of her despair in hospital. It was where she'd grown up, gone to school, married, had two of her children; where her parents and childhood friends lived. But she wasn't going to see any of them that night.

All she saw during the one-hour stop was the inside of Malton Airport (now Pearson International), Canadian customs and immigration officials, and airline attendants briskly pushing her gurney outside to the Montreal plane. She couldn't even call her parents to tell them how and where she was, or where she was going. They were probably at home, perhaps making final arrangements for Grandma's trip to Argentina, and still desperately worried about what was happening to their daughter. They were completely unaware that she was just a short drive from their apartment on Avenue Road.

I've often wondered why my mother didn't take that opportunity to contact her parents, to speak with them by phone for even a few minutes. I can't believe she didn't try. The answer may lie somewhere between her deeply debilitated condition and my father's powers of persuasion. We'll never know for sure.

ON ARRIVAL AT Montreal's Dorval Airport (now Trudeau International), shortly before midnight on July 22, Carol was moved in her stretcher from the airplane to an ambulance, then driven through the dark streets to the Montreal Neurological Institute (MNI).

Her MNI case history gives us a bare-bones report of what happened next. The wording is clinical and distressingly incomplete. But sixty years later, it's the closest thing we have to an eye-witness account.

CASE HISTORY OF CAROL BLACKSTOCK

THE ABOVE PATIENT WAS ADMITTED TO THE MONTREAL NEUROLOGICAL INSTITUTE ON JULY 23RD, 1959 AT 12.30 A.M. SHE WAS ABLE TO GIVE HER OWN HISTORY AND TOLD US THE FOLLOWING STORY.

SHE HAD BEEN WELL UNTIL MAY 1959 WHEN SHE HAD A SUDDEN ONSET OF DYSPNEA [DIFFICULT OR LABOURED RESPIRATION] AND COUGHING AND CHOKING, WITH SOME VOMITING AND SLIGHT FEVER. SHE WAS TOLD SHE HAD ASTHMA THOUGH THERE WAS NO PREVIOUS HISTORY OF ALLERGY. VOMITING CONTINUED AND SHE WAS ADMITTED TO HOSPITAL IN BUENOS AIRES WHERE SHE STOPPED VOMITING AFTER 2-3 DAYS AND SEEMED TO RECOVER.

The doctors who treated her in Montreal had been given Dr. Mercer's clinical record of Carol's treatment in Buenos Aires, including the interviews conducted with her at La Pequeña Compañía de María and Dr. Mercer's interpretation of the psychosomatic "neurotic element" in his diagnosis.

EXAMINATION IN THE NEUROLOGICAL INSTITUTE REVEALED A THIN, TENSE YOUNG FEMALE WHO ANSWERED QUESTIONS IN A FLAT UNINTERESTED MANNER. SHE WAS DEMANDING ATTENTION ALL THE TIME. THE SKIN WAS DRY BUT THERE WAS NO EXCESSIVE PIGMENTATION. SHE VOMITED TWICE DURING THE FIRST EXAMINATION. . . .

. . . TOUCH AND PAIN SENSIBILITIES WERE DIMINISHED OVER
THE LOWER THIRD OF BOTH LEGS AND THERE WAS A QUESTIONABLE
LOSS OF POSITION AND VIBRATION SENSE OVER THE LOWER EXTREMI-
TIES. . . . IN VIEW OF THE SEVERE ELECTROLYTE IMBALANCE,
THERAPY WAS DIRECTED PRIMARILY TO REMEDY THIS.

ON JULY 23 THE VOMITING HAD BEEN CONTROLLED BUT THE
PATIENT WAS CONFUSED AND RESTLESS. THE NEXT DAY, "SPASMS"
WERE SEEN INVOLVING THE FACE AND ARMS AND, IN ADDITION, SHE
DID NOT RESPOND TO QUESTIONS READILY.

The MNI case history provides no indication that Carol Blackstock was dying. It contains no sense of urgency, no suggestion that the doctors struggled to save her life, except at the very end. Perhaps the physicians' apparent lack of urgency reflected their interpretation of Carol's behaviour: the loss of sensation in her lower extremities was "questionable"; she answered questions in a "flat uninterested manner"; she was "demanding attention all the time"; she had "spasms" (the quotation marks suggest they may have been real or imagined); she was "confused and restless" and did not respond to questions readily. If only she'd been more helpful.

If she was demanding attention all the time, it was simply because she was fighting for her life.

CAROL'S VOMITING WAS brought under control on July 23, the same day she arrived at the MNI. While this no doubt moderated her suffering somewhat, it's not clear what else it achieved. Vomiting is, of course, the body's way of expelling toxic substances.

But what was making Carol Blackstock vomit in the first place? She'd been vomiting, with the occasional brief respite, for nearly three months, since the onset of her sickness at the beginning of May. And what was causing the polyneuropathy, which had afflicted her for almost as long? Why weren't these the primary questions in the big diagnostic picture?

Knowing the urgency and gravity of her case, the doctors at the MNI would presumably have wanted to brainstorm and conduct a complete battery of tests, including screening for the presence of toxins. Carol was in the institution's care for more than fifty-five hours, nearly two and a half days. But sadly, the MNI case history contains no diagnostic picture of what was making her so critically ill. Instead, the focus was on the treatment of her electrolyte imbalance—an important symptom, no doubt, but viewed in isolation from the vomiting and the polyneuropathy, it appears to have been a distraction from diagnosing the real problem.

The case history is silent about the presence of our father during Carol's last moments, although he is mentioned elsewhere. It does provide graphic details of the indignities of her condition, some of which will not be repeated here. The hospital record notes her saying that there were "people attacking her." Whether this was a function of the hallucinations also recorded, we don't know, though it seems likely.

With a dull, sickening thud of finality, like the door of a mausoleum sliding shut, the case history describes what happened next in two stark sentences.

THE LEVEL OF CONSCIOUSNESS DETERIORATED, AND THERE WAS A PROGRESSIVE RISE IN THE PULSE RATE, WITH A FALL IN BLOOD PRESSURE AND CARDIAC ARRHYTHMIA. SHE DIED ON 25 JULY.

That is the only account I have ever seen or heard of how our mother died. Our father never told Doug, Julie, or me anything about it. He didn't say whether she died without pain. He didn't tell us if he was by her side, as people are when a loved one dies, as husbands and fathers are. Did she ask after us before losing consciousness? Did she see a clergyman? All unknown.

I can only imagine that if Dad had been with her, he'd have mentioned it. It would have been a comfort to us to know that she wasn't alone, that he cared about her to the last.

But as far as I know, she died already unconscious, with hospital personnel as her only company.

LATER THAT DAY, a cable went from Ottawa to Ambassador Bower.

> TO: THE CANADIAN AMBASSADOR,
> BUENOS AIRES
> JULY 25, 1959
> FOR BOWER CAROL BLACKSTOCK DIED THIS MORNING.
>
> **BROWN**

Clearly, Assistant Deputy Minister Leslie Brown was on top of the situation. He must have been informed of Carol's death by someone other than George—otherwise, he would have known his message was redundant. George, in fact, sent the following cable on the same day.

> TO: CANADIAN AMBASSADOR,
> BUENOS AIRES
> JULY 25, 1959
> CAROL DIED THIS MORNING AT NEUROLOGICAL INSTITUTE STOP CAUSE
> STILL UNKNOWN STOP WILL ADVISE PLANS SOON.
>
> **BLACKSTOCK**

George's message differed from Brown's only by adding pointedly "cause still unknown."

Many years later, Dr. Bernard Graham, one of the doctors who treated Carol in Montreal, told Julie and me that her medical team was deeply puzzled by her death. As physicians at a research and teaching hospital, the doctors regarded her case as a professional challenge. According to Dr. Graham, an MNI neurologist and the institute's registrar, they convened a post-mortem round-table discussion and did some brainstorming.

After they had run through the range of possible reasons for her death, one of the doctors looked at his colleagues and said, "This is the sort of thing that happens with heavy-metal poisoning." With that stroke of intuition, the pieces began coming together—and with hindsight, her strange combination of symptoms started making sense.

The doctors immediately conducted a careful and detailed physical examination of the body. Their post-mortem findings supported their suspicion. As obligated by law, they called in the coroner, and Carol Blackstock's body was transferred to the Montreal city morgue for an autopsy.

8

BURIAL

TWENTY YEARS LATER, Julie and I would learn how our mother's parents found out about her death.

On the morning she died in Montreal, Saturday, July 25, 1959, the telephone rang in our grandparents' Toronto apartment. Grandma answered.

"Hello?" she said.

"Hello. It's George."

"George! Where are you? Where is Carol?"

"I'm in Montreal."

"Oh—but what are you doing there? We thought you were in Argentina. Where's Carol?"

"Carol died this morning."

Grandma immediately dropped the phone and collapsed onto the floor.

TWO DAYS LATER, a terse death notice appeared on page 32 of the Monday, July 27, edition of the Toronto *Globe and Mail*.

BLACKSTOCK, CAROL JANICE GRAY – *Suddenly, at the Montreal Neurological Institute, Montreal, Que., on Saturday, July 25, 1959, Carol Janice Gray, dearly beloved wife of George E. Blackstock, mother of Jeffrey, Douglas and Julia, daughter of Mr. and Mrs. F. Howard Gray, Toronto. Funeral arrangements later.*

It is virtually certain that George would have written or approved this. For anyone who knew Carol, the news must have hit like a bomb. How on earth could she be dead? The word *suddenly* in a death notice often implied suicide. Could Carol have killed herself? And yet she'd been young, healthy, beautiful, popular, married with three small kids, and with everything to live for. Not only that, but hardly anyone knew she'd been seriously ill in Argentina—let alone that she'd been flown back to Canada on a stretcher.

With no information about the funeral, those who wanted to make arrangements to attend would have been bewildered.

What Carol's family and friends in Toronto didn't know was that the unusual circumstances of her death had required an autopsy—hence the delay in announcing her funeral. It was held two days after her death, on the same day as the death notice appeared. The pathologist conducting the autopsy was Dr. J.P. Valcourt of Montreal's Medico-Legal Institute (Institut de médecine légale et de police scientifique). Also present, and observing with intense interest, were several MNI physicians, including Dr. J.B.R. Cosgrove, head of the team that had treated Carol.

It appears that George failed, then or later, to tell anyone that this was the reason for the delay in bringing Carol's body home to Toronto. As I would learn, George, along with his cousin Mary and her husband, Sam (a doctor himself), with whom George was staying in Montreal, were pressing hard for release of the body. In fact, Dr. Valcourt would tell us, the delay apparently made George and his relations feel "quite hard done by."

Evidently, Dad's impatience was rewarded. On the day after the autopsy, Tuesday, July 28, the same death notice appeared again in *The Globe and Mail*, with the addition of the funeral details. The visitation at the funeral chapel in Toronto would take place that very same evening. Carol's parents and friends received only a few hours' notice to attend.

The funeral service would be held the next afternoon at Grace Church on-the-Hill, an Anglican church in Forest Hill attended by the Blackstock family. Interment would be in the Mount Pleasant Cemetery—in the Blackstock family burial plot.

The arrangements were all handled by senior Blackstock family members on behalf of George and his mother. Grandma was prostrated with grief, and Grandpa was looking after her amid his own emotional devastation, so they had little involvement in the arrangements for their daughter's funeral.

Events moved so swiftly that Carol's parents scarcely had time to arrange for their own family or their daughter's friends to attend her funeral. Joan Clark, for example, Carol's best friend, was out of town and didn't hear about her death until well after the funeral had taken place.

Carol died on Saturday; the autopsy was performed on Monday; she was transported more than three hundred miles to Toronto on Tuesday; and by Wednesday afternoon she was in the ground.

WHEN GEORGE ARRIVED in Toronto from Montreal, he'd have been picked up at Malton Airport by Aunt Kay and her husband, Grant. They always picked George up for the drive into the city. As his big sister, Kay was never shy about telling him exactly what was on her mind. She'd have asked him, "George, what in heaven's name happened? Why didn't you let us know you were bringing Carol to Canada? Mother is very upset. What can we tell her?"

I'm sure George told them what he later told Julie, Doug, and me: that the doctors couldn't discover what was wrong with Carol; that it was her idea not to tell anyone they were travelling to Canada, so as not to upset her parents.

My grandparents asked George similar questions. They were disbelieving and hurt when he told them their daughter hadn't wanted them to know she was returning to Canada. That wasn't like Carol at all. If she'd thought there was a chance she might die, she'd have wanted to see them right away. If she'd thought she was going to get better, she'd have had no problem telling them she was there. Why hadn't George, under such life-and-death circumstances, taken it upon himself to notify them, even if it meant overriding Carol's wishes? His insistence that she simply didn't want to worry them was very hard for them to hear.

George's mother would surely have asked questions too. So would friends who had been close to George and Carol as a couple. Others would have not asked, for fear of intruding, but would have wondered nonetheless.

I write "surely" and "would have" because Dad never told us anything about the circumstances of Mom's death. He told us nothing about the funeral, nothing about who was there to say goodbye to her, or about who had expressed condolences to us as her children. Nothing. Some of what I know about all this came from my grandparents, for whom the recollection of these events was very painful. The rest comes from documents we acquired later.

I asked a cousin of George's who had attended the funeral to describe it for me, but I was stonewalled. Like many others in the Blackstock family, she didn't want to talk about it. And yet, I have a pretty good idea what it must have been like, having attended services at that church and having known most of the people involved.

At the visitation, Carol's closed coffin would have concealed the ravages of her sickness and the pathologist's scalpel. Grandpa,

Grandma, and Carol's friends would have arrived at the funeral home in a state of helpless confusion. They'd scarcely had time to catch their breath. What could possibly explain Carol's sudden death? George would have responded that he'd asked the same question, but there were no answers. The doctors simply didn't understand why she'd died. He always said that, then and afterwards.

At the funeral service at Grace Church on-the-Hill, family and friends were still in shock, whispering among themselves, hoping somebody knew something, anything. It was understandable, but nonetheless unsettling, that Carol's young children weren't present.

At the tea following the service, conversation would have been muted, an awkward silence prevailing. With so many things unknown, what was there to say?

The guests would have stayed briefly, paid their respects to the bereaved husband and parents, and departed. Grandma told us that she and Grandpa, greatly outnumbered by Blackstock relatives and other strangers, soon left to go home. Grandma was so overwhelmed by sorrow that she couldn't attend the interment. Largely bedridden for the next two months, she would lose a considerable amount of her hair and wore a hairpiece for the rest of her life.

Carol was laid to rest in the family plot of George's ancestors at Mount Pleasant Cemetery, in midtown Toronto. Years later, Grandma told me she was upset by the coldness and anonymity of Carol's nameless grave. There is no visible memorial to her. Even George asked, in a note to himself that we found among his papers after his death, "Who else is buried there?" Grandma and Grandpa had no say in the matter.

I never visited Mom's burial site, not even with my grandparents. And Dad never took me there. Not once.

THE HASTE SURROUNDING Carol's funeral might have been more understandable if George had needed to fly straight back to

Buenos Aires to be with us, and to tell us of Mom's death before we learned about it from others—his embassy colleagues, perhaps, or the household staff. A cousin of George's told me later that she'd said confidently at the time, "Oh, George will be on the next plane to Argentina."

But he wasn't. Instead, he spent the next seven weeks in Canada—in Toronto, Ottawa, Montreal, and points in between. He had paperwork related to Carol's death to attend to. He had departmental business in Ottawa. Between appointments, he visited his friends at their summer cottages north of Toronto. It was August and September, and the warm weather, rocky shorelines, and blue waters of Muskoka beckoned. According to the cousin, even his best friends asked whether he didn't want to get back to Argentina to be with his children.

In the troubled, anxious silence hovering around Carol's death, there were things George undoubtedly didn't mention. These included the fact that, after the initial findings of Dr. Valcourt's autopsy, George had been summoned to an interview by the Montreal police.

Around the same time, the Montreal medical authorities met with Assistant Deputy Minister Leslie Brown, called in from Ottawa on short notice. Apparently, George was ordered—either by the police or his superiors in the federal government, or both—to remain in the country until further notice.

Those government officials, particularly Brown, now found themselves in a tricky position. The wife of a Canadian government representative abroad had just died under unusual circumstances—circumstances that had attracted the interest of the police, which suggested the possibility of foul play—leaving behind three children in the family home in Buenos Aires. The Montreal Neurological Institute doctors, the coroner, and the chief prosecutor for the province of Quebec, to whom the case had been referred, technically had no responsibility for those children—for us. And the Montreal police had no jurisdiction outside of Canada. But the Government of

Canada, specifically the Department of Trade and Commerce and the Department of External Affairs, certainly did have responsibility, and they knew it, as shown by their swift reaction a month earlier to our grandparents' inquiry about their daughter's health.

If anything were to happen to us children—for example, because someone still in our house, perhaps one of the domestic staff, might possibly do us harm— Brown and other federal officials would be held responsible. They'd be found derelict in their duty if they hadn't seen to it that the children were removed from the house or the staff dismissed, the usual courses of action in such circumstances.

Yet nothing of that sort was done. Instead, a cable from the Canadian embassy in Buenos Aires assured Ottawa, "children not been told [about their mother's death] but being well taken care of." Apparently, suspicion hadn't fallen on any of the household staff.

TOWARD THE END of his apparently enforced seven-week stay in Canada, George was required to return to Montreal. He'd been called to another meeting at the coroner's office on September 11. Years later, he would tell us it was an uneventful meeting that involved merely filling out some routine paperwork.

The next day, he attended a meeting at the MNI, where he picked up two typed letters addressed to "H. Leslie Brown, Assist. Deputy Minister, Dept. of Trade and Commerce." Both letters were from Dr. J.B.R. Cosgrove.

Later that same day, George travelled to Ottawa and delivered the two letters to Leslie Brown. In turn, Brown provided him with a handwritten receipt for the letters and for bills George had submitted for Carol's medical and hospital expenses. Since he'd undoubtedly read the letters (we found copies in his papers after his death), George knew that Carol's doctors had considered "the possibility of an unknown toxin" as the cause of her death, resulting in the call to the coroner to conduct an autopsy. Brown also knew. And each knew that the other knew.

We don't know exactly when, or from whom, George got the green light to leave Canada and return to Argentina as a free man, but it must have been right around this time.

GRANDMA LATER TOLD me that George telephoned before he left for Buenos Aires, partly to thank his in-laws for the presents that Grandpa had dropped off at Granny's for us. It was a very short conversation. Grandma couldn't come to the phone, and between Grandpa and George there wasn't much to say. There had never been much to say at the best of times, and now there was really nothing. The main link between them was gone, suddenly and without explanation. What brief words passed were about us children, with assurances from George that the Grays would be kept in touch. Of course, he stressed, we children knew nothing of what had happened, so it was out of the question for Grandma and Grandpa to call us.

Around September 15, George left Canada to return to Buenos Aires. But first he made stopovers for a few days in New York and Mexico City for visits with friends, shopping, the theatre, and sightseeing. He sent a postcard to his mother from Mexico City showing the beautiful new Central Library building at the University of Mexico, with its Aztec-inspired murals.

Saturday Sept 19, 1959

Dear Mother:

Arrived here Thursday night after a fairly uneventful stay in N.Y.C. (saw "My Fair Lady," did a little shopping, went out to dinner with a friend from the Consulate). I'm enjoying my stay with Dick Willemsen and his wife tremendously. Mexico City is beautiful; about

3 ½ million population. We drove out this morning to see the Aztec pyramids and ruined cities. This afternoon we went to see the University of Mexico – 50,000 students. This is the library on the Campus which is all new – a tremendous number of ultra-modern buildings. Leaving for BA tomorrow evening – will write from there – Love George

P.S. The statue is not Stalin but the founder of the University

It had been nearly two months since our mother had died, and still no one had told us.

9

LIFE WITHOUT MOM

MARÍA LET DOUG and me stay up late for Mom and Dad's long-awaited homecoming. It was the evening of Monday, September 21, 1959. We were already in our pyjamas with our teeth brushed, Julie fast asleep in bed. My brother and I were excited to be awake past bedtime on a school night. We couldn't have slept anyway. Mom and Dad had been gone two whole months, and we were hopping with anticipation over seeing them again.

Keeping watch through the front window, we leaped off the couch when a car with bright headlights pulled into our driveway. María opened the front door and told us to wait just inside. She stood behind us, her hands resting gently on our shoulders. It was pitch-black outside and cool—early spring in Buenos Aires.

Dad stepped out of the car first, wearing an overcoat, followed by Dwight Fulford from the embassy.

"Hi, Dad," I said, trying to keep my voice normal. "Where's Mom?"

"Mom isn't here right now. Wait for me upstairs, boys—I'll explain in a minute. Good night, Dwight. I'll see you at the office tomorrow."

"Good night, George," came the sombre reply.

A few minutes later, Dad came into our bedroom. I guessed he'd been talking to María.

"Where's Mom? When's she coming back?" I asked.

"Mom's not coming back," Dad said.

"Not coming back? Why not?"

"Well, Mom's gone to heaven."

"You mean she's dead?" Even as I said the words, I couldn't believe it was possible. But I knew what *dead* meant, and so did Doug.

"That's right. Mom died in Canada," Dad replied, his eyes unfocused and glassy.

"*Why? What happened?*"

"Well, she died of the sickness she had here in Buenos Aires. The doctors in Canada couldn't save her."

Doug and I burst into tears. It was a long time before we were able to stop crying.

Dad sat there, maintaining his self-control, waiting for us to finish. I'd never seen him cry, and he didn't on this occasion.

For some reason, the next thing I asked was, "What will we do with all her things?"

"We'll have to remove them. They're not going to be needed anymore."

"Oh," I replied.

Dad didn't offer, then or at any time afterwards, to give us something of Mom's to remember her by—a photo, a lock of her hair, some favourite books, a bracelet for Julie—nothing.

He said, "I have some presents for you boys from Canada."

"Okay," said Doug. "Can we open them?"

Dad produced the presents—some of our favourite home-baked cookies from Grandma Gray, a penknife for me, a ball and glove for Doug.

WE COULD HAVE no inkling that on September 22, the day after George's return to Buenos Aires, a forensic chemist at the Medico-Legal Institute in Montreal named Bernard Péclet made a "Preliminary Toxicological Report" based on his chemical analysis of Carol's organs. His findings were that her liver, kidneys, brain, and toenails contained significantly large doses of arsenic. The subsequent completion of the toxicological analysis would also show a massive dose in the ileum (small intestine), which she hadn't fully digested. The preliminary report's one-sentence conclusion read, "The toxicological analyses have shown that the viscera of Mrs. Carol Blackstock contained some large doses of arsenic, the values of which are situated in the limits of those observed in poisoning cases."

This is the only one of several autopsy documents which is dated, providing tangible evidence that the cause of death was known within a relatively short time (less than two months) after Carol's death.

THE FOLLOWING WEEKS and months in Buenos Aires were a blur of sadness, pain, and confusion. I struggled to comprehend the idea that Mom was gone from our lives forever.

Complete strangers who knew Dad would come to our house and put their arms around Doug and me, expressing sympathy for our loss. They only bewildered and annoyed me. Who were these people anyway? Had they even known Mom? María told me to stay away from one stranger in particular, because he was "a dirty old man." My teacher excused me from writing a composition in Spanish for Mother's Day. A nice, thirtyish Argentine lady, the teacher gave me a hug and said how sorry she was. It was very kind of her, but I still felt uncomfortable. Mrs. McKenney, the mother of my pals Michael and Danny, also told me how sorry she was, adding, "I guess God just needed another angel." I thanked her, but didn't believe what she said.

Dad's social life in Buenos Aires carried on unabated. It was as if nothing had happened. He was out of the house most evenings, but fortunately the household staff were always around. They were caring and affectionate toward us and provided some sorely needed continuity in our lives.

I know George saw the Krapfs around this time. Louise Krapf would tell Julie years later that he regaled them with stories of his visits in Canada, New York, and Mexico City. After that, apparently, Louise and Rolf lost their appetite for seeing him. As we confirmed later, George didn't put a memorial service announcement or even a simple death notice in the *Buenos Aires Herald*, the English-language daily read by the expatriate community, or *La Nación*, the leading Spanish-language daily—a courtesy that would have been appreciated by the Krapfs and, no doubt, by Carol's many other friends in Argentina. I can say with confidence that there was no memorial service, because it is highly unlikely that I would not have been included or would not remember attending it. I do not.

Dad was around on weekends sometimes. He played kick the can in the garden with Doug and me. We enjoyed that. At the dinner table, he'd laugh heartily while reading *Pogo* cartoon books or perusing a newspaper.

"What's so funny, Dad?" I asked. "Can we read *Pogo* too?"

"No," he replied, without looking up. "*Pogo* is really for adults."

I stopped asking about *Pogo*.

More than ever, María became our surrogate mother. She was always there when we needed her—when we scraped our knees or needed to buy new clothes, since all three of us were outgrowing our old ones. She made the arrangements for our birthday parties. More and more often, she and Martín took us on Sundays to the house they were building in Boulogne, which now had a working toilet. With Julie in tow, María and Cristina would entertain neighbours who dropped by to share *mate*, the local sweet tea sipped from a gourd through a metal straw. Martín would always be working at the back of the house.

Julie later told me that at three years old she still didn't understand Mom was dead and never coming back. Every time a plane passed overhead, she'd wonder if that was *Mamá*. She doesn't remember anyone actually telling her that Mom had died. The toddler who "never puddles," as Carol wrote from the SS *Argentina*, was now wetting the bed.

As for me, I would just lie on my bed for long stretches of time. The bedroom had become my sanctuary, a place to escape from the false and intrusive condolences of strangers who purported to know my mother but didn't, and pretended to know how I felt but didn't. They didn't have the right. My feelings were private. Though I was alone a lot, wondering what had happened to Mom and struggling with the realization that she was gone, I didn't like the attention of other people on the subject. I've always been a person who keeps his feelings to himself.

Even though my mind was co-operating with this approach, my body revolted. I guess the body gets to a point where it says it's not going to take it anymore. On November 23, 1959, I had an epileptic attack while walking to school. My feet started dragging, my hands turned spastic, and as hard as I struggled, I couldn't walk. I wound up lying on the sidewalk on my side, confused and frightened. I had no idea what was happening to me.

A young, well-dressed Argentine gentleman passing by on the other side of the street was my good Samaritan. He saw I was lying helpless on the ground and came to my assistance, asking me where I lived. I said I was okay, but he could clearly see I wasn't. He picked me up and carried me home, where María thanked him and took charge.

I was taken to the British Hospital. I stayed there for three days while the doctors ran tests on me, putting sticky pads all over my head with wires running to machines. It was messy, but it didn't hurt.

I still have the hospital admission form, which states, under "Diagnosis," "*Ataque Epileptico.*" One of the referring doctors was Dr. Mercer.

After I left the hospital, I was all right again. I'd never had an epileptic attack before, and I've never had one since. Now I understand that they can be triggered by extreme emotional stress.

DAD'S FAMILY IN Toronto hadn't been hearing much from him. On December 15, 1959, replying to an evidently rare and overdue letter from Dad, Aunt Kay complained about his failure to write home earlier.

> *Dear George:*
>
> *Thank heaven you wrote at last. For weeks [we] heard nothing else from Mother – why don't you write? It really is a great wrong to her. . . .*
>
> *She wishes you would write to the Greys [sic] too. If you do not want to, why not have one of the children write? Children normally like to do this esp. at your dictation more or less and the Greys would be so thrilled and also they would know that you had gone to the trouble of getting the kids to do it.*

Naturally, Grandpa and Grandma were also upset by my father's lack of communication after he had promised to keep in touch about us. I know he was busy filing medical expense claims after Mom died, on top of his workload at the office and his demanding social schedule. But Aunt Kay wasn't thinking about all that. She'd been reflecting on other matters.

> *I've been thinking a lot about your problems myself and I feel that if you are so sure you have something to offer the children that is better than what the Greys can offer (and don't forget they have a lot to offer in the way of love and devotion which is what children thrive on) you*

must be with them in order to impart anything to them. It isn't even
enough just to take them to someone else's house but I'm sure you
realize this yourself.

Evidently, George and Aunt Kay had been discussing which living
arrangements would be best for us kids. What amazed me on finding
this letter among my father's papers was Kay's seeming suggestion
that he consider giving us up to our grandparents to raise. Maybe she
was trying to illustrate her point that it wasn't enough "just to take
them to someone else's house." Or maybe she realized that the Grays
would have been better parents for us.

BY A CURIOUS coincidence, George received another letter dated
December 15, 1959, the same day as the letter from Aunt Kay. It came
from Santiago de Chile and was written by someone I'll call Ingrid.
Since her letter was mostly in Spanish, I've translated those parts into
English and put them in roman type. The italicized parts were written in English, a language Ingrid evidently hadn't yet learned to speak
with complete fluency.

Hotel Carrera
Santiago de Chile

15-12-59

Dear George!
I'm in the wonderfullest hotel I have ever seen. Big rooms, and a
swimming-pool on the roof. The trip through the Andes was very
nice and interesting, but too long. You need to make this trip by
plane or by car. The trip from Buenos Aires to Mendoza was fantastic. Pullman car with air conditioning. – Santiago, the hotel

and everything so nice that I needed to write to you right away. If I can I will write to you again from Chile, if not soon after from Bariloche. *In the meantime, I wish you mery [sic] Christmas and Happy New Year for you and your children.*

"Ingrid"

My address in Bariloche is: Hotel Llao-Llao.

Clearly, Ingrid wasn't writing to a complete stranger. To judge from her familiar, eager tone and her implicit assumption that George wanted to continue their correspondence, she and he had already known each other for a while.

We don't know exactly when George met Ingrid. My parents' friend Bibi Fischer later would tell George's mother in a letter that she and her husband, Peter, "brought them together." After Peter met Ingrid at a party, he opined to Bibi that Ingrid would make a perfect wife for George and a mother for his children. Nevertheless, Bibi wrote that it was "quite some time" before she and Peter introduced the couple.

The problem with Bibi's version of events is that between George's return from Canada on September 21 and Ingrid's exuberant letter dated December 15, fewer than three months had elapsed. Depending on one's interpretation of "quite some time," there were scarcely enough weeks in the calendar to constitute what most people would consider an appropriate pause between George's return and an introduction to Ingrid occurring well before she wrote her letter of December 15.

Perhaps Bibi was stretching the truth to obscure from Granny the apparent precipitousness of a relationship that the Fischers took credit for encouraging—a relationship that may have begun shortly, perhaps very shortly, after George returned from burying his wife in Canada. We have no evidence, however, to say exactly when it began.

CHRISTMAS WAS EMPTY without Mom. Dad handed out the presents from under the Christmas tree and helped us with them, keeping a list of who had received what from whom. There was no lively laughter, no animated Mom saying excitedly, "Jeffrey, look what you got. Aren't you a lucky boy!" or, "Oh my, Julie, isn't that a nice dress for you from Grandma. Won't you look pretty in it!" or, "Dougie, a new cowboy outfit from Grandpa! It will be fun to go riding with Mummy in that!" I could still hear her voice all the same.

María, Cristina, and Martín were away visiting family and friends. Alejandra was still there to do the cooking. Doug and I will never forget her ruining the Christmas brunch by putting too much salt in the scrambled eggs.

Alejandra was a strange bird. At first, instead of speaking to Doug and me, she'd call us to dinner by motioning with her bunched fingers toward her mouth. When she saw me naked after a bath, she'd point and say, "What's that?" in Spanish. I complained to María, who told her to stop making fun of me. I didn't like Alejandra much, but I didn't have a lot to do with her. After dinner, she'd wash up and disappear to her flat above the garage.

Shortly after she started with us, Alejandra had had a set-to with Mom in which she demanded a huge pay raise and other concessions, including no cooking. Mom said no, telling Alejandra she could pack her bags. The result was that Alejandra backed down and begged to stay. Mom relented and kept her on, and Alejandra was fine afterwards. Mom used to refer to her fondly as Alex and sometimes entrusted her with Julie's care.

According to my father, Alejandra had come with the house after working for the previous occupant, Jorge Antonio—"crook number 2" in the Perón regime, as Mom had called him. Much later, for reasons of his own, Dad would make a great deal out of this.

TEN DAYS OR so after Christmas, George received another letter from Ingrid. It was written from Nahuel Huapi National Park, near Bariloche, in the Patagonian Andes, where she was staying with her parents. Ingrid taught kindergarten while living with her well-to-do, conservative, and very class-conscious mother and father in Buenos Aires. She was travelling with them on the same trip she'd mentioned in her previous letter.

Ingrid wrote this letter on New Year's Eve—on the same hotel letterhead as Mom's letter to Grandma seven months earlier, when Carol and George had made their trip to the Andes. When I first saw Ingrid's letter, I did a double take, thinking there must be some mistake. No: she'd been staying in the same hotel as Carol and was writing to George on the same hotel stationery. However much this may have been a coincidence, it still left me with a cold, queasy feeling.

Except for the opening salutation, Ingrid wrote this letter entirely in Spanish. Below is my translation.

31.12.59
Hotel Llao-Llao
Parque Nacional
Nahuel Huapi

Dear George!
It's a week today now since your letter arrived, right on Christmas day.

You can't imagine how happy it made me. I thank you very much for it. It is now 5 in the afternoon and I think you will be leaving your house now to go to the Fischers' ranch. I hope that you have a very nice time and that you enjoy yourself. I am happy that the kids can spend their vacation there. Here, there is the most beautiful sunshine every day. The lakes are still too cold for swimming. However, I went horseback riding and I played golf. My parents have golf classes every day, and I take advantage to learn a little. We made some excursions

*to get to know some nice spots. Everything is very pretty and interest-
ing here, but not much fun, since there is nobody my age. There are
a lot of people 40 and over, and kids 12 and under. I will tell you the
rest of it when I get back. Next Thursday, the 7th of January, we are
taking the plane and we will be back at home that night. Well, then,
I hope that you have a good start to the new year in which your
wishes come true.*

Best wishes

"Ingrid"

Best wishes to the kids and to Peter if you see him.

If there were any doubts that Ingrid and George had known each other
for some time before her previous letter, they were dispelled by reading
the second sentence: "You can't imagine how happy it made me." It
seems safe to say that this was already more than a casual friendship.

Just how long they'd known each other remains uncertain. Many
years later, María told Julie that Ingrid started appearing at our house
almost immediately after George returned from Canada.

I don't remember seeing her then. But as I've said, there were a
lot of strangers around the house, and I tried to avoid them as much
as possible.

AFTER NEW YEAR'S 1960, Dad took us to the Fischers' estancia
for our vacation. It was the height of the Argentine summer, and we
were off school for a couple of months.

We kids and María drove with Bibi in the Fischers' car, and Dad
flew with Peter in their light plane. Bibi got us singing along to songs
she knew in English, like "This Old Man," as the paved highways out
of Buenos Aires turned to dirt roads in the late afternoon, and we
drove into the vast grasslands of the pampas.

Of the Fischers' two estancias, the one I remember better was located about four hours by car south of the capital, and it was huge. The Fischers raised beef cattle, some dairy cows and chickens, grew potatoes, and kept horses, some for cattle work and others for pleasure riding. They had a large Spanish Colonial house with maids' quarters and a saltwater outdoor swimming pool. Beyond the main house stood a lonely laurel tree and a hollow Martello tower, a roost for pigeons. Farther out on the pampa was the runway for the plane.

There was a separate set of dwellings, shacks really, for the extended family of caretakers who worked the ranch and the stables. Like the Fischers, the caretakers were of German heritage, with blond hair and blue eyes, and they spoke German as well as Spanish. But that is where their common ground with the owners ended. The caretakers spoke Low German and lived in squalid conditions. One of the men used to shave outside with a knife, no shaving cream. I'm sure they too had immigrated before the war.

I was fascinated by the caretakers. I went with their raggedly clothed kids when they milked the cows and hosed down the horses. I wondered why they put up with such a shabby way of life, especially when the luxury in which the owners lived, just a stone's throw away, was so plain to see. Nevertheless, food was plentiful, and everyone ate well. They probably remembered worse from the old country.

I had a double perspective on the way of life there, which has largely disappeared now. Because I was a nine-year-old boy, I was accepted by both the *patrón* (the owner, or boss) and the *campesinos* (hired hands). And because I could communicate in both English and Spanish, I could understand what was happening in both camps. I enjoyed hanging about with the workers and their kids. It was a welcome distraction from my lingering sorrow over Mom, which was never far away.

I was out riding one day with the *campesino* kids when one of the girls' horses bolted, taking off in my direction. With the girl holding on for her life, horse and rider galloped past me at full speed. She was screaming in fright as she struggled to get the animal under control. Later, I saw her back at the estancia hosing down the sweat-covered horse, which must have eventually slowed down from sheer exhaustion.

Sometimes, I'd go with one of the boys to the pigeon house literally to bag supper. The birds lived in their pigeonholes in the wall inside the Martello tower. Most would fly off when we approached, but some would remain hunkered down in the wall; they were easily captured in a bag and wound up as a savoury dinner.

The Fischers' lead field hand had a rather bestial-looking wife. I once watched her stalk a chicken in the dirt backyard of their tiny house. Sneaking up behind the hapless bird, she grabbed it amid a frenzy of feathers and clucking, and, chicken in one hand and axe in the other, chopped off its head. She let it run around headless for a minute or two before taking it into the kitchen, where she plucked the feathers off the still-twitching carcass. Another day, I helped the *campesinos* with the potato harvest, digging the biggest potatoes I've ever seen out of the rich black soil with my hands.

The days were hot and sunny on the pampa, and we swam in the saltwater swimming pool. But it was very quiet too. In addition to missing Mom, I missed my friends back in the city. Lassie had been left there too. Fortunately, María was with us throughout our visit. Dad and Peter flew back to Buenos Aires for their jobs during the work week, but we kids and María spent over a month at the estancia.

Bibi Fischer was very nice to us. Her sister-in-law and a girlfriend came to visit and spent some time with Julie and Doug, reading them stories and playing with them. This spelled off María, whose time was mostly spent looking after my brother and sister. I was now grown up enough, or so I thought, that I didn't need much minding.

In her letter to Granny, quoted earlier, Bibi gave her account of the situation.

*I told you before how much the children missed their mother. Jeffrey
was very quiet and serious, all inward. Douglas was trying to make
friends with young women. We had them out at the Estancia once and
Douglas formed such an attachment to the girlfriend of one of our
friends that he asked if he could sleep in her room. He wanted to be
near her all the time. And Julia somehow attached herself to my sister-
in-law, maybe because she had 3 little girls already – she called her
Mummy and only she could dress her and put her to bed. It was so
moving to see how each in their way tried to find a substitute.*

Bibi's description of me as quiet and serious was accurate, and an
acknowledgment that she really didn't know what I was thinking or
feeling. I avoided the other guests at the estancia, just as I'd avoided
the strangers who'd been around our house. The idea of looking for
a substitute for Mom certainly wasn't on my mind. Perhaps that's
why Bibi's account was short on my behaviour and focused on Doug
and Julie.

Bibi was about to bring someone new into our world. She and
Peter had introduced George and Ingrid, or so she suggested in the
letter to my grandmother. Now, having in her words "brought them
together," she and Peter arranged for them to be together with us
kids. As she said in the letter, "Later on we invited them all to the
Estancia to see how it would work with the children." The relationship between George and Ingrid had obviously advanced quite a lot.

So in early February, toward the end of our visit, Señorita Ingrid
arrived. She was a beautiful young German woman in her twenties,
with long blond hair, freckles, and a charming manner. And with her
arrival, everything changed.

Señorita Ingrid seemed to take a lot of interest in us. She obviously took a lot of interest in Dad too. We all went horseback riding
and played games together in the swimming pool. She helped Julie
get dressed and came into our room to say good night to us. She told

us about the little kids in her kindergarten class. She even brought to
life the romantic history of the Argentine cowboys, the gauchos, telling us how they used *boleadoras,* a throwing device made of leather
and stone, to ensnare ostriches on the pampas.

When I got a stomach ache from eating too much honeycomb
from the apiary on the property, Ingrid took care to get me some
medicine and give me a hug. She read stories to Doug and Julie. She
only stayed for a week, but by the end of her visit, Señorita Ingrid
had made a big impression. We soaked up all the attention she lav-
ished on us.

Bibi wrote in her letter to Granny,

> . . . – *and this was most wonderful to see – how well everything
> worked out. The children liked [Ingrid] and she liked them, she
> knew how to talk to them and play with them and showed immense
> patience with Julia and Douglas.*

I liked her well enough. But I had no idea how that would be used to
imply something far greater. Doug and Julie couldn't have known
either. Although we didn't understand it, we were still mourning
Mom and hadn't come to terms with losing her. Those things take
time and patience. Dad didn't have a lot of either.

Later, I'd learn that Señorita Ingrid's family had immigrated to
Argentina from Germany some fifteen years earlier, at the end of
the Second World War. The details were a bit vague. Apparently,
they'd migrated through Switzerland, where Ingrid's parents left her
for two years with family friends because she'd become too sick to
travel. There she learned excellent French before travelling the rest
of the way to South America. Much later, Ingrid told me that her
parents were prominent enough in German society—the family
owned a big industrial corporation—that her father had had to join
the Nazi Party. How they managed to slip out of war-torn Germany,

when many of the most powerful Nazis could not, is still a mystery to me. Ingrid's mother came from French nobility by way of Neuchâtel, in Switzerland, so I was told, and perhaps her family connections provided them with safe passage. Her parents would later return to Germany in their retirement.

Because she'd lived in Buenos Aires for almost half of her life, Ingrid spoke perfect Spanish with an Argentine accent. That accent, really Italian in origin, is very pronounced and distinctive in the Spanish-speaking world. She also spoke some English with a bit of a German accent —although she was obviously not yet comfortable in writing English—and French and some Italian too. She was clearly a natural when it came to languages.

AT THE END of our visit to the estancia, I developed a sore throat and was taken to see a doctor in Buenos Aires. María cheerfully told me I needed to go to the British Hospital to have my tonsils taken out; they were going to do it the very next day. I'd been in that hospital recently because of the epileptic attack, and María knew it wasn't a fun place for me. She tried to dispel my worries, saying I'd be able to eat lots of ice cream, and off to the hospital we went.

That night, I begged María to stay in my room, and she agreed. The next day, I was excited, smiling from ear to ear as the nurse wheeled me into the operating room and told me, in an English accent, to breathe into a mask like a jet pilot. I soon stopped smiling when I realized how horrible the gas smelled, then passed out. They used ether as an anesthetic in those days.

After the operation, I was wheeled out of the operating room with my head still spinning. When I fully came to, María was there, and to my relief she agreed to sit up all night in my room again.

IN BUENOS AIRES, Señorita Ingrid increasingly became part of our lives. Sometimes, she came to our house from her parents' home, ten minutes away in San Isidro, to meet Dad after work before they went out for the evening.

One afternoon, when Señorita Ingrid came to the gate, Lassie barked at her, as usual, and Dad told me to take her to the far side of the yard.

"Who's *that*?" my pal Michael McKenney asked, frowning, when he saw Ingrid talking to Dad, glamorous in a cocktail dress and heels and smoking a cigarette. With her beautiful long blond hair, Ingrid attracted attention wherever she went.

"My Dad's new friend," I replied quietly, sensing Michael's discomfort.

After Dad changed his clothes, he and Señorita Ingrid went off for the evening to the Teatro Colón. She'd replaced me as his companion at the opera on Mom's season ticket.

I wondered what Michael told his mom when he got home. I was a little worried she might disapprove and question me about this new woman in our lives. Mrs. McKenney had been very fond of Mom. Everyone had been.

One day, Señorita Ingrid came to the house to take me shopping downtown before meeting Dad after work. As a treat, she bought us hot dogs for lunch. When we met up with Dad, she told him they were "the best-tasting hot dogs ever." They were good, I thought to myself, but to call them the best-tasting hot dogs ever was an exaggeration.

In early April 1960, Dad asked us where we'd like to spend our Easter holidays: we could go to the Fischers' estancia or to Córdoba again with María. We all wanted to go back to the estancia. I could see María was disappointed—she'd wanted to go to Córdoba so she could see her family. When Dad announced later that Señorita Ingrid would be joining us for the holidays, it was to the general delight of us kids. Doug and Julie liked all the attention she showered on them, and I thought she was fun to have around.

At the Fischers' place, the days were growing cooler and shorter with the onset of fall, but the romantic relationship was heating up between Dad and Ingrid. There was no mistaking the meaning of the giggling emanating from the bathroom as they washed each other's feet after an afternoon of horseback riding.

One evening during the Easter vacation, Dad and Señorita Ingrid sat us down in the estancia's living room. They had something important to announce: they were going to get married. Ingrid told us she loved Dad, and she loved us too.

On the drive home after saying goodbye to the Fischers—Ingrid had already left—Dad told us that he wanted us to start calling her "Mum."

"I know you've been calling her Señorita Ingrid, but now that she's going to be your mother, I want you to start calling her Mum. Do you understand?" he said intently.

Doug and I listened quietly and said, "Yes, Dad." Seeing our obedient unanimity, Julie chimed in, "Yes, Dad."

I was surprised Dad wanted us to call her that so soon. It felt awkward, not genuine. At least it didn't sound exactly the same as "Mom," as we'd always called our real mother. I wasn't sure why this was so important to Dad, but he'd made it very clear that it was, and I knew we had to do what he told us. I don't think Julie understood what was really going on, but at seven, Doug understood very well: Señorita Ingrid was our new mother, and that was that. Doug also knew that a spanking was just around the corner if he said anything out of line on the matter.

In my mind's ear, I can hear Dad shouting over the phone from Buenos Aires to Granny in Toronto, "And the kids are already calling her Mum!" Though I can't actually remember hearing him say those very words—he was much too smart to allow that to happen—it was exactly what he would do. Our calling Ingrid "Mum" gave him the trump card he needed to convince his family in Toronto of the rightness and urgency of marrying Ingrid, all for the sake of his children. I know this in my bones.

When María heard about Dad's marriage plans, she was horrified. She took me aside on the stairway of our house and spoke to me in Spanish about it.

"Do you agree with your father and Señorita Ingrid getting married?" she asked sternly, holding me by the shoulders so I looked her in the eye. María was a big woman and had an imposing personality when she was serious about something.

"It's all right, I guess," I replied, feeling conflicted between María's understandable concern and Dad's orders.

For a domestic in Argentina, even one as indispensable as María, to question her *patrón*, even implicitly, to his son's face was taking a huge risk. If it had ever got back to my father, she'd have been fired on the spot without a reference, and she and her family thrown off the property. I didn't want any kind of conflict over this, and probably María knew that, but out of concern for us she'd still taken the risk.

On Easter weekend, Dad and we kids had dinner at Señorita Ingrid's parents' place in San Isidro, a big two-storey, red-brick suburban house with a large lawn. Ingrid's father, Herr Engelhardt (a pseudonym), was a slim, greying middle-aged man, and Frau Engelhardt was as tall as Dad, who was six feet, and carried herself with an aristocratic bearing. They enjoyed petting their two dachshunds. Maids in black-and-white uniforms served the dinner.

The Engelhardts had plenty of space, so we all spent the night there. The next day was Easter Sunday. There was an Easter egg hunt in the yard for us and Ingrid's nieces and nephews. Although we didn't realize it, we were being introduced to the family, as they say.

WE NEVER RETURNED to the Fischers' estancia, and it would be years before I saw Bibi again. But shortly after Easter, Bibi wrote the letter to George's mother quoted earlier.

"Dear Mrs Blackstock," she began, "It is a year ago you came to my house for lunch with Carol—only one year and so many changes! Had we ever thought that then?"

Granny's visit to the Fischers' house must have been one of the many social activities Carol organized during her mother-in-law's visit. Carol couldn't have known that by introducing her to Bibi, she would inadvertently occasion such a letter a year later.

Bibi went on to mention what needed to be acknowledged before anything else: Carol's death.

> Somehow one is not prepared that such a young beautiful girl should pass away – it makes us all reflect how happy and grateful we must be for every moment we have with our dear ones – and that the children are healthy and happy, what a joy we have been given.

After giving her version of us children missing our mother and trying "to find a substitute," Bibi revealed that she and Peter had brought George and Ingrid together. Finally, she addressed the real purpose of her letter.

> I wanted to write you this letter to tell you that as a mother and grandmother and so far away you are probably concerned and maybe a bit worried about the type of a girl George would marry and probably also think it is too soon to think of marriage.

Bibi didn't actually mention that by the time she was writing the letter, on May 3, George and Ingrid were already engaged to be married. I wonder whether George hadn't yet told his mother about the engagement, and this letter was supposed to smooth the way for her acceptance; or he'd already told her, and Bibi's letter was intended to allay concerns Granny may have expressed. George remarrying so soon after Carol's death would have been the last thing Granny expected or wanted. On her traditional scale of values, it would have been out of the question.

Bibi moved on to make her closing argument.

> *Therefore (since we have a hand in this) this calms any fears [since] George could not have found a sweeter and nicer girl – from so many points of view [she] is the best to fill that empty space and I further-more believe the children need a new mother the sooner the better. [Ingrid] is also the right one to help George in his job of representa-tion and entertaining – she is capable to run a house, is intelligent and knows how to talk to people and last but maybe most important – she loves George as well as she loves the children.*

Furthermore, Bibi claimed, even María was onside.

> *María has expressed that she would be happy to have her as patrona and she has also seen how well the children like [Ingrid] as a younger mother and María is still María to them.*

That is categorically untrue. It's not the way María told me she felt about the impending marriage. In any case, it would have been pre-posterous, in that place and time, for a *patrón* to be concerned with a servant's opinion on such a private and personal matter. No one would have known that better than Bibi. And only George would have known about Granny's belief, instilled in her by Carol, in María's importance to her grandchildren.

Bibi ended on a lighter note, encouraging Granny to revisit Argentina—as unlikely as she was to do that.

It was an extraordinary letter: skilfully and artfully composed, with its not-so-hidden agenda. It was also remarkably well written (if not entirely idiomatic) for someone who wasn't a native English speaker. However, I don't think it was really Bibi's letter at all. She may have written it in her own hand and signed it, but I believe the content of the message came straight from my father. There was no way Bibi would have written such a personal letter to Granny without being asked—pressed, more likely—by him.

There was no letter from George himself to his in-laws informing them of his impending marriage —at least none that we ever found in their papers. The Grays were going to have to swallow the fact of George's new fiancée whole, without any sugar coating.

AFTER THE EASTER holiday, we went back to school. The routine felt good. I was doing better and better in my studies at St. John's and even got first place on some Spanish-language math exercises. Thanks to my increasing fluency, I now had no trouble handling the classes conducted in Spanish.

I found new ways of escaping into my own world—drawing my own comic books, riding my bicycle, helping build an "addition" to Freddy Brander's pool house by laying down bricks in the dirt, attending to my collection of marbles, organized by colour, type, and size. Boys have their own non-verbal ways of dealing with their feelings.

I didn't want to go to the places we used to go with Mom. Dad wanted to take us to the Club Hípico, where Ingrid was supposed to meet us. I told him I didn't want to go, but he insisted. He didn't take us to the church where Mom had taken us, or to any other church for that matter, and I didn't mind. I didn't like going to church anyway.

María was busy getting us and the house organized for our move back to Canada. Dad had told us we'd be leaving for Toronto at the end of the Argentine winter and would be staying there until December, when we'd move to our new posting in New Orleans.

"Are we going to have snow in Canada?" I asked María in Spanish.

"I don't think so," she said uncertainly.

I was bewitched by the idea of seeing snow again after such a long time.

GEORGE'S SISTER, AUNT Kay, didn't feel at all the same as Bibi Fischer did about his forthcoming marriage. On July 22, 1960, Kay wrote George a long, anxious letter—the first paragraph ran on compulsively for four tightly spaced pages—revealing deep disquiet in the family about his plans. She was speaking for herself, of course, but her frequent references to their mother and her "nerves" showed also that Granny was upset about George's wedding in general and the demands it would make on her in particular.

After a brief nod to George's good fortune in "finding such a nice girl as she sounds to be," as advertised in Bibi's letter, Kay described their mother's emotional state.

> Mother spills out with emotionalism all over the place with every letter you write and then forgets to transmit it to you, I gather. . . . She forgets a lot these days and perhaps doesn't give you a true picture of her feelings in her letters.

Kay aimed to remedy that. She saw difficulties ahead resulting from George's not being able to serve out his full term in Buenos Aires, as he'd wanted. The posting was supposed to last for three years, and when George had taken Carol to Montreal, he had stressed to the ambassador that he wanted to complete it. But now the department had cut it short.

This meant that George and Ingrid would marry between postings. We'd all be moving to Toronto on the way to New Orleans, his new assignment, and would require temporary accommodation while George and Ingrid were away getting married. They'd decided to hold their wedding in the ancestral hometown of Ingrid's family in West Germany, followed by a six-week European honeymoon— leaving us kids behind in Toronto.

George wanted us to stay at Granny's house, something Aunt Kay foresaw as difficult and disruptive. There was a "desperate" shortage of maids in Toronto to look after us, she explained, and, as George ought to know, "kids get on Mother's nerves."

Somewhat plaintively, Kay urged her brother to ask the department to reconsider its decision.

> I don't suppose you could persuade the department to leave you there till the end of your term. This would probably be best for the children and for [Ingrid]. You must remember she is totally unprepared for the life of the North American housewife & the care (physically every day – not kindergarten) of 3 children.

In fact, Aunt Kay wanted George to reconsider his wedding plans altogether.

> Let me just say that you & she have seen each other under ideal conditions so far. Also it is not recommended to marry someone with such a different background. You think you know her but do you talk together seriously about important matters such as religion, politics, the upbringing & education of children – aims and ends of life?... Everybody is "nice" on casual acquaintance – to meet socially. Remember how you liked the Grays at first (granted you were younger). [Ingrid] is... more set in her ways of thinking and acting [than Carol], not so likely to adopt your ways.... Mother feels... that if [Ingrid] sees the household... with Mother & 3 children & inadequate help – if any – it might put her off altogether.

Aunt Kay must have known she wasn't going to persuade her brother to change his mind. She turned to offering him sisterly (and no doubt unwanted) advice on how to make the best of his situation.

> *Be prepared <u>now</u> to make allowances . . . if you want your marriage to be a success because with your a) difference in nationality & background b) the children & c) moving around you are putting a great strain on marriage which can be a difficult situation even under the most ideal circumstances.*

Aunt Kay was probably speaking for the family when she suggested that she wasn't thrilled with the "nationality and background" of George's choice of bride. She then moved on to a more promising subject for counselling her younger sibling, a subject she cared about sincerely: his children and their emotional needs. "I am most worried that [the marriage] should be a success on account of the children," she wrote. Even though Carol had once referred to her differences with Kay in a letter to her mother, she would have been heartened that *someone* in the Blackstock family was standing up for her kids.

> *Mother thinks sending a maid would be good although she feels María would be best of course. Mother feels, and I agree, that separation from her at this stage (even a year later would be better) will be an awful blow to them – more than you realize. No matter how much they love you & like [Ingrid] it is the person who looks after their everyday needs as Carol did here & as María does now that they really depend upon emotionally.*

Granny and Aunt Kay understood how important María was to us. But the idea of María travelling with us to Toronto was completely unrealistic. Neither George nor Ingrid would have wanted it. And

María herself, no matter how much she cared about us, wouldn't have wanted to leave her own family and move to a strange country.

Kay pulled out all the stops trying to persuade George at least to consider altering his wedding plans: "How about marrying [Ingrid] down there, getting on the boat with your goods & chattels & the kids and all coming up here together for a visit?"

That wasn't going to happen either. George and Ingrid marrying in Buenos Aires? Where so many people remembered Carol on the heels of her mysterious death, with her three children hanging around as reminders to everyone? Nevertheless, Kay persisted: "The more I think of it the more I wish you would just marry [Ingrid] down there quietly with the children all present. They would have a pleasant memory of it all their lives."

Of course, we were never going to be included in the wedding. Someone had to make the suggestion, however, and Kay stepped up. But she still had to contend with the big European honeymoon that George and Ingrid had planned, entailing the problem of looking after us kids in Toronto.

> Give up your idea of a European honeymoon till later. . . . You have all
> your lives for this six weeks trip in Europe and in your job a good
> chance of getting it. You might consider it a sacrifice but one under the
> circumstances you might make for your children.

Anyone familiar with George knew he wasn't going to give up his chance for a romantic six-week jaunt in Europe. I'm sure Kay knew it too, but she tried to persuade him anyway, for our sake. She knew better than even to hint at Toronto as a venue for the wedding, given our parents' ties to their hometown. A fresh start with Ingrid was more attainable in Germany, with the added benefit that they could tap into her family fortune to finance the whole extravaganza.

Finally, Aunt Kay urged George and Ingrid to send thank-you notes to Grandma and Grandpa Gray for sending them their best wishes on their engagement. Grandma and Grandpa knew that however distasteful it might be, they had little choice but to ingratiate themselves with their grandchildren's new stepmother. George and Ingrid, for their part, apparently saw no urgency to reply and acknowledge the Grays' gesture.

BEFORE OUR RETURN to Canada, Dad told us "Mum" would take us on the plane while he stayed behind in Buenos Aires to tie up loose ends. I asked if María was going to come with us, and Dad said, no, she needed to stay in Buenos Aires.

"Why can't you come with us, María?" I asked in Spanish.

"I need to stay here to look after Martín and Cristina," she replied.

So attached were we to María that I'd almost forgotten she had her own family to look after.

Dad said we were going to have a new maid. Her name was Irma, and she'd be going with us on the plane.

I felt sad about losing María, Martín, and Cristina. At the same time, I was excited about the trip. I loved flying and the adventure of travel, and still do. And we'd get to see Grandma and Grandpa again in Toronto.

María told Doug and me to go say goodbye to our friends Michael and his brother Danny, and Freddy Brander. I knew we'd never see them again. Mrs. McKenney took a snapshot of me with my arm around Michael and gave me a hug.

I walked over to the St. John's boarding house, even though I didn't have fond memories of the place, because María had said I should see Mr. Legge, the headmaster. He was feeling sad himself, because his wife had just died of cancer. I told him I was sorry about Mrs. Legge, as María had reminded me to. She had been kind to me.

Mr. Legge crouched down to give me a handshake, and I could see the sorrow in that tough British headmaster's face.

On the morning of our departure, María got us all dressed up, Julie in a pretty dress, Doug and me in bow ties. We needed to look smart when we saw our grandparents, María said. We said goodbye to Martín. We said goodbye to Lassie. She would join us later, Dad told us.

We all got in our car, with Dad at the wheel. Doug and I sat in the back seat on either side of María, who had Julie on her lap. Cristina also squeezed in beside us. The new maid, Irma, rode in front with Dad.

María and Cristina cried all the way to Ezeiza Airport. We were María's babies, and we wouldn't be coming back. Doug and I consoled her by snuggling up close. Ingrid's parents drove her to the airport separately in their own car.

For us, the posting in Argentina was over.

10

UPROOTING

INGRID — "MUM" TO US — didn't like flying. But I loved it, so on the first leg of our trip from Buenos Aires to Toronto, I got the window seat on the port side, next to Doug. Julie and Ingrid sat across the aisle from us, and Irma was behind them. It would be a four-hour flight to São Paulo, Brazil.

Irma was a thirty-something Argentine *morena* (a woman with dark hair and tan complexion) and had a kind disposition. She and Ingrid would spell each other off looking after Julie. It was understood that Irma would be on call twenty-four hours a day, to ensure that Granny wouldn't be overburdened when we stayed with her in Toronto. Ingrid would have insisted on having someone like Irma in any case. One thing Ingrid always required was a live-in maid. Another was her afternoon beauty sleep. There were other needs, but these were requirements.

As the plane climbed away from Buenos Aires, I looked down wistfully at the Rio de la Plata. Two and a half years earlier, the great river had welcomed us to Argentina. Now it looked small from twenty thousand feet. In that moment, a deeper realization sank in:

our life in Argentina as over. Mom was dead. María was left behind. I'd never see my friends again. We had a new mother. So much had happened that it was hard to take it all in.

The flood of memories passed as we left the river behind and flew over the cattle country of Uruguay and southern Brazil. Dusk descended, and we settled in for the long journey to Toronto.

After refuelling in São Paulo, we took off again into the night. Our next stopover would be Caracas, Venezuela. I settled into airplane reverie and fell asleep to the drone of the four DC-6 engines.

I awoke with the morning sun. Ingrid, who was unusually quiet throughout the flight, was staring straight ahead. It was nothing like travelling with Mom, who had always pointed out landmarks to us in her animated way. I noticed that the number-two propeller on the port side wasn't moving. When I mentioned this to Ingrid, she replied, without looking for herself, that it couldn't be true—the propeller was probably just going so fast that I couldn't see it. Then the pilot announced that one of the engines on the left side had been shut down. We shouldn't be alarmed, he said; there was no danger. At midday, we landed without incident in Caracas.

WHEN WE ARRIVED at New York's Idlewild Airport (now Kennedy International), it was the second evening of our journey. As pre-arranged by Dad, airline ground staff met us at the arrival gate and led us to the Trans-Canada Air Lines terminal. The summer evening was so warm that the gates to the tarmac were left open, filling the air with the smell of aircraft fuel. While we waited for our flight to be called, Ingrid took a break to smoke a cigarette, leaving Irma to mind us.

By the time we were airborne again and on the final leg to Toronto, we kids were already well frayed. Doug and Julie slumped over asleep in their seats, but I was too tired to sleep. My attention wandered to Ingrid, seated across the aisle from a young, athletic-looking black man. He turned out to be a Triple-A baseball player, and I heard him offering her tickets to a game in Toronto. "No, thank you," she said, with a stiff, uncomfortable smile, and stuck her head in an airline magazine for the rest of the flight. Afterwards, she told me it was unthinkable that she would have accepted the tickets. It went without saying that this was because the man was black.

We touched down at Toronto's Malton Airport at 10 P.M. and staggered into the terminal building. When we reached the arrivals area, I saw Grandma and Grandpa waiting anxiously in the crowd. I waved to them, and they waved back. Now, I imagine how they must have felt—their stomachs hollowed out as they watched a pretty blond stranger carrying Julie in her arms, with Doug and me alongside.

Excited to see them again, Doug and I ran toward their open arms. They crouched down and gave us big warm hugs. "My goodness, boys, it's so *good* to see you!" Grandma exclaimed. "Welcome home!"

Grandpa reminded us to say hello to Aunt Katherine and Uncle Grant, who were standing by patiently, letting our grandparents be the first to greet us. Then Ingrid walked up, still holding Julie.

"Hello, Mrs. Gray. I'm Ingrid."

Grandma managed to smile and say hello. But before Ingrid could reply, Julie called "Grandma!" and practically leaped out of Ingrid's grasp.

Grandma took her in her arms and hugged her tight. "Why, Julie, how much you've grown!" She passed Julie to Grandpa and shook Ingrid's hand. "It's nice to meet you, Ingrid."

Turning to Grandpa, Ingrid said, "Mr. Gray, it is nice to meet you also."

Grandpa very formally shook Ingrid's hand while Aunt Kay and Uncle Grant looked on. They, at least, would have understood how difficult this moment was for our grandparents.

Granny would see us when we arrived to stay at her house.

INGRID'S STAY IN Toronto would be short. For Grandma and Grandpa, this was probably just as well. It was going to be an awkward relationship on both sides. My grandparents' natural inclination was to keep their interactions with Ingrid polite and to the minimum. But since this woman was going to be our stepmother, friendly relations would be essential—whatever it took for our sake.

As for Ingrid, she knew her place, and it wasn't at the bottom of the pile. Coming from a family of wealth and prominence in Germany, and more recently from a highly stratified Latin society, she was accustomed to being catered to. She let it be known that she was inclined to be toured around Toronto, and Grandma and Grandpa knew better than not to oblige. During a round of sightseeing, they took Ingrid and us kids to a baseball game—so she saw the black player on the Triple-A Toronto Maple Leafs after all. Included in the party were Grandma's aging aunt and uncle. All this must have seemed strange to Ingrid, who had no interest in baseball and even less in the Grays' family.

Grandma and Grandpa invited Ingrid and some of the Blackstock clan for a buffet dinner at their apartment. I played translator between Irma and Aunt Kay, who aspired to learn Spanish and was thrilled to hear me speaking it. "*Mi tía dice que le agradece mucho a usted por venir al Canadá con sus sobrinos y su sobrina*" ("My aunt says she is grateful to you for coming to Canada with her nephews and niece"), I told Irma, who nodded and smiled graciously at my aunt.

Grandma even took Ingrid to tea at the upscale Royal York Hotel, a cavernous fixture of Old Toronto, so the two of them could get better acquainted. She gave Ingrid a five-year diary for keeping a record of this new chapter in her life. In a letter to Dad, Ingrid said what a nice gift the diary was. I wonder if she understood that Grandma's hope was to encourage her to share news of us when we were far away. Ingrid talked to Grandma about her and George's wedding plans. Later, Grandma told me she declined Ingrid's request to be taken on a shopping expedition to pick out her trousseau. She felt it wasn't appropriate for her to help her daughter's successor with that particular task—in fact, she found the request in very poor taste.

Aunt Kay hosted a dinner at her home for Ingrid, Granny, and us kids, all of us crowded around the dining room table—it had been decided there was no room for Grandma and Grandpa. Ingrid sat quietly in the tiny living room with a drink and cigarette in hand while Kay, who hated smoking in her house, attended to the roast, boiled potatoes, and green beans. Uncle Grant doubled as assistant cook and host in the living room. Grant was a brick, a family soldier, who seemed unfazed by whatever circumstance threw his way. Here he was playing waiter to his mother-in-law, still and forever "Mrs. Blackstock" to him, and his soon-to-be sister-in-law, who was already addressing Granny as "Mother."

To George's family and friends, Ingrid's arrival in Toronto was a big deal. Other Blackstock family members did their share of fêting her. Granny took her for drinks at the Badminton and Racquet Club and gave her a brooch. A group of aunts and cousins took her to lunch at the Toronto Women's Club, where they gave her a silver maple-leaf pin. Another cousin invited both Ingrid and Granny for drinks at her house to meet still more cousins and still more aunts. Some of George's friends dropped by Granny's house to be introduced to his new fiancée.

In retrospect, it was probably fortuitous that most of the socializing didn't involve me and my siblings. Ingrid vastly preferred to be the star of the show, and besides, I doubt all those family members and friends who had known and liked Carol would have felt comfortable hearing us call Ingrid "Mum."

With us safely deposited at Granny's, Ingrid soon escaped to West Germany, where she would meet up with Dad for the wedding. A small entourage saw her off at the airport. Instead of Uncle Grant playing chauffeur, this time it was my godfather, Bill Dafoe. Even

Grandma and Grandpa went to the airport. Granny, totally in character, didn't go. There probably wouldn't have been room in the car for her anyway; Ingrid had a lot of baggage.

DOUG AND I needed to start the new school year in Toronto, which wasn't synchronized with the Argentine school calendar. In Buenos Aires, I'd been halfway through the equivalent of fourth grade when we left. So, in September 1960, I skipped ahead half a year to start fifth grade at Brown School, a turn-of-the-century, red-brick public school on Avenue Road, a few blocks from Granny's house. Doug too was moved ahead, into third grade.

Because Granny usually preferred to stay uninvolved with our doings, I was surprised when she took us to school to meet our new teachers and help us get settled. I listened quietly in a chair next to my teacher's desk, while my prim, grey-haired, sixty-year-old grandmother, large black leather purse in her lap, told the teacher my story, or part of it: I had just arrived from Argentina, my parents were away, and I needed to be at the school until Christmas, after which I would be joining my parents in New Orleans.

The school building was huge compared to St. John's. The classes had twice as many kids in them, but, of course, they were all strangers to me. No uniforms. No Spanish. Over the following weeks, I learned some Canadian geography and some French-Canadian songs, such as "Frère Jacques." I felt out of place. There was no Mrs. Toppie to help with homework, so once again I was barely passing.

We stayed at Granny's during the week, Doug and I in one bedroom on the third floor, Irma and Julie in adjoining bedrooms. Most of the time, Irma was occupied with Julie, so Doug and I fended for ourselves. We explored the dank, dark basement, which looked as if it hadn't seen a human being in fifty years. It still had the original coal chute, and moss grew on the walls between the bricks. There were cobwebs in all the corners, rusted-out iceboxes, and other household relics. I missed Lassie; she would stay in Buenos Aires until Dad decided it was time to send her to Toronto. I felt lonely for Grandma and Grandpa. Mrs. Pike, Granny's long-time housekeeper, overheard me telling Grandma on the phone that I missed her and said to me afterwards, "But we love you too."

Luckily, we got to spend the weekends with Grandma and Grandpa. Their apartment was cramped for three kids and two adults, but that was fine with us. Grandpa and I watched Harry Jerome run the hundred metres for Canada at the 1960 Rome Olympic Games. Grandma had Doug mixing ingredients in the kitchen while she was cooking or gave him crayons and colouring books to keep him amused. She took Julie along to the grocery store, sitting her in the cart while she shopped. Doug and Julie spread toys all over the living room floor and turned the place into a romper room, and Grandma and Grandpa didn't mind at all.

Grandma showed me mementoes of Mom: some of her books, a favourite doll, a dress that Grandma couldn't bear to part with. I was especially drawn to the wonderful pastel portrait of my mother hanging on the living room wall. It portrayed a beautiful, unsmiling, almost sad young woman with wavy mid-length dark hair and a strong and determined bearing. Every time I looked at the portrait, it made a powerful impact on me. She looked so *alive*, her deep, pene-trating brown eyes gazing directly into me. She'd have been only nineteen when it was done, but she looked more mature than that—almost timeless—and regal.

The artist was the well-known portraitist Audrey McNaughton, a family friend, who had also painted former Prime Minister Louis St. Laurent for the House of Commons of Canada. Grandma prom-ised she'd ask Audrey to make a copy of Mom's portrait for us, and I told her we'd love to have it. I didn't realize what a time bomb this promise would become.

ON SEPTEMBER 1, 1960, shortly after she arrived in West Germany, Ingrid wrote George a letter. He was still in Buenos Aires. She wrote him partly in English, partly in Spanish; I've translated the Spanish excerpts, which appear below in italics.

She'd had to deal with a lot of last-minute errands in preparation for the wedding, including registering at the local police station. She gave George his marching orders on the matter of the formal attire required for the festivities.

> *All the men are coming in black or cut [cutaway] suits. Papá went to see what it costs for cut suits here, but they are so expensive here that he decided to buy them in London. . . . If you don't wish to buy one . . . there is a shop here which rents brand new cut suits. One thing that is very* <u>*important*</u> *for you to bring is a* <u>*smoking*</u> *jacket. My Uncle . . . and his wife . . . are hosting a formal smoking dress party for us the night before.*

Ingrid wanted his tacit approval of the wedding venue. Then there were the post-nuptial arrangements. For the wedding luncheon "we invited only 50 people more or less," she wrote, and some guests still hadn't confirmed their attendance. For their wedding night, "My parents booked us a very nice room (according to them) in a hotel (old castle) nearby."

Ingrid signed off, "Well my love, I'll go to sleep and dream about you. I love you very much and I can hardly *wait* to see you. Come soon. Many hugs, kisses and love to you."

Julie and I found the letter years later among Dad's papers. I've quoted it because it's the only document we have describing what was happening between him and Ingrid just before their wedding. There wasn't a single mention of us, his three kids, even in passing— nothing to let him know we were all right when she'd been with us in Toronto. It was as if we didn't exist.

A peculiarity of the situation was that George never showed up in Toronto to introduce his fiancée, the stepmother-to-be of his children, to his family and friends. Ingrid had to manage all the social visits, gifts, luncheons, and dinners entirely without him. He was waiting in Buenos Aires while bureaucrats of two nations processed the legal paperwork he needed to get married. The Canadian embassy required certification of certain documents: the birth certificate of George Edwin Blackstock, the marriage certificate of Carol Janice Gray and George Edwin Blackstock, and the death certificate of Mrs. George Blackstock, *née* Carol Gray. George received the embassy certification stamps on what may have been, from his perspective, the earliest acceptable date: July 26, 1960, exactly one year and one day after Carol's death. An earlier date would have made him appear in unseemly haste to remarry. A later date could have jeopardized his wedding arrangements, delaying the remaining paperwork required for the wedding to take place at all.

For some reason, the involvement of the West German embassy in Buenos Aires was also required. Once the documents had been approved and stamped by the Canadian embassy, they needed to be seen and approved by West German authorities as well. This could only be because Ingrid was a German national. It wasn't until August 29, 1960, over a month later, that the West German embassy put its *"Visto Bueno"* ("Approved") stamp on all the documentation that the Canadian embassy had already certified. This was just nineteen days before the wedding.

It must have been a very tense time for George. His fiancée was already in Germany awaiting his arrival, with relatives and friends scheduled to fly in from Argentina, Canada, and various points in Europe. The church, hotels, and restaurants were booked, the all-important smoking jackets and cutaway suits ordered, the honeymoon suite reserved, the honeymooners' travel plans made. The stage was set, and curtain time was fast approaching. But for the many weeks while he stayed on in Buenos Aires, George didn't have all the stamps and approvals he needed to get married.

It wasn't the first time he'd found himself in a close-call situation, and it wouldn't be the last. Most people would feel so stressed by the prospect of something giving way in this house of cards that they'd allow more time, letting the wedding take place in a more relaxed atmosphere. Most people would have followed Aunt Kay's advice about holding a quiet wedding in Buenos Aires. Not George Blackstock.

He had so little time between getting the West German stamp of approval, on August 29, and the date when his presence was required that he flew directly from Argentina to West Germany. No brief stopover in Canada to see his kids.

I wonder what Ambassador Richard Bower and Assistant Deputy Minister Leslie Brown thought about all this. Only a year earlier, they'd been exchanging cables about the difficult family situation George faced. Bower, describing himself as close to tears, had written Brown an emotional appeal for departmental financial assistance for George. Shortly afterwards, there had been still more cables, containing the sombre news of Carol Blackstock's death. Now, barely more than a year later, George was about to remarry in Germany. How had this new relationship evolved so quickly? What had happened to the financial hardship he'd been facing only a year ago?

Brown knew about the Montreal doctors' initial concern over "the possibility of an unknown toxin" in Carol Blackstock's body, and without a doubt he knew about the autopsy findings of arsenic. For him, George's wedding plans must have been—or should have been—horrifying. Here was George, who not long ago had been under suspicion in his wife's death, and whose behaviour the police had been observing, getting remarried already. Not only that, but his new bride had been living in Buenos Aires throughout his posting.

It would have been disturbing enough for Carol's parents to see George remarrying so soon, even without knowing about the "unknown toxin." What must it have been like for Brown to be burdened with that knowledge? What was he thinking about Carol? What was he thinking about her children?

Did Ambassador Bower suspect something? If nothing else, Bower must have felt confirmed in the wisdom of not allowing George to complete his full term in Buenos Aires. His early remarriage after Carol's sudden and mysterious death could have made him an object of unwelcome speculation and an embarrassment to the embassy.

GEORGE MANAGED TO escape the labyrinth of paperwork and board a flight to West Germany in the nick of time. I don't know much about the great event itself, however. Neither George nor Ingrid nor anyone else told us kids anything about it. Except for Granny and Aunt Kay, who managed to make the trip, the occasion was attended exclusively by Ingrid's family and their friends.

All I have by way of a souvenir is a group snapshot taken, I believe, on the night before the wedding. It shows my father in a smoking jacket and striped pants looking as pleased as the Devil himself; Ingrid in formal dress and jewels, turning to smile with satisfaction at the camera; Granny in a fur jacket and pearls, cigarette in one hand, drink in the other; Ingrid's father keeping to the background, his face mostly hidden by Ingrid; and Aunt Kay in a dark nondescript dress, looking slightly shell-shocked. Kay had probably never been to a formal dress soirée like this one in her life, and this certainly wasn't the quiet wedding with children she'd envisioned in her letter to George. No Uncle Grant. Granny must have sprung for Kay's ticket.

The wedding took place in Ingrid's early childhood hometown and site of the family business, the large industrial firm that had prospered during the Nazi era. Like many other companies, it had survived the war and was now growing again as West Germany recovered economically. The company remained the basis of the family fortune.

Unlike my parents' modest civil marriage before a Justice of the Peace in Toronto, George and Ingrid's wedding was a full-dress church ceremony. We know from Ingrid's letter quoted earlier that the venue was a traditional Protestant church for the local English-speaking community, a nice cross-cultural touch. I don't know if any children were present, but there must have been; Ingrid had lots of nieces and nephews.

Back in Toronto, we hardly thought about Dad and Ingrid, and their grand doings. Doug and I knew they were off in Germany somewhere getting married, but we didn't wonder why we weren't included. Nor did we hear from them while they were gone.

After all the festivities, the newlyweds embarked on their six-week honeymoon touring Europe. Where they went, I don't know. Nor do I know for sure who paid for it all, but it certainly wasn't George. I'm quite familiar with a junior foreign service officer's salary. I expect Ingrid's parents paid; my father would continue tapping them for money for years to come. And no doubt he'd already put the bite on Granny to cover airfares and various other expenses he'd incurred.

AFTER THE HONEYMOON, George and Ingrid returned to Toronto for a week or so. They gave us a big toy elephant on wheels, the kind kids could sit on, with a handle for steering. I thought it was an odd present to bring from Europe—if they'd been to India, it might have made more sense. Now I realize it's unlikely they brought it all the way across the Atlantic on the airplane. Dad must have had Uncle Grant pick it up at a Toronto department store.

I'd been waiting anxiously to ask Dad and Ingrid when we'd be getting Lassie back from Argentina.

"Oh, Lassie died there," Dad replied casually, without any explanation.

It was only after I broke down in tears that he offered a token expression of sympathy: "Yes, that's really too bad about Lassie," he said. Years later, Cristina told me that after we left Buenos Aires with Ingrid, Lassie appeared to be ill. The vet said there was nothing medically wrong with her; she was just despondent because her family was gone. So Dad had Lassie put down.

On December 5, 1960, María wrote a letter from Buenos Aires to Julie, Doug, and me, care of Dad, to say hello. She was working for our former neighbours, the McKenneys, she said, and she saw my old friends Michael and Danny regularly. They remembered us, and so did Freddy Brander down the street. Her new house in Boulogne was looking very pretty. María hoped we would write back to her, and she sent hugs from her, Cristina, and Martín. She said she would never forget us. Dad never gave us the letter. When Julie and I got in touch with María, it was many years later, and it wasn't in response to her letter. We only found it in my father's papers after he died.

Following their brief visit to Toronto in late October, Dad and Ingrid took off to New Orleans together so he could start his new job at the Canadian consulate. They stayed at a downtown apartment hotel while looking for a home. We kids stayed behind in Toronto and wouldn't join them until the Christmas school break.

Once again, George was setting off on a new posting. He must have felt a rush of triumph at bringing off all his plans so successfully. Within a little over a year, he'd buried Carol, avoided further unpleasant inquiries by the authorities or the consequences thereof, moved out of Argentina, remarried, enjoyed a long European honeymoon, and stayed on track for his second foreign posting. Even better, he'd arranged to have others foot the bill. It's a marvel that he managed to get away with it all. I wonder what Mom would have said about his *tour de force*.

In our worst nightmares, Doug, Julie, and I couldn't have imagined what was coming next.

11

TERROR IN NEW ORLEANS

"NO, MUMMY! NO, MUMMY! NO!"

I could hear the terror in six-year-old Julie's pleading voice. She was in her bedroom down the hall. Not again, I thought. Scared as I was, I couldn't help myself; from the study I shared with Doug, I bolted down the hallway toward the sound. Through my sister's open doorway, I saw her standing naked, shivering with fright, her ribs protruding, hands by her side after Ingrid had instructed her to remove them from protecting her buttocks. As she later recalled the scene to me, she heard the whistling of the riding crop before it struck her. She remembered wanting to die in that moment, anything to escape the pain. Struggling for air, she felt to her horror a trickle of pee down her legs. And the punishment carried on, blow after blow. When it was over, Ingrid told her to stop crying immediately. It seemed impossible to stop her sobs, but the threat of more punishment was all it took. Almost worse was having to accept a hug from Ingrid, who felt it was important to be magnanimous and show she was now able to forgive the transgression.

Doug had run out into the hall behind me. He knew exactly what was going on and scurried down the stairs. After catching a glimpse of my sister, I was right behind him. We both knew better than to be anywhere near Ingrid when she was seized by one of her fits of rage.

The reason for this particular outburst is long forgotten—Julie had stained her blouse, lost her pink barrette, left her cupboard in a mess—but her degradation and shame are not.

Julie thinks Doug got it even worse than she did. It's possible. Doug could be a mischievous little devil, raiding the cookie jar, fibbing about getting his homework done, lying about losing his pencil set. But all three of us felt the fear, a fear instilled by the unsparing fury of Ingrid's attacks with the riding crop, the belt, the coat hanger, the bamboo cane, a length of garden hose, tools deliberately chosen.

Doug, to his credit, was as stubborn as a donkey. And since he wasn't a gifted pupil in school, he kept getting it. Julie was going to keep getting it no matter what—and for much longer than Doug or me, because she was the youngest. And because she was a girl.

As for me, it took only a couple of Ingrid's beatings before I figured out my avoidance strategy: say as little as possible to her and stay as far away from her as I could.

The beating I remember best was the time I melted lead in one of our kitchen pots. At that point we had been in the house for some time, and Ingrid had recently had her first baby. My friend Steve and I had been experimenting with chunks of lead to make weights for shot-putting. He'd been melting lead at home, and I decided to do the same. Steve took me through the process over the phone, telling me how to melt down a piece of lead pipe in a pot on our gas stove.

The next evening, Ingrid called me up to her bedroom. Dad was away on a business trip somewhere.

"What did you do last night, Jeffrey?"

"I melted lead in the kitchen."

"And what did you use to do that?"

"A pot."

As her interrogation continued, her voice became lower, more and more deliberate and restrained, and I could feel the terror rising within me.

"And what pot was that?"

"A milk pot, I think."

"The same pot that I use to boil the baby's milk."

"I don't know."

"And you melted lead in that."

"Yes."

"And you know that lead is poisonous."

"I guess so. I didn't think of that."

The whole time, I was highly conscious of the riding crop lying on the bed beside her. She told me to turn around and proceeded to hit me furiously on the head, shoulders, back, and legs. I was then sent to bed.

In retrospect, my little chemistry experiment in the kitchen was a dumb and possibly dangerous thing to do. Of course, I had no clue that, beyond the household safety issue, what I'd done probably resonated with a special significance for Ingrid. I was completely ignorant of the fact that my mother had died of poisoning. But it's as if Ingrid *thought* I knew and was going to beat the notion out of me.

JULIE, DOUG, AND I had arrived in New Orleans in December 1960. At the time, we had only the vaguest idea what was going on. We knew Dad had married our new mum and we had to start a whole new life in a totally strange place. That was about it.

Our life in New Orleans began with a pervasive homesickness. Nothing was familiar. When we left Toronto, winter had set in, so it felt very odd to wake up in the morning to mild temperatures. In Buenos Aires, even after Mom had died, there had still been our house, María, our friends, Lassie. In Toronto, there had been Grandma and Grandpa. Here, there was no one, and nothing at all to make us feel at home.

At first, we lived in the Claiborne Towers, a downtown apartment hotel about eight blocks from the French Quarter. Dad and Ingrid had already been living there for several weeks. They were on one floor, we kids and Irma on another. We'd ride the elevator up to our parents' apartment for meals and a TV program before bed. I was disappointed when Dad and Ingrid told us we couldn't watch my favourite program, *Perry Mason*, because it was for grown-ups. I enjoyed the crime stories and the drama, which offered an escape from our barren new existence. Instead, we could watch *Sprechen Sie Deutsch?* on public television.

New Orleans had its charming areas, but the neighbourhood around us wasn't one of them. It was populated by an odd mix of homeless people and men in business suits. In front of our building was Canal Street, a huge boulevard with palm trees, wrought-iron lampposts, quaint streetcars running down the median, and ugly billboards. A block or two away was a raised freeway with layered concrete ramps.

No sooner had we arrived, it seemed, than Doug and I were whisked over to the school we were to attend. École Classique was a midtown private school on Napoleon Avenue, not far from the Garden District. It was favoured by local professional families and expatriate foreign service people. The school receptionist tested us to make sure we could read and write. In her mind, I gathered, Canada was a wasteland of ice, snow, polar bears, and the Royal Canadian Mounted Police, ruled over by the Queen. As far as she was concerned, we might have been illiterate—and Argentina might as well have been on another planet.

The school was racially segregated: no "coloured" students, the polite term for African-Americans in those days. Most white people put their kids in private schools if they could afford it, especially after the public schools became racially integrated in the early 1960s. Yet I was impressed by the huge black presence in the city—about 50 percent of the population—after living in Canada and Argentina, where at that time there were few black people. I was also struck by how badly they were treated, stuck in the most menial and lowest-paid jobs: house cleaning, gardening, garbage collection.

I was put into a fifth-grade class, as I'd been in Toronto. I felt spaced out and lost. For the first week, I kept forgetting to take my homework home with me. I was sent to detention hall for an hour after school and required to do my homework there. Ingrid and Dad had to wait outside in the car until I'd finished before we could drive home. After a few days of this, Ingrid gave me the bus fare, put me on the public bus, and told me to find my own way home—which I did. She also set a rule for Doug and me: there would be no after-school play until we finished our homework.

After a couple of months, we left the hotel and moved into the house Dad and Ingrid had found to rent. It was a two-storey, five-bedroom villa built in the 1940s. A staircase at the front led to a covered patio with a panoramic view of Bayou St. John, just across the street. Beyond the water, there was a statue of General P.G.T. Beauregard, a native son and prominent commander in the Confederate army during the Civil War.

The most distinctive feature of the property was a huge, moss-covered, three-hundred-year-old oak tree known as the "Traders' Oak," said to have been a meeting place for merchants in bygone times. Inside, the house had a spacious living room that did service as an entertaining space, a dining room, a study for Dad, a big kitchen with breakfast area, and a bedroom for Doug and me, where we had bunk beds, and our own bathroom. Ingrid and Dad's bedroom was upstairs, containing a huge king-sized bed and his-and-hers walk-in closets. Ingrid's was jammed full of dresses and more pairs of women's shoes than I've seen in my life. There were bedrooms for Julie and, a little way into the future, the two daughters who would be born to Ingrid and Dad. An upstairs storage area the size of a bowling alley, with two desks and no air conditioning, served Doug and me as a study space. There were also maid's quarters to the rear and another covered patio.

The abuse that had begun in the Claiborne Towers ramped up in earnest once we had a house. It was decided we kids needed "discipline," which Ingrid provided in spades. We soon learned this meant, above all else, obedience to her authority.

Julie was taught to say "Yes, Mum" whenever Ingrid told her to do something. Doug was instructed to put down his toys, stand up, and look at her when she spoke to him. And, of course, the same rules applied to me. Whenever I failed to follow them, I could feel the hair on the back of my neck prickling when Ingrid lowered her voice and intoned, "Jeffrey, do you want to be smacked?"

"No, Mum. I'm sorry," I answered, in the contrite tone she demanded.

Ingrid put Julie into ballet school. She was gangly and awkward, Ingrid declared, and needed to learn how to be more graceful. I was set to practising the recorder. Julie and I were both hopeless at these activities and never were able to come up to Ingrid's high standards.

We all did learn proper manners, however. At the dinner table, you helped the ladies with their chairs and waited until they were seated before sitting down yourself. You never left a piece of bread on your side plate with bite marks in it; you broke off a bite-sized piece instead. You put your folded hands on the table but never your elbows, nor your hands in your lap. You waited until the hostess started eating before you ate. You wiped your mouth before drinking, so as not to leave a mark on your glass. You never spoke when an adult was talking, and you never interrupted. You finished what was on your plate. In that connection, we were told several times about the terrible privations in Germany during the war, and how Ingrid's father had to slaughter their pet rabbit to feed the family. Ingrid showed us how to ring the little bell summoning the maid to clear the table and bring in dessert. You asked to be excused from the table before getting up, but only after you'd folded your napkin in the proper fashion and put it inside its ring.

Dad got into the spirit too. "Douglas, don't eat with your mouth open. And Jeffrey, it's *Captain* Wedekind"—who was one of their friends—"not Mr. Wedekind. He was a ship's captain. That's his proper title. Get it right," he said, pointing a finger at me.

We were enlisted to help clean up the kitchen. Doug got a smack on the head if he tried to deke out of kitchen duties. Julie got a yank and a push if she got in Ingrid's way. Ingrid said she'd learned how to stay out of the way from her mother, who had once pushed Ingrid's face into a pot of hot soup when she'd tried to sniff it as a child. It was like something out of *Grimm's Fairy Tales*. And so we grew adept at staying out of the way, while remaining ever vigilant for Ingrid's instructions.

Normally, Irma did the cooking, with us helping her clean up. Irma was a kind, submissive person, and Ingrid walked all over people like that. Irma put in long hours slaving away to please Ingrid, but she still didn't last very long in our household.

When Dad came home from the office, Ingrid liked to take over in the kitchen, donning an apron and striking a pose by the stove. After saying his usual "Hi, kids," and dropping his leather billfold on the kitchen table, where we were sitting, he'd walk over to Ingrid, and for a couple of minutes they'd make out passionately in a way one would expect only in the privacy of the bedroom. Dad wanted us to see this display. I thought it was kind of gross.

Dad was away on business trips a lot. His assigned territory covered sixteen states across the South. He'd tell us about the Neiman Marcus department store in Dallas; show us photos of the Georgia State Capitol, with the golden dome, in Atlanta; recount his visit to the military base in Alabama, where to his delight he was made an honorary colonel. He was always flying off somewhere.

Sometimes, I'd overhear Ingrid on the phone with Dad when he was travelling. "It's so lonely here without you, *Schatzi*. Please come home. Why can't you come home?"

Ingrid was expecting a baby. She'd become pregnant back in September 1960, the month they got married. I only became aware of it after we moved into the new house, when Dad and Ingrid announced they were having a child. No wonder she was lonely with Dad away, which was always when the hitting got worse.

When Ingrid went out on a Saturday night during one of Dad's absences, Doug and I snuck out of bed to watch a movie on the television in his study. When we heard the car pull into the driveway, we turned off the movie and hightailed it back to bed. Ingrid went into the study, put her hand on the set to check if it was warm, then came into our bedroom. She smacked us both and banned us from watching TV for a week.

I still think Julie got the worst of it. It would start with verbal abuse. A guest at our house had told Julie she was big for her age—a harmless remark that Julie repeated proudly. This met with a tongue-lashing from Ingrid in front of the entire family, including Dad. Ingrid repeated sarcastically, "I'm big for my age, I'm big for my age."

But a lot of the abuse was physical. Ingrid would chase Julie down the hall with a belt in hand for spilling or breaking something. At age seven, Julie told me later, Ingrid put her in her closet for an afternoon as punishment for some infraction, first allowing her to recover from being winded when Ingrid tried to knee her in the stomach. Another of Ingrid's favourite methods was to lead Julie by the ear or her hair to the site of her transgression, yell at her, then yank her by the hair back and forth.

With the benefit of hindsight, perhaps some of Ingrid's behaviour shouldn't be completely surprising. She was a young, relatively inexperienced woman living in a foreign country, suddenly responsible for three young children born to another woman, and engaged in a passionate relationship with her new husband while trying to start a family of her own. Not only that: she had a sheltered, upper-class background and was living apart from her parents for the first time. Being required to adapt to life in a supposedly classless society (except where "coloured" people were concerned), where she had no status apart from her husband, must have been stressful for her.

I suppose that little Julie, being a girl, was Ingrid's chief reminder of her husband's dead wife and lover. Nevertheless, Ingrid had known from the start that if she wanted George as a husband, three children came as part of the package.

If Ingrid was trying to beat our memories of our mother out of us, the strategy backfired. Her cruelty only made me think of Mom all the more. Lying awake in my bed, once again my only refuge, I'd ask myself why Mom wasn't there to protect us. Doug and I would plot our escape—running away to Canada to our grandparents' place—but, of course, we never did. We were too young and knew we wouldn't get very far.

WHEN THE NEW baby was born, things settled down a bit. One day, Dad took us up to his and Ingrid's bedroom to watch what he called "the miracle of breast feeding." There was Ingrid, lying in bed with her entire freckled breast exposed, nursing the baby. We watched with our eyes popping out.

Sometime later, Ingrid received a gift of a golden retriever puppy from Bob and Jenny Borden in Toronto. Ingrid called him Whiskey, because he was the colour of Canadian rye. She took up obedience training with Whiskey and became good at it. She took us to obedience trials in which she and Whiskey were entered, and they won many first-place trophies.

Eventually, Ingrid became Louisiana state obedience champion. The crowd would laugh with delight when Whiskey snapped to heel with alacrity. Ingrid loved that dog. Owners would sometimes discipline a dog at the trials by smacking it with the leash. They'd be disqualified for this, and I asked Ingrid why. She told me it was because hitting the animal showed the owner had failed to teach the dog true obedience.

For Ingrid, teaching obedience paid dividends with us as well. Before long, she had me doing the family's grocery shopping at the A&P supermarket. This could be awkward for me. As a diplomatic family, we didn't have to pay local sales tax, so every time I went to the A&P checkout, I had to produce our tax card and request "no tax." Ladies in line behind me would protest that everybody else had to pay tax, so why was this kid getting away without paying? The manager would have to be called. It made a big fuss and was very embarrassing.

My chores also included mowing the lawn and cleaning up the yard after Whiskey. Ingrid bought a scoop and showed me how to pick up the dog shit and put it into a plastic bag. After a while, she'd come out to make sure I'd done a thorough job. Ingrid was a great believer in one of my father's favourite sayings: "A job worth doing is worth doing well." He'd say it when he showed us how to wash his car. Ingrid applied it to cleaning up dog shit.

One Saturday morning has remained vivid in my memory. Ingrid came out to the backyard while I was cleaning up. She and Dad had slept in and had just got out of bed. For once, she didn't seem too concerned about the dog shit. I had the scoop and bag in my hands and was all prepared to tell her that I hadn't finished, so please not to make any judgments yet. Instead of threatening me, Ingrid had something completely different in mind.

"Jeffrey, let me tell you something. Never let a woman trap you by getting pregnant."

"Okay," I replied.

I had no idea what she was talking about. Now I know exactly: my mother. There must have been some pillow talk going on between Ingrid and Dad, in which, perhaps, she'd pressed him for answers.

TO PEOPLE IN New Orleans, we must have looked like an ideal family: a handsome young couple with three well-behaved, well-scrubbed children, and now a new baby. We were instructed to greet Dad and Ingrid's guests at their cars when they arrived at our house for cocktail parties, our hair combed, clothes pressed. The family Christmas cards were adorned with photos, snapped after much prodding from Dad and Ingrid, of everyone smiling, sort of. We kids didn't smile much otherwise. If we made jokes or carried on laughing in Dad's presence, he called us smart alecks. "The loud laugh that spoke the vacant mind," he used to say. Dad sure knew his *Bartlett's Familiar Quotations*.

Julie never smiled. Dad made a joke out of her blank expression, empty of feeling. "Simper, Julie, simper," he'd say in a sing-song tone.

"I had never seen children so cowed," an aunt of ours remarked later in Canada.

Aunt Kay came for a visit. She and Ingrid got along like oil and water. From the back of our Pontiac Parisienne convertible, I heard Kay, in the passenger seat, tell Ingrid, who was driving, "I still love my children, even if they misbehave." That was quite a rebuke coming from one's sister-in-law, with us kids within earshot.

When Granny visited, Dad and Ingrid threw a cocktail party for her. (There had been no cocktail party for Kay.) I overheard Ingrid making a pitch to her mother-in-law to support her desire for another child. Apparently, Dad wasn't co-operating. "Well, why doesn't he get busy?" replied Granny in an indignant tone, however contrived, to accommodate her daughter-in-law. It's amazing what kids take in that adults think they don't understand.

SOMETIMES, PEOPLE WHO knew us recognized our plight, consciously or unconsciously, and helped us out in little ways. Our landlady, Mrs. Lauer, who lived next door, gave Doug a worktable and tool set.

"Wow, Doug, are you ever lucky to have a friend like Mrs. Lauer," Dad said. "Say thank you to Mrs. Lauer,"

"Thank you, Mrs. Lauer," said Doug.

One of Doug's teachers, Miss Federico, took a shine to him. She was a nice lady, perhaps a bit lonely, and used to take us to the sea lion pool in nearby City Park. She drove us in her late-model Cadillac down to the French Quarter, where she'd buy us ice cream while she had tea. Over the years, Doug seemed to attract the sympathies of older women who picked up on his obdurate rebellion toward his stepmother. Maybe it brought out the mother in them. It must have appeared a little strange for a teacher to be taking us on excursions on Saturday afternoons, but Ingrid didn't seem to mind; it freed up her nap time. Grandma later thanked Miss Federico for all the attention she'd paid us, just as she'd thanked María previously.

I found some consolation in talking to Francisca, our new live-in maid after Irma disappeared from our lives. (I didn't know what had happened to Irma and used to wonder if Dad and Ingrid had assisted her in returning home to Argentina.) Francisca was an attractive *morena* from Guatemala who lived in an un-air-conditioned bedroom off the kitchen. She had a Latino boyfriend who irritated Ingrid when he picked up Francisca on her days off. He'd pull up to our house in his car and honk his horn, which Ingrid considered uncouth. I can understand how she felt.

Francisca and I would sit in the kitchen speaking in Spanish, sharing complaints about Ingrid. She told me she was particularly offended when Ingrid gave her the dog's bowl to eat from. It was clean, of course, but Francisca flatly rejected the insulting gesture. She worked very long hours: her day began before dawn and didn't end until 8 P.M., after she'd finished washing up in the kitchen with our help. But the day after her day off would last even longer, because Ingrid let all the housework pile up until she came back. Ingrid considered housework beneath her. Francisca couldn't leave her job whenever she wanted to, because Ingrid and Dad held on to her passport.

We were also fortunate in having Daisy, our African-American babysitter. Daisy was affectionate and would talk and cuddle with us on evenings when Dad and Ingrid were out. Ingrid didn't like that. Since Daisy was "coloured," Ingrid told us, we shouldn't be hugging her. "You should be proud of your own race," she would say. "We don't want to wind up with everybody *café con leche* [coffee with milk]." She even used the N-word a few times, which in those days was common practice in the Deep South.

With that kind of influence surrounding us, I don't know how we avoided picking up the pervasive local racism. Maybe our family situation gave us sympathy for the underdog. Maybe it was because of values we inherited from Mom and her parents.

I told the mother of a friend that I was disturbed by the racial prejudice in New Orleans. Kids at our school threw garbage at African-American ladies walking by on the sidewalk and yelled "niggah" at them.

"Why do white people treat black people that way?" I asked her. She had no answer for me. But to her credit, she was ashamed of it.

When President John F. Kennedy was assassinated, I was twelve and in seventh grade. On the day it happened, one of the more liberal-minded teachers interrupted our class. "The President has been shot," he announced grimly. "School is to be closed for the rest of the day. If anyone cheers, there will be consequences." Many white people in New Orleans hated Kennedy for advancing the civil rights of African-Americans.

By that time, it had begun to bother me when the Pledge of Allegiance was recited every morning in school. Because I wasn't

American, I was the only student in our class who didn't have to recite it. But apart from that, I thought it was hypocritical for Americans to say they believed in "liberty and justice for all," considering what I saw around me every day.

(New Orleans is a very different city today, nothing like what it was then. When I went there in 2015, many mixed-race couples were strolling along Canal Street, suggesting a far more racially integrated society. The airport is named Louis Armstrong International Airport. The city had ordered the removal of Confederate monuments I used to see. The statue of General Beauregard near our house has since been taken away.)

LIFE WITH INGRID was all about finding ways to avoid her. She terrorized us so much that when she was at home, the only peace we found was in our beds at night. It wasn't a question of being hit for any deliberate wrongdoing. We were always in fear of being hit, at any time, for any reason.

Fortunately, I could escape sometimes by going for sleepovers at friends' houses. I also got some satisfaction from getting better grades in school. Driven, ironically, by the discipline instilled by Ingrid, I put in long hours slogging away in the study room. I received the help and encouragement of some sympathetic teachers and made the honour roll in sixth grade.

One year, after school finished in early June, we drove to the beach at Dauphin Island, Alabama, for a family vacation. Dad drove us in the Parisienne with the top down. On car trips like this, he'd share some of his ideas, which have stayed with me. He didn't agree with certain attitudes prevalent in American society, such as the obsession with handguns. "Why would anyone want to have a handgun unless they were prepared to shoot somebody?" he'd say. The prohibition against abortion was another of his sticking points: "Of course, there are circumstances where abortion is the right thing to do. How can anyone say that an early-stage fetus is a person?"

That holiday remains in my mind as one of the rare family occasions I enjoyed. But our greatest respite from Ingrid's tyranny came when Doug and I went to Toronto in the summers to spend long stretches of time with Mom's parents.

After our mother died, Grandma and Grandpa had told us, "You kids are all we have now." They doted on us. They took us on picnics, helped us with our summer book reports, took us fishing, treated us to baseball games, taught us checkers and cribbage, and made us feel we had a home where we were wanted and we belonged.

I told Grandma about the beatings. Horrified, she said I should call the police when I saw Julie being hit. But I never did. Who, I thought, would believe a kid?

After a couple of years, Julie would no longer be allowed to go to Toronto with us. Dad and Ingrid kept her away from our grandparents. Instead, she went to Buenos Aires with Ingrid to visit *her* family, even though she wasn't considered one of them. On those visits, Julie told me, she didn't have to sit up straight and smile while family photos were taken: she got pulled aside and told to sit nearby.

In New Orleans, I'd go over to my friend Steve's place across the Mississippi River in Timberlane, a housing development with a golf course and country club. We played with Steve's pump-action BB guns, went go-carting, hung around the pool at the country club, and did other things that twelve-year-old boys enjoy.

During a sleepover at Steve's, I told him about my problems with Ingrid. Steve too had a stepmother, but they seemed to have a normal enough relationship. After some emotional conversation up in Steve's bedroom, he encouraged me to call my grandparents from the phone in his room. I took him up on it. I told Grandma and Grandpa I didn't want to live with Ingrid anymore. They already knew about the beatings, but they were understandably alarmed.

My grandmother again said I should call the police when I saw Ingrid striking Julie. But I knew the police would do nothing about it, and it would just result in more trouble from Dad for me and my grandparents. They must have felt terrible not knowing what they could do to help us. I still regret having put them through so much worry. I was desperate.

When his parents saw their phone bill, Steve must have had to explain the reason for the expensive call to Toronto. They never mentioned it to me, and they mustn't have mentioned it to Dad and Ingrid either, who would have punished me if they'd known.

Later, Steve and I got into trouble when he came for a sleepover at our house. We went out after dark and roamed around the neighbourhood throwing stuff at cars. The police picked us up and delivered us to my house. Dad gave me a thrashing and grounded me for a month. Steve's parents just grounded him.

WITH DAD AWAY on business a lot, Ingrid was lonely with no one but kids for company. Since I was the oldest, she'd sometimes tell me things as though I were an adult and not a twelve-year-old. I had a very ambivalent, two-sided relationship with Ingrid, especially as I got older—I was still a kid to be disciplined, but also a quasi-adult when it suited her.

She told me about a colleague of Dad's from the South African consulate who was making sexual advances to women in their circle. Ingrid and her female foreign service acquaintances were all talking about it, and one of them said jokingly, "Maybe we should give him a try." She also told me about a male guest at one of the cocktail parties she and Dad gave who wanted to dance cheek to cheek with her, which she permitted. The next day, he showed up at our door to tell Ingrid he knew "a place where we could go." She sent him on his way. Dad would have been very upset about Ingrid having male friends. I once heard him tell her he expected her never to go out to dinner on her own with a man.

Ingrid got everything she could ask for in material terms—clothes, jewellery, maid service, travel—but Dad also ordered her around sometimes. "Why don't you do something with your hair instead of wearing it straight and long like a teenager?" he told her in front of me. The next thing we knew, Ingrid appeared in a stylish bouffant hairdo. One night, after we all arrived home late from shopping, she didn't feel like cooking (the maid was away) and wanted to feed us a dinner of cold cuts. Dad overruled her. He said that wasn't enough to eat for growing children, and she had to prepare something more substantial.

Dad and Ingrid had a big row after Grandma and Grandpa sent us, as promised, the copy of the pastel portrait of our mother. At first, all we knew was that Ingrid was furious about something. Dad pursued her along the upstairs hallway into their bedroom, where she slammed the door shut behind them. We could hear their argument escalating behind the door. Ingrid was yelling, and Dad was trying to get her to keep her voice down. We couldn't hear what they were saying, but we knew better than to hang around trouble like that.

Later, Grandma and Grandpa phoned and asked us if we'd received Mom's portrait. That's how we found out about it, and how we realized Dad and Ingrid were reading our correspondence from our grandparents. Having learned the painting was on its way, they'd intercepted it without telling us. Their argument had been over what to do with it.

When we asked them if they were opening our mail, they confirmed it without hesitation—as though it were a normal thing for parents to do. Dad told us Ingrid had wanted to give us the portrait herself, but she'd now put it away for us "for safekeeping." Grandpa's reaction was that the painting wasn't hers to give. In the end, Ingrid and Dad held on to it.

IN THE WAKE of this furore, I was surprised when Dad and Ingrid announced that Grandma and Grandpa were coming to see us in New Orleans. They made it sound like a big treat they'd arranged themselves.

The tension between our grandparents and Dad and Ingrid was apparent to us. We knew we were not to talk about our mother—Dad and Ingrid had never come right out and said so, but we knew—yet Grandma and Grandpa were a constant reminder for them of Carol. I also knew our grandparents had been upset about my phone call telling them I didn't want to live with Ingrid anymore. And I knew they were very worried about the mistreatment of Julie. Somehow, it seemed unlikely the visit would go well.

But there was a lot I didn't know. I didn't know that Grandpa had been pressing Dad hard for information about the cause of Mom's death, and that Dad had been putting him off, claiming ignorance, which only made Grandpa more frustrated and suspicious.

With all these fears and anxieties gnawing at them, Grandma and Grandpa drove down from Toronto to New Orleans in their old Ford Mercury Meteor. Its high roof and metal sunshade over the windshield made it look ancient beside the newer, sleeker cars on the streets of New Orleans. This was in February 1964, just before Mardi Gras. I'd turned thirteen two months earlier. We always had school holidays on Mardi Gras so we could watch the parades on Canal Street.

Grandma and Grandpa stayed in a motel, and at first everything seemed to be going surprisingly well. When Grandpa took me out for ice cream, he made a point of telling me he appreciated Dad's taking him to his favourite oyster bar. Both men liked oysters on the half-shell. I learned later that Grandpa was trying to smooth things over for now, so that he and Grandma could enjoy spending time with us kids.

But Grandpa and Dad didn't talk just about oysters. A couple of days after the visit began, Dad and Ingrid abruptly took off for

Acapulco. On their return, Ingrid told me the tension had been running so high they simply had to get out of there. Dad just told me about the magnificent view they'd enjoyed from the balcony of their hotel room, high on a hill overlooking Acapulco Bay.

While Dad and Ingrid were away, Grandma and Grandpa took us to see the Mardi Gras parades. Crowds twenty-deep lined the route, grasping for cheap trinkets tossed from the floats by women in flamboyant costumes and headdresses. Trash lay in the streets everywhere. Sailors on leave climbed the lampposts on Bourbon Street to steal street signs as souvenirs. Returning to the parked Meteor, we passed on old drunk collapsed against a wall with a stream of urine running between his knees. Grandma turned her gaze aside. Mardi Gras was one giant, exotic piss-up.

Things weren't so much fun for our grandparents at the house. At first, Frau Adler, one of Ingrid's frequent babysitters—I don't know what happened to our beloved Daisy—helped out with the baby, our little half-sister, now two and a half. One evening, Frau Adler wasn't there, so we and our grandparents collectively fed the baby. She had quite a set of lungs, which she put to maximum use when she wanted her favourite security blanket at bedtime. Grandma left the house that evening leaning heavily on Grandpa's arm, her nerves completely frayed.

From that point on, the visit was a disaster. Poor Grandma became very ill and finally had to be flown back to Toronto. She was suffering from severe nervous exhaustion over seeing first-hand how difficult and unhappy our home life had become. Her stress was compounded by the frustration of being unable to do much about it. I'm sure Dad would have said Grandma was "acting out," one of his favourite put-downs.

In the wake of our grandparents' sadly shortened visit, Dad sat down to talk with us. Ingrid had departed with her daughter to visit her parents in Buenos Aires. Either he'd finally seen how miserable we were or he'd got the message from his own family, maybe from Aunt Kay, that things were just not right. One way or another, he seemed to understand we deserved a hearing.

The three of us were sullen as we sat on the couch in Dad's study.

"I guess you kids think Mum is pretty strict," he said.

"Yes, we do," I said, speaking for all of us.

"Why do I get smacked every time I open my mouth?" Doug blurted out, wiping away a tear.

"We want you to *protect* us, Daddy," Julie pleaded—then she too broke into tears.

Dad was taken aback by this spontaneous barrage from his normally submissive children. Briefly at a loss, he paused for a minute so we could calm down and he could regroup.

"All right, I know it's been an adjustment for you—a new mother, moving to a new country, starting at a new school. But it's been difficult for *her* too, you know, taking on you three kids as your new mum. I think she's done a pretty good job. A bit of discipline is good for kids, especially with all the confusion of starting out in a new place. We needed to make sure there was order in your lives, that you got your homework done, learned to do your chores, settled into a routine. And darn it, you *have*. When I see all of you with Mum, I see real love between you and her. And let me tell you, that gives me a lot of satisfaction. Now run along and get ready for bed, I'll be right there to say good night."

Dad sounded pleased with himself, satisfied he'd set us straight. But we knew better. We didn't believe a word of it.

12

PANDORA'S BOX

DAD CALLED ME into his study after the other kids had been put to bed. Ingrid too had gone to bed, so the house was quiet. It was spring 1964, a few months after I'd turned thirteen.

He was sitting behind his desk putting his "New Car" folder in order. Whenever he was going to buy a car, he'd set up a new file folder and cram it full of automotive brochures and yellow legal-sized notepads. The folder was already as thick as a telephone directory.

"Hi, Dad. You wanted to see me?"

"Oh, hi, Jeff. Come on in. Sit down."

While he continued tidying up his papers, I looked around the study. Behind him were shelves stuffed with books—dictionaries, *Bartlett's Familiar Quotations,* P.G. Wodehouse novels (I think he'd collected the entire "Jeeves" series), numerous Agatha Christie murder mysteries, the *Encyclopaedia Britannica,* paperbacks about the Second World War. Next to me on the wall were certificates, signed by the now late President Kennedy, appointing George E. Blackstock Vice-Consul of Canada to Louisiana, Texas, Mississippi, and other Southern states. On one corner of his desk sat a wood carving of a Spitfire fighter and on the other a photo of Ingrid. Copies of his favourite magazines, *Sports Illustrated*, *Time*, and *Life*, lay on the coffee table behind me. A chess table was set up between a love-seat and a leather Moroccan pouf footrest. (In one of my favourite photos of Mom, she is playing chess with Dad on a similar board.)

He stapled some paper, closed the file with a rubber band, and sat back in his high-backed, almond-coloured wooden chair, which matched his desk. He clasped his hands behind his neck, stretched back, and peered at me through his tortoiseshell glasses, as if sizing me up.

"Well, Jeff, you're graduating from grade eight soon, going off to boarding school in Canada. So I thought this would be a good time for us to have a little talk, man to man, as they say."

Not *the* man-to-man talk, I hoped.

"You've got the brains in the family, Jeff."

This was news to me. Nothing in the way Dad treated me had ever suggested he thought this. He mostly just ignored Doug, Julie, and me. When any of us did have something to say, it was usually squelched by Ingrid, and that was that.

"I've looked at your last report card and it's pretty good. Well done."

"Thanks, Dad."

"So have you thought about what you want to do in the future?"

"I don't know, Dad. I only just turned thirteen."

"You'll want to go to university, of course."

"I guess so."

"And perhaps do post-graduate work. I could carry you through graduate school." He mused for a moment. "Then a PhD? I don't know whether you're really PhD material."

"I hadn't really thought about it, Dad."

"What about other things in life you might want?"

"Like what?"

"The good things in life, for example. Nice house. Nice things. The good life. Everyone wants that."

"Oh, yeah . . ."

I wasn't sure what he was talking about. All the "nice things" my brother and sister and I got were hand-me-down clothes, measly allowances, Saturdays filled with chores. My clothes came to me from Dad himself. He was such a pack rat that he still kept golf shirts, jockstraps, and other attire from his Upper Canada College days, which had shrunk in the dryer, so they no longer fit him. Ingrid, on the other hand, had a closet replete with fashionable outfits for every conceivable occasion, a jewellery box overflowing with gold bracelets and pearl necklaces, and maids, and us, to clean up after her. She and Dad were out at parties all the time. They paid us so little attention—positive attention, that is—that we might as well have been the hired help. Doug couldn't get the bicycle he'd wanted for his birthday. He would go through his childhood hoping for a bike. Julie's wardrobe was the bare minimum. Was this the good life? For Dad and Ingrid, yes.

"How do you feel about having a family someday?"

"I don't really know."

"You won't understand this until you're older, Jeff. But having a family is the most satisfying thing you can do in life. Love makes the world go round. I loved your first mother very much, and I love your second mother very much. You know, I still have pictures of your first mother. I take them out sometimes and look at them."

I thought this was very odd, especially after the fraught incident with Mom's portrait. We still felt we weren't allowed to talk about her.

But Dad seemed to be in a conversational mood, so I worked up my courage to ask him something that had been bothering me for a long time.

"Then why weren't we given the picture of our first mom that Grandma and Grandpa sent us?"

My father, George Blackstock, circa 1937, with his father, George Sr., who died when the boy was 12.

My mother, Carol Janice Gray, about two years old, circa 1936.

Carol, bottom row, 4th from left, at age 15 in grade 10 just before she married George.

Carol, 16, and George, around his 18th birthday, with the author, 1951.

Carol's portrait, a source of acrimony with my father and stepmother.

George and Carol, probably in their late teens after they married.

Carol's diplomatic passport for Argentina, found in our father's papers after his death.

Our family on our lawn
in Buenos Aires, 1959.
Carol would never return
to Argentina.

DEPARTMENT OF EXTERNAL AFFAIRS

INCOMING MESSAGE

| FROM: | THE SECRETARY OF STATE FOR | BROWN |
| | EXTERNAL AFFAIRS, CANADA | OTTAWA. |

TO: Canadian Ambassador,
.... Buenos Aires.................

Security Classification

UNCLASSIFIED

File No.

| Priority | Air Cypher | Code | No. | Date | July 25,1959 |
| | En Clair | Cypher | | | |

| Internal Distribution: | Reference: |

Subject:

FOR BOWER CAROL BLACKSTOCK DIED THIS MORNING.

BROWN

Done SL..............

Date July 27/59....

Copies Referred To:

The cable from Ottawa to Argentina on July 25, 1959, the day Carol died in Montreal.

George Blackstock at the party for his wedding to Ingrid in Germany, September 1960.

María, our nursemaid and Carol's confidante, with Martín and their daughter Cristina.

Portrait photo of George Blackstock as a Canadian foreign service officer.

Doug, Julie, Grandpa, and I in our grandparents' apartment, about 2 years after our mother's death.

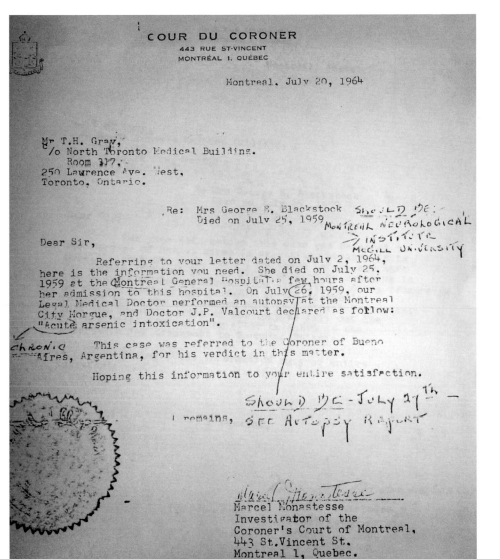

COUR DU CORONER
443 RUE ST-VINCENT
MONTRÉAL 1. QUÉBEC

Montreal. July 20, 1964

Mr T.H. Gray,
c/o North Toronto Medical Building.
Room 317,
250 Lawrence Ave. West,
Toronto, Ontario.

Re: Mrs George E. Blackstock _Should be:_
Died on July 25, 1959 _Montreal Neurological_
→ Institute
McGill University

Dear Sir,

Referring to your letter dated on July 2, 1964,
here is the information you need. She died on July 25,
1959 at the Montreal General Hospital a few hours after
her admission to this hospital. On July 26, 1959, our
Legal Medical Doctor performed an autopsy at the Montreal
City Morgue, and Doctor J.P. Valcourt declared as follow:
"Acute arsenic intoxication".

chronic ← This case was referred to the Coroner of Bueno
Aires, Argentina, for his verdict in this matter.

Hoping this information to your entire satisfaction.

Should be - July 27th -
I remains, _See Autopsy Report_

Marcel Monastesse
Investigator of the
Coroner's Court of Montreal,
443 St.Vincent St.
Montreal 1, Quebec.

The Montreal coroner investigator's letter to my grandfather stating the cause of Carol's death. As my grandfather's notes indicate, key details are inaccurate.

My grandfather's poem in memory of Carol with her photo that he
kept in his wallet.

From left: Doug Blackstock, Julia Blackstock, and the author in
Mérida, México, 2019.

"That was a misunderstanding, Jeff. Mum and I decided to keep it for you because Mum wanted to give it to you herself. When your grandparents tried to give you the picture directly without speaking to Mum and me first, they created a lot of bad feelings. We felt they were going behind our back with our children."

"So what's going to happen to the picture?"

"We're keeping it for you children so that you'll have it someday."

Though this made no sense, I felt emboldened to take another chance.

"And what about reading our letters between us and Grandma and Grandpa? I don't understand why you and Mum have to read our letters."

"Well, Jeff, you won't understand this until you're a parent yourself. Parents want to protect their children. Your grandparents have been difficult. They've done things that interfered with our family. You know, Mum has had a hard enough time as it is, moving away from her parents in Argentina, coming to a new country to be with us and look after you kids. She'd never been a mother before and now she has four children. She's doing the best she can. I know you kids think she's strict, but we believe children need strong parenting."

"But what about—"

"Your grandparents should be supportive. They should be helpful. They need to talk to Mum and me about you kids before interfering. But they don't. We're worried about what they might say to make things worse in our family. I don't really expect you to understand this until you're older. For now, you'll just have to trust me."

IN FACT, GRANDPA'S patience with Dad was now completely exhausted. As I later learned, he had made repeated attempts to get a straight answer from him about the cause of Carol's death. He'd never received one. In his frustration over George's evasions and stonewalling, he'd launched his own investigation.

When Grandpa contacted the Montreal Neurological Institute, he was put off at first, given the runaround. Then a breakthrough occurred. In September 1963, my mother's medical case was presented, ostensibly under the cloak of anonymity, at the annual meeting of the Canadian Society of Forensic Science, in Quebec City. A few months later, in 1964, the society published the presentation in its journal, along with the related autopsy and toxicology reports. As before, the identity of the deceased was disguised under the moniker "Mrs. C.B." But given those initials, as well as other details cited in the case study, there could be little doubt that it was based on Carol Blackstock's autopsy. Although it wasn't explicit enough to reveal her identity to the world, this development must have made it difficult, if not impossible, to block or ignore Grandpa's enquiries any longer.

Grandpa finally worked his way through to the Montreal coroner's office. There, he learned the truth about the cause of Carol's death. His discovery must have occurred roughly around the time I had my "man-to-man talk" with my father in New Orleans.

Of course, I, and the world at large, knew nothing of this. And as it would turn out, my grandfather was not in a good position to reveal it. I can only imagine my grandparents' pain and anguish.

AS DAD HAD announced to me in his study, a new chapter was opening in my life. That summer, he took me to visit Ridley College, the boarding school for boys in St. Catharines, Ontario. Ridley had accepted me as a student, and I'd be boarding there, far away from New Orleans, for the next four years.

When Canadian foreign service families are on posting, to ensure the children continue to receive a high quality of education, the government offers them a choice: their kids can attend, at public expense, either a local private school in the host country or a boarding school back home. Dad and Ingrid elected the boarding school option, which meant eventually Doug, Julie, and I would all be living away from home as children.

Dad had arranged for us to meet an assistant headmaster at Ridley, who gave us a walkabout tour of the extensive grounds. Since the decision that I'd attend Ridley had already been made, our visit was just a pro forma introduction, and a chance for Dad to establish his presence with the school. During my four years there, he'd visit me no more than three or four times.

By September, Dad was back in New Orleans, and it was Grandma and Grandpa who drove me from Toronto to start the fall term at Ridley. Grandma packed me some sandwiches and cookies, as she always did. Grandpa gave me some pocket money.

I was installed in the Lower School in ninth grade. At first, it was lonely living in a dorm with linoleum floors, sleeping on steel-frame beds with thin mattresses on wire mesh, and sharing one toilet with eleven other boys. When the bell would ring at 7 A.M., I'd wake up wondering what I was doing there. That bleak feeling was familiar from the days when I'd boarded at St. John's, in Buenos Aires, but then I'd known I was staying only a short time, until we found a house. The duration at Ridley was going to be far, far longer.

Most of the other boys were from Toronto, less than two hours' drive away, where they had networks of friends and family. I didn't have any friends in Canada, and the only family that really mattered to me were my grandparents. There were some boys from the United States and Latin America, but they were mostly returning students, already familiar with the place.

Academically, I got off to a slow start—something that seemed to happen whenever I moved to a new school in a new country. But I was a determined kid and took pride in my accomplishments. After a period of adjustment, I began doing much better. I made friends and enjoyed playing on the soccer, swimming, gymnastics, and cricket teams. I participated in some theatre productions and represented Ridley in a discussion forum with public school students from the region. In twelfth grade, I studied tirelessly to wind up near the top of the class and get accepted at Neuchâtel Junior College, a Canadian school in Switzerland with high academic standards.

One Sunday, when Dad was on a business trip to Canada, he visited me at Ridley. It was the day after my sixteenth birthday. I was in eleventh grade. He took me out to lunch and, while we sat in his rental car, he gave me a birthday card, along with fifty dollars and some little presents such as comic books. The gifts would have been more appropriate for a much younger boy. I don't know whether Dad actually believed I was still a child or just wanted to believe it. It had been a long time since we'd seen very much of each other.

THROUGHOUT THE YEARS at Ridley, my real home base was my grandparents' place in Toronto. Every year, I'd spend the Thanksgiving long weekend and Easter holidays there. For the Christmas holidays, I went at first to New Orleans, where Dad and Ingrid stayed on for another two and a half years. Their next posting was Bern, Switzerland, in summer 1966, and after that I spent Christmases in Toronto. Dad considered it too expensive to fly me to Bern; I think the government paid for only one trip "home" a year.

As before, Doug and I had our summer holidays with Grandma and Grandpa. Doug joined me at Ridley in my second year, but he didn't like it much. Julie continued living with our parents throughout their six years in New Orleans, then three more in Bern and another in London before she could get out of the house—where, in her mind, she was living as a hostage—and away from Ingrid to attend an English boarding school.

My grandparents loved to play bridge and socialize with friends. Grandma taught me the basics of bridge: "Length before strength," she'd tell me, a tenet of the game I've retained ever since. Grandpa showed me how to use the tools in his basement workshop in their apartment building, took me to baseball games, and regaled me with his First World War stories.

My grandfather was my mentor and role model. He was kind and big-hearted, with a great sense of humour, but he was no pushover and could be tough when necessary. I admired his toughness, just as I admired his work ethic. Although retired from his corporate job, he still prepared tax returns for individuals as a chartered public accountant and managed a medical building for business clients. He told me about one client who insisted on paying him less than his normal fee, on the grounds that Grandpa was retired and therefore shouldn't charge the going rate for his services. Grandpa sued him in small claims court and won.

Grandpa didn't like phonies and was very frank in expressing his opinion of my father. Dad had told me he sent Grandpa "fat cheques" to pay for our room and board during the summers. Grandpa told me flatly this was false.

I liked it when Grandpa gave me adult responsibilities. On the first of the month, I'd take my grandparents' rent cheque for $170 to the landlord in the apartment below. Sometimes, Grandpa would ask me to go to a nearby store to buy Grandma some stockings or perfume she liked.

My friends were always welcome at my grandparents' place and appreciated their openness and kindness. My Ridley roommate came from a small town in Northern Ontario, too far away for him to go home at Thanksgiving or Easter, so he'd have to stay at school during the holidays. Instead, my grandparents were glad to have me bring him along so he wouldn't be lonely. I also brought my first girlfriend, a cute, petite, smart blond girl who attended a public high school in

Toronto, for dinner at my grandparents' place. She fell in love with them, as all my friends did.

From Ridley, I dutifully sent letters home to Dad and Ingrid, reporting on my exploits on the soccer team or the cricket pitch. In twelfth grade, I bowled a hat trick (three outs in succession off three balls) playing for the second cricket team against Upper Canada College. "Have you ever bowled a hat trick in a game before?" my coach asked incredulously. Dad wrote back, "Well done," while also expressing his annoyance that, since I'd failed to send my letter by airmail, it had taken weeks to reach Switzerland.

Doug and I visited Dad and Ingrid in Bern one summer. He took us summer skiing at Zermatt, beneath the towering Matterhorn. It was our first time on skis, and Doug and I slipped and fell so much in the slushy snow and ice that we swore a blue streak in our frustration. Offended, Dad told us, "You know I don't like to hear that kind of language."

The subject of Mom arose from time to time, at first obliquely, later more directly. Doug and I were always at a loss when completing school medical forms requiring us to state the cause of our mother's death. Dad told me to write "Cause unknown." On one occasion, Doug asked Dad straight out why Mom had died, and Dad replied testily, "She just stopped breathing."

Doug knew better than to ask that question again.

So what transpired when the subject came up next was a big surprise.

I WAS NOW seventeen and spending the summer holidays with my grandparents as usual. At the medical building where Grandpa was business manager, he got me my first job, working as an attendant in the parking lot.

Grandpa and I would chat from time to time during my shift, sharing jokes, some of them off-colour. He kept a fifth of rye in his office desk and would take a nip on occasion, though he wasn't a big drinker. I had to laugh when he said Grandma had asked if he had a bottle in his office: "Noooo, dear," said Grandpa, shaking his head in earnest denial as he told me the story.

That summer, Dad was back in Canada on one of his business trips. While in Toronto, he stayed at Granny's house, and I'd visit him there. He refused to come to Grandma and Grandpa's apartment. I was unaware of the greatest cause of their antagonism, but I did know that Grandma and Grandpa worried about us grandchildren, especially about Julie still being under Ingrid's control. "We don't want Julie to be just a handmaiden for Ingrid," Grandpa told me.

Before one of my visits to Dad, Grandpa gave me a note to deliver to him. It was unsealed so that I could read it, which I did.

"George, it is imperative that you come and see us while you are in Toronto," Grandpa had written.

I handed Dad the note in Granny's kitchen, where he'd been reading *The Globe and Mail*. After scanning the note, he looked up at me from his chair.

"Your grandfather wants to see me. What do you think it's about?"

"I don't know exactly," I replied.

"He says it's 'imperative' that I see him."

"I think there may be trouble," I offered.

"Well, I hope not. It really doesn't do any good when they make trouble."

"I think they're worried about Julie."

Dad let out a sigh, as if it was all too tiresome. "I can understand them being concerned about their grandchildren. But they forget it's the *parents* who have responsibility for them."

"I think they're concerned that Mum is too strict with her."

"Well, you know, we all understand how hard it was for them when your first mother died. But your grandparents are meddle-some—they've created more problems for everyone and for them-selves by interfering rather than accepting the circumstances."

"Meddlesome?"

"Yes, meddlesome. Your grandmother is a worrywart and a busy-body. She doesn't have her own daughter anymore and has taken to meddling in the lives of her grandchildren—and in *our* lives, quite frankly. Of course, we all know about the reputation of stepmothers. Mum has two black marks against her from the start—and with your grandparents probably three. Instead of working with us, they create problems. Instead of understanding that you kids have a new mother, who has done a pretty good job in a challenging situation where she could have used their support, they've just made things more difficult."

I listened in silence.

"Let's sit here for a minute," Dad said, and motioned me into Granny's living room.

"Mum came into the family and right away had to take responsi-bility for you kids," he continued. "She realized that a little discipline was needed. You hadn't had a mother for a while and our home needed some order. Your grandparents have chosen to cast this in the light of the wicked stepmother, which is of course nonsense, all twisted around. As you're aware, people who know us know that's just not true.

"Jeff, the road to hell is paved with good intentions. You may sympathize with your grandparents—but just remember they're being very destructive. That whole business with your first mother's picture created a lot of bad feeling. Mum wanted to give you the picture herself, and her plan was ruined by your grandparents' inter-ference. In spite of that, I look at you all and I see love, real love. Whatever you do, don't let your grandparents spoil that."

He was so persuasive, I could almost believe him—even though the image he was presenting was far from the reality I knew. He must have been talking about some other family, not ours. We hadn't felt any love from, or for, Ingrid, let alone "real love," since she'd become our stepmother. Maybe my grandparents *were* interfering. But they were doing it out of love for us. We felt they were the only people in our lives who truly cared about us and were ready to defend us against Ingrid's physical and emotional abuse. But it was a lot more complicated than that—far more complicated than I knew.

Even so, I certainly didn't want to get into an argument with my father. What would have been the point? I wasn't going to win, and he wasn't going to change his mind.

I WAS AT my grandparents' apartment when Dad arrived for the meeting. He came up the stairs and met them in the living room.

"Hello, George."

"Hello, Howard. Hello, Gladys."

After Mom died, Grandma and Grandpa had asked Dad to call them by their first names, instead of "Mom" and "Dad."

It was arranged that I would go out for a while so I wouldn't witness the confrontation. Over the next few days, however, I heard bits and pieces from both sides, affording glimpses into what had clearly been a bitterly contentious meeting.

"Your father is a ruthless man, Jeff," my grandmother told me.

My grandfather was even more specific: "You probably know this, Jeff, but I think your father is a bastard. We are not prepared to have Julie be mistreated."

I also got Dad's version.

"Your grandparents have it in their heads that Julie is a prisoner of her evil stepmother," he told me. "They actually want me to sign over custody of Julie to *them*. Well, no parent is going to do that.

From now on, I think Mum and I are going to have to limit our contact with your grandparents to a bare minimum. We tried to accommodate them, but they returned our goodwill with nothing but problems.

"You know," he continued, "your grandfather and I have had an understanding, a sort of unwritten gentlemen's agreement, if you like, about you kids. I realized that since your mother died, you're pretty much all the family they have left. I also wanted you to have a place to stay in Toronto, where the family is based. But that was on the understanding that they'd behave as normal grandparents would."

"What do you mean by that?"

"Oh, you know, grandparents are there to spoil their grandchildren, but they leave the role of raising the children to the parents."

And then Dad said something completely out of the blue.

"You know how you've asked about your mother's death? I've always told you they never found out what she died of. Well, they never *did* find out."

This seemed very strange to me. I simply didn't know what to make of it.

Dad didn't tell me what he was going to do about my grandparents, except to limit his and Ingrid's relationship with them. As it happened, he never did anything about my grandparents' contact with Doug and me, which continued the same as before.

But that wasn't all there was to it. Grandpa still hadn't told me the whole story. I suspect he knew that, as a young adult, I was aware of this.

He must have been horribly conflicted about what to do. I think he didn't want to impose on me a terrible revelation about my mother's death because he feared it would burden me for life. But neither did he want to deprive me of what I was entitled to know: the truth. In the end, he told me just enough so that I could decide for myself how much I wanted to know.

When I finished my shift at the parking lot, Grandpa fetched me, and we got into his car.

Before starting the engine, he turned, looked me in the eye, and said, "Jeff, we found out how your mother died. It wasn't a tropical disease, like your dad once said. And when I tried to talk to him about what we know, he told us, if we didn't keep quiet, we were never going to see our grandchildren again."

So this was my grandfather's take on the "gentlemen's agreement," as my father had termed it: talk about Carol's death to *anyone* and you won't see your grandchildren again.

"Nevertheless, if you ever want to know what your mother died of, I'll tell you."

Grandpa was prepared to tell me the truth, even at the risk of being cut off from his grandchildren.

I struggled desperately to take this all in, to understand fully what it meant. This was my *mother*, and my grandfather was hinting to me—no, telling me—that she'd died of something ugly and terrible. Yet deep down, I didn't want to know. It sounded very much like it implicated Dad.

I loved my dad. He was a godlike figure who still towered over my life.

I loved my grandfather too.

I didn't want my world to come crashing down. I remained silent, unable to accept my grandfather's invitation.

13

MY ENGLISH SUMMER

THE AIR CANADA DC-8 began its descent over the lush green fields of Southern England. It was the summer of 1971, and I was twenty. The trip from Toronto had been uneventful. I'd managed a couple of hours' sleep before North American night fast-forwarded into North Atlantic dawn. Groggy and dishevelled, I felt nonetheless content, as always, to be embarking on an international trip promising escape and adventure.

I breezed through Customs, collected my suitcase, and stepped outside the Gatwick Airport terminal. Although it was the end of June, the early morning air was chilly. I spotted my father behind the wheel of the family station wagon in a lineup of vehicles waiting to meet arrivals.

I was happy to see Julie in the back seat as I climbed in beside Dad.

"I just got this new jumpah. D'yuh like it?" she asked me.

"A new jumpah. D'yuh like it?" I replied, echoing her recently acquired English accent.

"Stop it!" she said, laughing.

Julie was now fifteen and attending boarding school in Guildford, near London. From her letters, it sounded like a typical English school for girls: masculine uniforms, straw boater hats, field hockey, luke-warm tea, and schoolmistresses bossing around students and parents alike. But Julie was happier living there than at home with Ingrid.

Of us three siblings, she was the one who missed our mother the most, yet ironically she had known her for the shortest time. Since Doug and I were several years older, we at least had substantial mem-ories of her, whereas Julie had only snippets of memories from when she was a toddler. It was nice to see that she now had the indepen-dence to buy herself a new sweater and hadn't been cowed into sup-pressing the accent she'd picked up at school.

"I really like your new sweater . . . uh, jumpah," I told her.

Turning to Dad, I asked how Doug was doing. Dad had sent him to a boarding school in Scotland, an ascetic institution where Dad had hoped the cold showers and hikes in the snow would improve my brother's academic performance. Wearing kilts and eating haggis may have built character, but the report cards were no better than they'd been at Ridley. Doug was now eighteen and wouldn't be returning to school in the fall.

"He's fine. He'll be home in a couple of days," Dad replied non-chalantly. Putting the car in gear, he pulled out of the lineup and headed for West Byfleet, the town in Surrey where the family home was now located, half an hour southwest of London by train.

Two years earlier, Dad had been posted from Bern to the Canadian High Commission, as the embassy in London is known, then on Grosvenor Square. He and Ingrid had bought a large, hand-some English country house with oak beams, leaded windows, and an expansive garden with a tennis court and swimming pool.

After completing my second year in arts at the University of Toronto, I was escaping from the drudgery of a two-month summer job as a dishwasher. I had no more profound motive for visiting

England than to have a good time. I was on holiday, and I was going to enjoy myself playing tennis, swimming, hanging out in the pub, chasing girls, and seeing a bit of Europe. I had no interest in learning more about our family life, from which I felt happily disengaged.

Since twelfth grade at Ridley College, much had happened.

I'd finished high school in Switzerland at the Canadian "junior college" in Neuchâtel. It was coeducational, a big change from a boys-only boarding school. I learned to speak French living *en pension* with a local family, and for a while I had a Spanish girlfriend. She and I were both outsiders in the closed society of *la Suisse romande*, though I had a Swiss girlfriend for a while too.

I enjoyed my year in Switzerland. I think I inherited a love of being abroad from Dad, who always showed his appreciation of local culture and history, no matter where we were. There were school trips to Spain, Morocco, and Italy. During the summers, I had fun working at an international camp in Davos, first as kitchen help, later as a counsellor to a group of ten-year-old European kids.

At the University of Toronto, I was back in the city where I was born, but had never lived for any great length of time. I had no established network there, except for my grandparents, whom I saw regularly, and some aunts and uncles on Dad's side, whom I'd see only occasionally. I was busy with my English and philosophy courses, getting together with some Neuchâtel friends, and the occasional romantic interest.

On the outskirts of West Byfleet, Dad pulled into the semicircular gravel driveway in front of "Longmoor," as their house was called. Flowers bloomed in the beds alongside the beam-and-stucco walls. The family's aging blue Volkswagen Beetle from Switzerland was parked near the front door. The tennis court and kidney-shaped swimming pool were in the back, complete with pool house and changing room, and a ninety-foot-wide lawn bordered by shrubs and oak trees. A rear gate gave access to the local golf course. Close by were a park and a pub. Beyond that lay the cafés, bookstores, and shops of West Byfleet. London was within easy reach, the Continent just across the Channel. I'd brought a few good books to read. What more did I need?

Over the following weeks, Doug and I enjoyed the use of the Beetle for making excursions around the area. We'd run over to the pub in Pyrford or into West Byfleet for shopping. I was a keen tennis player and would practise my serve with a bucket of balls on the court. I'd swim in the pool when the weather was warm, read in the alcove off the living room overlooking the garden, play croquet, and go to parties. While Doug enjoyed a dalliance or two, I had a couple of short-term girlfriends.

Ingrid still had designs on controlling my behaviour. But I disabused her of that idea early in my stay, easily rebuffing her by saying, "You have no reason to speak to me like that." I wore my hair shoulder-length, in the style of the times; this wasn't popular with either Dad or Ingrid, but they had to live with it.

FROM TIME TO time, we went into London as a family, usually to a play or concert in the evening. The first production Dad took us to see was *The Mousetrap*, by Agatha Christie.

I drove Julie, Doug, and Ingrid in the station wagon to meet Dad at a West End pub. He took the train to work in the mornings, so by bringing the car we could all drive home together after the play. For Ingrid, in her evening clothes, the car was more comfortable than the train. There wasn't as much of a role for her in London as there had been in New Orleans or Switzerland, and nothing like the social whirl of Buenos Aires. As a result, she stayed home a lot. An evening at the theatre gave her an opportunity to dress up and wear some of her jewellery. Dad would be in a business suit, so we all dressed up. Our two younger half-sisters were at home with their German au pair.

We were in the West End to see a play, but for Dad the pub itself was a stage. It was one of his favourites, and with his family on display he was in his element.

One of the barmen came over to escort us to our table.

"Hello, Mr. Blackstock. How are you this evening?"

"Very well indeed, Jerry. You have a table for us?"

"Your usual, sir. Right over here."

The pub was fitted out with leather banquettes and lots of old-world oak and brass. The lighting was more subdued than in the raucous, smoke-filled East End pubs, where the drinkers would fall off their stools if a barman greeted a guest at the door. But this wasn't the East End, and Jerry knew he could count on a duty-free bottle of Canadian Club at Christmas if he treated Dad right.

Ingrid ordered a gin and tonic, Julie a shandy, and Doug and I both emulated Dad by having a pint of best bitter. After giving us newcomers a discreet once-over, the regulars settled back into their Scotch-and-waters, *Financial Times*, and quiet conversations.

The bill arrived face down on a small black tray, and Dad enacted his customary ritual, studiously examining the bill like a poker player with a newly dealt hand, replacing it face down on the tray, withdrawing his billfold from his breast pocket, and removing some pound notes while shielding them from view with a conjuror's sleight of hand. Folding the vulgar pound notes, he carefully tucked them under the bill so they were invisible. Julie, Doug, and I looked at each other with expressions that said, "Not again!"

I didn't know which was more entertaining: Dad's performance at the pub or the play afterwards.

As we settled into our seats at the Ambassadors Theatre, in Covent Garden, Dad expressed his long-standing admiration for Agatha Christie. "She's *tremendously* clever," he exclaimed, marvelling at the incredible nineteen-year run *The Mousetrap* had already enjoyed in the West End. He loved the way Christie was able to fool audiences, misdirecting them so they didn't realize who the killer was until the trick ending. He also admired her dedication to her work. "Writing books for a living like that requires not only discipline," he said, "but self-discipline." Mrs. Christie had probably killed off more characters than any mystery writer ever, Dad enthused. We all enjoyed the play, but not half as much as he did.

During the hour-long drive home, Dad at the wheel this time, we had a lively talk about theatre. If he hadn't been obliged to earn a living so early in life, I'm sure Dad would have preferred the theatre as a profession. He told us he'd have liked to be a director. "It would be wonderful to stage a play exactly as *you* see it," he said wistfully, recalling his days in college drama.

I'd directed a play myself in my second year at university: *The Bald Soprano*, by Eugène Ionesco. That summer, I also took a theatre studio course in London and wound up dating a fellow student. I was still trying to emulate Dad—though he'd never have chosen to direct an absurdist play by someone like Ionesco. For her part, Julie was reading English literature at school, and it didn't take long for the conversation to turn to Shakespeare.

Dad, Julie, and I had all read Shakespeare, and Dad was fond of quoting him at the drop of a hat. Somehow, we got on to *King Lear*. Dad expanded on the timeless simplicity of the story: A king gets duped by two of his daughters, Regan and Goneril, who are scheming and deceitful and claim to love him, but just want his power and money. In his folly, he fails to see the value of his third daughter, Cordelia, who turns out to be the truly loyal and honest one. His initial failure to recognize Cordelia's love becomes his undoing and leads to his downfall.

"But why couldn't Lear recognize the duplicity of Regan and Goneril?" Julie asked. "After all, he was the king—supposedly a great man."

Pausing thoughtfully for a moment, Dad replied with one of the most self-revealing things I ever heard him say: "Well, do you ever really know *anyone*?"

Uncertain whether he was talking about himself or someone else, I put in, "Cordelia certainly got the short end of the stick."

To which Dad said, "Shakespeare knew that it's not a rational universe."

WE HAD A string of visitors all summer. A pal from my Ridley days flew over from his home in Bermuda to stay for a month. We played tennis and competitive croquet, swam in the pool, went to the pubs, drove around Britain in the Beetle, and had a good time. We visited my Scottish relatives, second or third cousins on my father's side, on their sheep farm near Perth, met girls, visited friends of his in Devon. Dad behaved as he usually did with my friends, treating him like the help. When he asked Dad for some advice about booking his return ticket, Dad responded helpfully, "Have you tried the phone?" It became a standing joke between my friend and me.

Guests of Dad's and Ingrid's, on the other hand, such as a Canadian cousin and family in Oxford on sabbatical, were accorded the full George Blackstock treatment: a candlelit dinner in the oak-panelled dining room, with roast beef, Yorkshire pudding, and a fine Burgundy, followed by a dessert such as bananas Foster, his favourite, and liqueurs. Julie was sent to fetch things from the kitchen. Doug helped mix and serve the aperitifs. We three older children all had the job of clearing the table.

Ingrid's younger cousin and his wife—let's call them Dieter and Traudl—visited from Germany. Keenly aware of his privileged status, Dieter helped himself to jumbo snifters of Rémy Martin from the sideboard. He and I played tennis, followed by a swim. Chatting by the pool, he was quite frank with me, in his European way, asserting that just because he'd found the right wife didn't mean they wouldn't take separate vacations from time to time.

Dieter's visit provided Dad with an opportunity to show off his prowess in German, a language he'd worked very hard to master while in Switzerland. "You don't know how much satisfaction it gives me to be able to speak to Mum's family in German," he told me. I picked up most of what was said; I understood a bit of German from having heard it around the house for so many years.

"Now, *there's* a smart guy," Dad said, as our entire family watched Dieter and Traudl pull away in their smart French rental car to continue their trip.

"He certainly is," Ingrid said.

"It's really too bad *we* don't have a professional in the family," Dad mused. Dieter was an engineer, in keeping with his family tradition.

"What do you mean?" Julie asked.

"Well, you know, it would be nice to have one of our kids be a doctor, a lawyer, a professor."

How sad, I thought—to tell your kids you're disappointed with them, because they'll never be doctors or lawyers or professors. And how insensitive, especially to Doug, who everyone knew wasn't going to make the grade by our father's yardstick of success.

Later on, Bibi Fischer arrived from Buenos Aires on her way to Denmark. What a flashback to the past—to another life entirely. Yet strangely, Bibi never mentioned, at least in my or Julie's or Doug's hearing, anything about Argentina, the estancia, or Mom, with whom she'd supposedly been friends. Some part of me hoped that she might have said how sorry she was about Carol's passing. It was as if our time in Argentina had never happened, as if Mom had never lived.

Bibi was, however, more than frank about other matters.

"Peter says hello. I know he still loves me, because he told me so from his girlfriend's apartment in Copenhagen," she said, as she waltzed into the dining room, where the rest of us were waiting.

"Oh, Bibi, really!" Dad said, in his disapproving, not-in-front-of-the-children tone.

"Terribly sorry. I forgot that Mr. Blackstock is a very proper and important man and doesn't appreciate these sorts of comments," Bibi said. All of us except Dad joined in a hearty laugh.

"Well, I have my own plan," Bibi continued. "On the plane to London, I sat next to an English radio show host, Roger Best. Perhaps you've heard of him."

"Roger Best!" Julie exclaimed. "He's the heartthrob of daytime radio—in the tabloids all the time. You don't mean you sat next to the most eligible bachelor in London?"

"I do mean it," she said, knowing she had us hanging on her every word. "He's *very* good looking and probably still in his early thirties. He asked if he could visit me here. I think he must be crazy—here I am pushing fifty!"

Bibi was being overly modest. She was still a tall, svelte, stylish blonde, and very sexy.

"Well, Ingrid. Do you think that would be possible? He gave me a newspaper article about his show, with his photo. Here it is."

Ingrid took a good look. "Wow, he *is* handsome. I'll have to get my hair done."

"Don't be silly, Ingrid!" Dad said.

"If you think I'm going to look frumpy for this guy, you're crazy."

Two evenings later, Roger Best (not his real name) showed up in his late-model Jaguar wearing a sports jacket, open-collared shirt, and jeans. Bibi and Ingrid were both dressed to the nines—makeup, jewellery, cocktail dresses, heels. They could have been going out to the West End. Even Julie got dolled up for the occasion. All three women looked pretty nice. Dad said hello to Roger Best, then retired to his study with an expression indicating just how tiresome he found all this fuss.

Dad was a contradictory mixture of propriety and even prudishness in public, libertinism in private. He had, for instance, some liberal, let's say European, views about nudity. Some evenings that summer, after the younger kids had gone to bed, he'd tell us it was "skinny-dipping time." With the lights dimmed appropriately, Ingrid and Dad, along with Doug, Julie, and me, would splash around the pool in the altogether before enjoying a nightcap.

Ingrid's English friend—I'll call her Marjorie—was an occasional visitor at Longmoor. Marjorie was a woman in her mid-forties, slightly older than Ingrid, who had worked as a secretary for years and was now completing her studies to become a barrister. Living in West Byfleet, a bedroom community for London commuters, Ingrid got lonely for conversation, especially girl talk. Marjorie was, in her own words, "Ingrid's confessor."

When I went to London, I'd sometimes meet Marjorie for a drink and get feedback about Ingrid and Dad. "George has worked very hard to become a somebody, and now he *is* a somebody. But Ingrid feels quite alone out there, and I'm the one she talks to," Marjorie told me over a martini at the Savoy.

"I guess Dad has some communication problems with my stepmother," I suggested.

"George doesn't communicate with *anybody*."

Later, I learned from Ingrid herself one of the subjects they weren't communicating about. She'd been trying to have another baby—a son, to be precise—but things weren't working out. She'd had a miscarriage. Extremely upset, she'd taken the fetus to her doctor in a jar. Evidently, the doctor had no bedside manner and even less empathy, and he told her bluntly to dispose of the fetus as she saw fit.

"But that was my *son*," Ingrid told me in tears.

I felt sorry for her and gave her a hug.

Why the baby needed to be a son, I didn't ask. But I could imagine. My mother had given birth to sons, while so far Ingrid had produced only girls. In her mind, she seemed to feel she had fallen short. Yet I'd never heard, and Ingrid didn't mention getting, a single word of regret or sympathy from Dad about the miscarriage. If he hadn't been in a hurry for more children in New Orleans, he certainly wasn't at this stage in his life.

As it turned out, there would be another child, some five years later, and a son at that.

Marjorie told me about another problem Ingrid was having with Dad. Ingrid had to pester him about giving her enough money for expenses—tradespeople whose bills were overdue, late school fees, kids' clothing, spending money for herself. I could certainly believe that. Dad always thought other people should carry the load where family expenses were concerned. In the case of Doug, Julie, and me, our relatives, especially Grandma and Grandpa, had taken us in for weeks and sometimes months at a time without any financial help from Dad. But he'd received plenty in handouts from his mother, and at one time the family trust used to pay his taxes.

Ingrid's family helped them out with creature comforts and far more besides. That summer, I got the first inklings of just how much help she and Dad had received from her relatives. The jewellery that had so impressed me in New Orleans, Ingrid confided, had been paid for by her family, not her husband. I also discovered they'd lent Dad the money to buy Longmoor. Ingrid's older brother, now the patriarch and chief custodian of the family fortune, had organized the transaction. Years later, he'd complain bitterly to me about the difficulties of trying to obtain repayment from Dad.

DURING MY VISIT I learned more about the family from Julie. She was worried about Doug.

"He tries so hard to please Dad and gets treated as if he's worth-less," she said. "Same with Mum, even though he can't stand her. It's so heartbreaking."

"How about you?" I asked. "How are you doing? How's life at boarding school?"

"Boarding school is boarding school. I'm just glad to be away from home. I have some girlfriends there. In a couple of years I'll write my A-levels and be off to uni [British slang for university] and out of the house for good. I can't wait."

"What about during the holidays?"

"Mum is constantly putting me down. The other day, the gardener was looking at me, and she gave me a tongue-lashing for wearing a skimpy T-shirt. I hadn't meant to do anything wrong. It was a warm day. This is supposed to be our house.

"And I overheard her say she thought I was going to be 'a giant.' I can't help it that I'm taller than her. I can't stand it. And Dad does absolutely nothing."

I didn't take that crap from Ingrid anymore, so I didn't need Dad's intervention. But at fifteen, Julie wasn't quite there yet, and she could have used some support from her father.

TOWARD THE END of that summer, Doug and I travelled in France. Dad had arranged for him to take a job in Provence providing personal care for an elderly man. Travelling on his own, Doug arrived to discover Dad's arrangements were much more tenuous than he'd been led to expect. After a couple of days, he was summarily dismissed and found himself on the street, suitcase in hand, in a strange village where he didn't speak the language.

It worried me when I heard this, and I travelled to the Côte d'Azur to join him. We met at the family villa of a recent girlfriend of mine. With a swimming pool high on a hill overlooking the

Mediterranean, it was an idyllic setting—idyllic and extremely boring. My friend had to spend most of her time completing an art portfolio for her studio class in the fall, while everyone else in the family sat around doing crossword puzzles.

Feeling trapped, Doug and I packed up and took the train to Cannes, where we spent a few days camping out on the beach. After the police searched and harassed us and other young travellers, we moved on to an abandoned house, where we squatted for a few days. I loved the adventure of it.

When Doug and I arrived back at Longmoor, we found brochures and application forms for the Canadian Army laid out neatly on Doug's bed. He'd end up spending the next two decades in the military. This was our father's formulaic way of dealing with Doug: if he wasn't, in Dad's opinion, showing an aptitude for anything, send him off to the army in his grandfather George's footsteps.

(As he'd prove later, Doug had a great knack for sales and marketing. With encouragement from friends and family, including myself, a little inheritance money from Grandma and Grandpa, and hard work, he'd parlay that talent into a successful real estate business.)

As I turned my back on Longmoor and flew toward Toronto, I was relieved to be putting my father and all his troubling contradictions behind me. From now on, I'd be my own man. I was going to keep my options open. The last thing I wanted was to get trapped—whether in a humdrum job, a house in the suburbs, or smothering family expectations. No thank you. I was going to live free as long as I could. Not knowing where I was going was a secondary consideration.

Of course, life wouldn't let me off the hook so easily.

14

JULIE'S DISCOVERY

MY LIFE CHANGED with a phone call from my sister.

It came in late fall 1979, eight years after my English summer. I was studying law in London, Ontario, and Julie was living in Kingston. She'd just been in Toronto helping Grandma sort out Grandpa's papers after his death a few months earlier. Grandma was having a tough time coping with his loss.

It was a very sad day for all of us when Grandpa died. Life had dealt him a shitty hand (I was yet to discover just how shitty), and he'd played it like a prince. He had shown unwavering love and devotion to us. He was in a coma for the last few days of his life, so I never had a chance to tell him how much he meant to me.

On the day Julie phoned, I returned to my apartment after classes to find a message from her on the answering machine. She didn't say why she'd called, just that she'd phone back later.

I made myself a mug of coffee and sat at the kitchen table to review my Christmas exam schedule. Still in my first term in law school at the University of Western Ontario, I was trying to stay focused on my studies. Even so, I found my mind wandering—to

Marie, my beautiful girlfriend of several years and soon to become my wife, currently off in New York City managing an art gallery. It was a dream job for a young curator, which we'd agreed she couldn't pass up. But I could hardly wait for the Christmas holidays, when I'd be staying with her in New York.

And I thought of Julie. I felt proud of her. At Dad's insistence, she'd had to spend a year at finishing school in Switzerland, where she'd learned how to make cocktail-party conversation, do the fox-trot, and boss the maids around. What a waste of time for someone who disdained everything that finishing school represented. Escaping to Canada, she'd completed her BA at Queen's University, in Kingston, Ontario, at twenty-three. While at Queen's, Julie gained a further measure of independence when she married a handsome chemistry graduate student, but not before Dad turned their wedding in Toronto into a grandiose affair at St. Paul's, on Bloor Street— known as having the longest aisle in Toronto—with limousines and a big reception at the family club. Grandma had recently sustained a fall, and with Grandpa gone, she was unable to attend her grand-daughter's wedding. Julie and her new husband went to see Grandma before the reception. According to my godfather, Bill Dafoe, Julie looked eerily like Carol herself walking down the aisle on George's arm. Perhaps it was just as well our grandparents weren't there.

After Grandpa died, Grandma went quickly downhill, becoming increasingly forgetful and less able to manage. This would turn out to be the early stage of Alzheimer's disease. With me in law school, and Doug newly married himself and posted to the Canadian military base in Lahr, West Germany, Julie would go to Toronto and help Grandma. She'd consult me on certain things, but she was doing all the work.

The phone rang, and it was Julie. I was glad to hear her voice. She was back home in Kingston, calling from the apartment she and her husband rented.

"I had quite a time talking to Grandma," she told me. "It was a challenge trying to sort through boxes and boxes of Grandpa's papers. And I found something really startling."

"Really? What?"

"There's an autopsy report. It shows how Mom died."

I felt my stomach lurch as though a trap door had sprung open beneath me. After twenty years of not knowing exactly what had happened to Mom, some dark hints from Grandpa, strange whispered rumours, and Dad's apparently definitive statement that no one ever discovered the cause, the question mark around her death had slowly faded from view. It had never totally disappeared, just receded into the background of my consciousness.

"Okay," I replied, feeling a distinct foreboding.

"Are you sure you're ready for this, Jeff? It's pretty shocking."

"Just tell me."

"It was arsenic poisoning."

I dropped the phone and ran to the toilet to retch over the bowl.

After a few minutes, I picked up the phone again. At first, I could barely speak. But as I regained my composure, one word came out.

"Dad," Julie and I said simultaneously.

Suddenly, a lot of things made sense.

Julie described for me what had happened. She'd been taking a break from tidying up, having tea with our grandmother in her living room, when out of nowhere Grandma said, "You know that Carol died of arsenic poisoning."

Dumbstruck, Julie asked, "What do you think happened, Grandma?"

"She was murdered. We're convinced your father did it. You kids weren't supposed to find out."

With Julie's prompting, Grandma explained. After Mom died, Grandpa repeatedly asked Dad for more information, only to be put off, over and over. Eventually, as Grandpa had told me when I was sixteen, Dad claimed—no doubt hoping to put an end to the questioning once and for all—that in the end, the doctors thought Mom had contracted some kind of tropical disease in Argentina.

Grandpa just didn't believe it, Grandma said. He conducted his own investigation by corresponding directly with medical officials in Montreal, without letting her know. Afterwards, Grandma found him increasingly morose and withdrawn. She asked him why, but he wouldn't tell her.

Months passed before Grandma persuaded him to say what was wrong: the coroner's office in Montreal had given him a copy of the autopsy report.

Julie listened as Grandma described her horror at her daughter's protracted suffering and painful death—a horror compounded by the certainty that she'd been murdered. Our grandparents could only conclude that Dad had killed her. This explained, as far as they were concerned, why he'd been lying to them. And it made them fear all the more for Julie and Doug, who were then, in 1964, still living with the man they believed was Mom's killer.

Julie said our grandparents' lives were never the same after that. We now realized the true extent of the anguish they had been living with all those years.

Grandma showed her the steel box where Grandpa kept his file of documents from Montreal, but it was locked, and Grandma couldn't remember where the key was. Anxious to see the documents for herself, Julie began what she described as "the most frantic search of my life." She spent the entire night rummaging through every nook and cranny in the apartment until finally, at 5 A.M., she found a key that fit the lock.

As soon as she opened the box, the words "arsenic poisoning" jumped out at her from one of the documents. Julie said her first reaction was to realize that she'd known it all along—seeing the words only confirmed her worst fears. The toxicology report was there too, and the exchange of letters in July 1964 between Grandpa and officials of the Montreal coroner's office. The correspondence made it unequivocally clear that, after performing the autopsy, pathologist Dr. J.P. Valcourt found that Mom had died of "acute arsenic intoxication."

In a note, Grandpa had written "Diefenbaker", the prime minister at the time Carol died, and the names of his ministers of trade, foreign affairs, and justice. While there is no evidence Grandpa thought they were complicit in a cover-up, he may have been contemplating taking his investigation to the top of the Canadian government.

After so many years of enforced silence, Grandma began speaking freely about what had happened. It was as if a dam had burst. Grandpa had wanted to tell me, she told Julie, but he'd been at a loss to know exactly when, and in how much detail. Should he come right out and say our father was a murderer? Then he'd died without being able to do so. Maybe this was Grandma's way of carrying out his wishes.

Sometime after learning the truth, Grandpa had taken the drastic step of seeking custody of Julie, then about twelve. Dad's response was to unleash the family lawyers on him. They threatened to "put him in jail," according to Grandma. I already knew from Grandpa that Dad had threatened to prevent our grandparents from ever seeing their grandchildren again. Finally, he and Grandma decided they had no option but to drop the matter.

During that period of struggle between Grandpa and Dad, Julie said, bizarre things happened that made her wonder at times if she was going crazy. Dad forced her to show him all the letters she'd received from our grandparents, claiming they were turning her against him. Julie would still write to them, but only from time to time, and only about superficial matters, so as not to arouse Dad's suspicions—just to let them know she was all right. During the occasional phone call from our grandparents, she'd be unusually guarded and withdrawn. I knew just how she'd felt. I used to feel the same way in New Orleans during phone conversations with Grandma and Grandpa. "You get so *quiet*," Grandma would tell me.

IT'S NOT SURPRISING that, on first returning to Kingston, Julie was torn between wanting to tell someone about the arsenic poisoning and fearing people would think she was crazy. At the same time, she felt she needed witnesses to her discovery. This may sound paranoid, but not to me: even when people are sympathetic, Mom's story can seem improbable to them, far removed from anything in their personal experience, and sometimes they think you're just imagining things.

The first person Julie confided in was her best girlfriend. Then she shared the story with her husband and his parents. They were all supportive. It emerged that Julie's in-laws had once heard rumours through the grapevine in Toronto of a scandal surrounding Carol Blackstock's death. Julie's mother-in-law said she'd always found it "unusual" that the cause of death had never been discovered. My girlfriend, Marie, had reacted in much the same way: surprised, even stunned, to learn that I didn't know the cause.

Despite her emotional distress at the time, Julie resolved that she wasn't going to let her discovery ruin her life—or her marriage. Within a year, she and her husband would be separated.

JULIE HADN'T WANTED to trouble me with her news so soon, knowing it would hit me hard, just as I was preparing for my first set of law exams. But then she realized she needed to tell me and, after our phone conversation, to speak with me in person.

When Julie arrived in London after the six-hour bus journey, I could see she was upset. I was too, but I was also very glad to see her. I wasn't going to be able to concentrate properly on anything, not even the upcoming exams, until she and I had figured this thing out together.

Naive as it seems, I hoped talking face to face would enable us to find a logical explanation for our mother's death. There had to be some circumstance, something we didn't know, to explain this mystery—or at least help us decide how best to approach our father to get his explanation.

Together, we pored over Grandpa's documents. The smallest detail might be a key to unlocking the truth.

When no such clue materialized, Julie and I did some brainstorming. How could Mom have died of arsenic poisoning? We ran through every scenario we could think of, plausible or not: she committed suicide; she ingested arsenic by mistake; she was a victim of medical malpractice; she'd been involved with the wrong people in Buenos Aires, who had killed her; she'd been having an affair but refused to leave our father, and her jealous lover poisoned her; she'd been a spy who knew too much and got executed; she'd been poisoned by the crazy cook, and by the time it was discovered, it was too late.

These were all wild and unbelievable ideas. In any of these unlikely scenarios, it was possible Dad had wanted to protect us by sparing us the terrible truth—so he'd invented his all-purpose explanation, which effectively put an end to further questioning. After all, if the esteemed specialists at the Montreal Neurological Institute couldn't determine the cause of Mom's death, who could?

To Julie and me, the idea that Mom had died from arsenic poisoning was itself unbelievable. But there it was, in black and white, staring back at us from the autopsy report. When he'd invented his story, Dad couldn't have known we'd come across this piece of paper many years later.

The problem we couldn't get around was that Dad had repeatedly said to us that no cause of death was ever found. Now we knew that wasn't true. He hadn't said, "*To my knowledge*, the cause was never found." He had always stated it with absolute certainty.

Over the next couple of days, while I was in class, Julie did some enterprising research. London, Ontario, is an affluent, mid-sized city, well stocked with professionals. She visited the office of a local criminal lawyer and outlined our quandary to him. He told her it was a very complicated matter, with no clear solutions in view. Later, I spoke to the lawyer on the telephone. "How do people deal with these situations?" I asked in desperation. Julie had told him I was a law student at Western. I guess it was quite obvious to him, even over the phone, that I was upset. He told me to pull myself together; if lawyers weren't able to deal with their own problems, they had little hope of being useful to others with theirs. True, perhaps—but in the circumstances, not helpful.

Julie also visited a private investigator, who suggested it would be necessary for him to travel to Argentina to interview people about the case. The expense would be out of the question for us. Apart from that, the investigator didn't speak Spanish, was unfamiliar with the country, and twenty years had passed since our mother's death. Even if Julie and I could have afforded his services, he wasn't the right person for the job.

Julie did some reconnoitring on the medical side too. She consulted with her own physician in Kingston. After reading the autopsy and toxicological reports, the doctor described the amount of arsenic found in Mom's small intestine as being "the size of a candy bar"—many times more than a lethal dose, which can be as little as one-eighth of a teaspoon.

While in London, Julie roamed the halls of the university's faculty of medicine. When she saw a nameplate that said "pathologist," she knocked on the office door and asked the doctor if she could speak with him. Amazingly, he was not only very familiar with our mother's case but had actually been working at the Montreal Neurological

Institute when she was there and had been part of the team that treated her. The doctor was probably as astonished as Julie was at this coincidence and took time from his busy schedule to speak with her.

During a post-mortem meeting on the case, the pathologist recalled, someone on the team remarked that Mom's pattern of getting sick at home, then better in hospital, was typical of classic slow poisoning cases in Victorian novels. He remembered that the post-mortem work was done with such meticulous care that the physicians thought the case was likely headed for court. Spectrometry technology, relatively new at the time, enabled the toxicologist to say that the cause of death was not only consistent with arsenic poisoning, it *was* arsenic poisoning. Our father, the pathologist told Julie, was under suspicion from the outset. The team didn't consider suicide a serious possibility, since the intoxication was not only acute but also chronic over a substantial period of time.

I spoke to a family friend, whom I knew well, who was living in London at the time because her husband was a senior faculty member at the university. I thought she might be able to shed some light on what had happened to Mom, especially since she knew the family history. I also thought that, as an older person I trusted, she might have some words of wisdom to offer.

When we met, I told her about the finding of arsenic poisoning and asked bluntly, "What do *you* think happened to my mother?"

"It was always a great mystery about your mother's death," she replied cryptically. She wouldn't elaborate.

The next day, she phoned to say that, because she'd seen I was so troubled, she'd spoken to her husband about my question, and he'd agreed to meet with me. When I saw him, he was taken aback, even affronted, by my speculation about Dad. He was positive there must be some innocent explanation and seemed genuinely convinced that such terrible things simply didn't happen in respectable families like ours.

"Well, Jeff," he intoned in his deep baritone, "I am certainly a lot more confident in your father than you are."

Clearly, Julie and I concluded, consulting professionals and family friends would only take us so far. To get to the bottom of this, we had no choice but to speak to our father. We needed to hear his side of the story.

DAD WAS LIVING in Minneapolis with Ingrid and their three children. He was head of the Canadian consulate there after his assignment at the consulate general in New York City. I told Julie I'd call him. I felt nervous about it; I wouldn't be able to disguise my suspicions about what we'd learned. Dad's keen instincts would pick up on that immediately.

What else could he expect? When a wife dies of arsenic poisoning, the number one suspect is always the husband. And when it takes twenty years for his children to learn the real cause of her death, which their father has always insisted was unknown, how could he not expect them to be suspicious? It was a phone call Dad must have been expecting for a long time—the knock on the door in the middle of the night. He'd had a long time to prepare for it.

Before picking up the phone, I ran through in my mind every conceivable way the conversation might go. But nothing could have prepared me for what happened.

"Hi, Dad."

"Oh, hi, Jeff. How are you? To what do we owe this call? Are you getting settled at law school?"

"I'm getting on okay, thanks. Lots of work. How are things in Minneapolis?"

"Oh, we're fine, enjoying the city and the new house. I'm liking the job. Is there something in particular you're calling about?"

"Yes, actually. Julie and I have been trying to sort out our grandfather's papers."

"Oh, yes."

"Julie found some material on our mother's death."

"Yes?"

"She found an autopsy report showing the cause of death."

"Yes?"

"It shows she died of arsenic poisoning."

There was silence for about thirty seconds. It seemed like an eternity.

"Dad? Are you there?"

"Yes." His voice was completely expressionless. As if he were still waiting for the punchline.

"Do you have any . . . comment?"

"No, I don't."

"Did you know about this?"

"No."

"You mean . . . you really didn't know anything about it?"

"No one ever told me."

"No one ever told you what Mom died of?"

"I never found out. As far as I know, nobody did."

For a long moment, I too was at a loss for words. Finally, I told him, "I find that amazing, Dad. I don't know what else to say."

"I don't know what to say either. No one ever told me about it."

TO THIS DAY, I remain astounded by that conversation. Intellectually, I realize it must have been a well-rehearsed set piece, prepared for a long-expected telephone call from *somebody*, probably Julie or me. And in hindsight, I also understand that Dad's response of total ignorance was carefully thought through—perhaps the best answer possible in his situation.

At the time, however, I was shocked by the utter lack of emotion in his voice. He expressed no surprise, horror, sorrow, disbelief, outrage—nothing. He offered me no emotional response at all. He certainly didn't sound like a man who had just learned that his wife had died of arsenic poisoning. How could he receive this awful news from me, his son, with such cool detachment?

Unless it wasn't news at all.

And if it wasn't news to Dad, if his response was a well-rehearsed act, then why didn't he go all the way and make it a convincing performance? Why didn't he express—fake—the kind of emotion that I, or anyone else, would have expected from a man in his situation? Surely that would have helped persuade me he was telling the truth.

Something else was missing, and I only came to realize it when Julie brought it to my attention: throughout our conversation, Dad showed no empathy at all—for anyone. Not once did he express any sadness over the manner of Mom's death or how painfully she suffered. Not once did he exhibit, even in a token way, any sympathy for me or my brother and sister, and how devastated we must have felt about what had happened to our mother.

With Dad, arrogance was inevitably in the mix too. Why should he put on an act for *me*? It was for me to accept whatever he offered up, and to believe it.

The magic explanation I'd hoped for wasn't there.

JULIE WAS MORE clear-headed about Dad's claim of ignorance. Her reaction was unsurprised and scornful.

"He said what!" she exclaimed over the phone. "How in the world could he not have known?"

Julie felt little doubt about Dad's guilt. For me, it was harder to believe conclusively one way or the other. In spite of the apparently damning evidence, I couldn't bring myself to condemn him outright. I needed to speak to him face to face. I needed to know if he could produce even one unexpected, as-yet-undisclosed piece of evidence that could put Mom's death in a different light and exonerate him.

I called him again to say I had to see him. At first, he suggested I come to Minneapolis for Christmas. I told him this was something that couldn't wait. He asked if I could drive there. No, I replied, the trip would take too long, and I didn't have the time because of the demands of law school. I had to fly, and I needed him to pay for the airfare, because I didn't have the money. He reluctantly agreed, but scheduling problems prevented me from going right away as hoped.

I spoke with Julie to rehearse what I'd say and to be sure I asked any questions she had. She didn't want to speak to Dad herself. She wasn't as ready as I was to keep an open mind. I asked her if she was comfortable showing Dad the documents we had from Grandpa's file. She wasn't. As I'd realize later, she was absolutely right to be cautious.

THE VISIT STARTED out normally enough. Dad picked me up at the Minneapolis airport with my three half-siblings in tow. He and Ingrid gave me a tour of their spacious suburban house. After supper in the dining room, Ingrid and the kids went to their rooms, as if on cue, and Dad and I sat down in the living room.

"Dad," I began, "I have to say, I was pretty stunned when you told me you knew nothing about our mother's autopsy or what it found. It really puzzles me, and . . . and it bothers me a lot, to be honest. I mean, didn't the hospital inform you?"

He didn't hesitate. "No. They never contacted me." He spoke in a flat, matter-of-fact voice, staring me in the eye with a look devoid of expression. He might have been telling me that, yes, it really was true that the dishwasher wasn't working, even though it was brand new — imagine that.

"Weren't they supposed to tell you? You know, something that important?" I felt foolish saying something so obvious.

"I don't know if they were *supposed* to. I guess I thought they would, if there was anything new to report." He looked off through the picture window at the large garden, which backed on to Cedar Lake. The wind was getting up, swaying the bare branches of the trees.

"You didn't follow up with them yourself?" My sense of disorientation was growing. I was struggling to get my bearings.

He turned back to me. "No, I didn't follow up. Why should I have? I had my hands full at the time. Dealing with your mother's funeral, the paperwork, family things, you kids. Then I had to get our lives back on track in Buenos Aires. When I didn't hear anything further from the hospital, I naturally assumed they had nothing more to report." He said this with grim determination, crouched over his knees, gazing at the floor. Then he raised his head to look straight at me, lips pursed.

Something in his defiant refusal to bend, to elaborate on his story, to give me anything whatsoever, made me determined to match his stubbornness. "You didn't *wonder* how Mom died?"

"Of course I did. But sometimes there are no explanations for these things. You can expend a lot of time and worry needlessly when what you really need is to get on with life—helping the living, like you kids."

"But Dad—"

He cut me off. "Anyway, what was I going to find out? As far as I knew, nothing. If there was anything new, they would have notified me. And what would have been the result of dwelling on it? Nothing. Nothing but a lot of pain and worry, at a time when the demands of life and work and family required me to try and put your mother's death behind me."

"Were the police involved?" This was a question I had to ask, and it was actually easier than I'd expected. It was perfectly obvious to anyone that, under the circumstances, the police would have wanted to know things from Dad, many things. He must have understood that, because he didn't miss a beat.

"Yes, they were involved. But it was just routine—a police clerk in an office ticking off boxes on a form. When someone dies shortly after arriving in the country, some formalities are required."

I was trying to get my head around Dad's portrayal of our mother's death as just a matter of "routine" and "formalities." I'd have felt less bewildered if he'd exploded with outrage, as I'd imagined he might, demanding, "How dare you ask me these questions!" Any show of emotion at all would have been welcome, instead of this hollow, unreal version of events.

I persisted. "I understand you told my grandparents about Mom's death by phoning them from Montreal."

"Yes. It was important they hear it directly from me instead of indirectly from someone else. You know, it was your mother's idea to go to Montreal. She didn't want to worry her parents. She was planning to let them know once she got better. We both thought this would be best—not only for your mother's recovery, but to spare her parents unnecessary worry. Your grandmother was a person who would fret and fret over things. The last thing your mother needed right then was to be dealing with her mother."

Dad said this in an eminently practical, sensible tone, looking thoughtfully aside.

"You've always told me Mom's doctors never discovered what it was." This was a loaded question. We both now knew for a fact that the cause of death had been established for years when Dad first told me that.

"Well, that's right. As far as I knew, they never did. I was staying with my cousin Mary in Montreal, and her husband was a doctor quite familiar with the hospital. I was sure he'd have heard if there had been anything to report."

My gut instinct was not to get into an argument over what he knew and when. He'd only have reduced it to a debate about semantics. And I realized a discussion of what Grandpa said about Dad's red herring of a tropical disease wouldn't be productive either. It was clear we'd reached the limits of Dad's willingness to discuss Mom's death.

He was, however, quite miffed that he'd had to spend $200 on my plane tickets. He took my questions about arsenic poisoning without blinking but got upset about the money I'd cost him.

I wanted to shout, "Come on, Dad! This is my mother—your wife—we're talking about!"

But I was beginning to doubt my ability to hold my own against him. Did he have ice water in his veins? Or was he just wiser and more mature than me? He sounded so reasonable, so confident, so sure of his facts, and I had no concrete proof he'd been officially notified of Mom's cause of death.

I was dealing with a situation beyond my comprehension or acceptance. There had to be a rational explanation, but I couldn't see it yet. I was stunned, uncomprehending, and fearful all at once.

Even so, my filial loyalty had been violently shaken. I wanted to believe my father. But what he'd told me made no sense at all.

When I returned from Minneapolis, the family friend I'd confided in earlier said she'd never seen me so disappointed and downcast.

15

INVESTIGATION

I DON'T REMEMBER exactly when I stopped believing my father. Even at first, I didn't really believe his story itself—it simply didn't add up. And yet I reserved judgment on *him*. I was hoping against hope there was something he wasn't telling us, perhaps couldn't tell us, which would finally emerge and explain everything—even why he'd had to concoct a false version of what had happened.

It wasn't until January that I'd been able to visit Dad in Minneapolis, two months after Julie revealed her discovery of the autopsy report. Dad had asked me who else knew what Julie had discovered. I just told him we had spoken to Doug before Christmas, at which point Dad would have realized that Doug had known about it during a skiing holiday with him shortly thereafter. Yet it would be three more months before Dad reached out to Julie about it, and five whole years before he discussed it with Doug.

Dad finally went to see Julie while in Canada on business. They met at her apartment. He must have rehearsed for the occasion as thoroughly as he would for a play, and his conversation with her was very different from his discussion with me.

Dad's story was basically the same: the doctors in Montreal had never told him, and he hadn't followed up with them because, after all, "What good would it do?" He claimed he'd thought about it but had dismissed the idea as fruitless: "It wouldn't bring her back," he lamented.

Julie noted that he seemed sincere, leaning back on her hide-a-bed sofa speaking about Mom's death. He said he felt remorseful that he hadn't done more to save her when she became ill. He was especially sorry he hadn't obtained a second medical opinion, remembering, with apparent regret, how his embassy colleague Dwight Fulford had urged him to consult another doctor in Buenos Aires and told him, "For God's sake, George, it's your wife's life we're talking about!"

Julie admitted she couldn't detect any evidence of duplicity or lying. I was very surprised to hear her say that. Equally astonishing, Dad admitted to Julie that it was now undeniably clear Mom had been murdered, based on the information Julie had found at Grandma's. He didn't even question that interpretation of the autopsy results. He told Julie he didn't believe that Mom had committed suicide, or that her death could have been the result of some accident. Perhaps he calculated that, by agreeing it was murder, he would make himself appear more credible. In any case, it was a huge admission for him to make, given his previous know-nothing stance, and the fact that suicide would have been such a convenient "explanation" by absolving him.

With hindsight, it's obvious Dad's position was contradictory, even preposterous. He now realized Mom had been murdered yet, unaccountably, the police hadn't considered it necessary to inform him of the arsenic poisoning, or even to conduct a criminal investigation. At the time, our grasp of this contradiction was overwhelmed by Dad's apparent sincerity and the power of his continuing authority in our lives. We *wanted* to believe he was innocent. And it was possible to cling to that belief, because we didn't yet know things we would discover later.

Dad also told Julie that, after returning to Buenos Aires following Mom's death, he became suspicious of our cook, Alejandra. He'd heard that the wife of the former owner of our house, Juan Perón's crony Jorge Antonio, had died mysteriously when Alejandra worked for them. He added that Alejandra had apparently adored *him*, George. But when he could find nothing to confirm his suspicions about her, he dropped the matter. He acknowledged that he kept Alejandra on as our cook for many months afterwards.

(Recently, however, a son of Jorge Antonio revealed that there never was a cook in the Antonio household, since his mother, Esmeralda Rubin, did all the cooking; that she did not die until 1987, when she was living in Spain; and that he didn't remember Alejandra being in the house at all. In addition, María's daughter Cristina told me that, in fact, Alejandra had a boyfriend at the time.)

Dad recounted what he'd done when Grandpa had accused him of poisoning Mom and later pressed for custody of Julie. He engaged the family lawyers, who told him to write a detailed account of his actions during and after Carol's illness. He did so, he claimed, and on the basis of his version of events, they opined there were no grounds for Grandpa's allegations. This was the first we'd heard of Dad committing any such testament to paper. Julie never saw it, and never would.

Julie asked whether he'd been interested in following up on the autopsy from a medical point of view, in case it revealed the possibility of a hereditary disease that could affect us kids.

Dad was less than convincing on this point. As Julie would observe later, "For someone who hadn't bothered to ask [the MNI doctors] for the autopsy report, he seemed very certain there was no potential value in knowing the results."

And yet after their conversation, Julie didn't believe that he had lied to her. To her own surprise, she felt as I had after my visit to Minneapolis: prepared to accept what he had told us.

True, Dad's story was jarring and bizarre, and left a number of loose ends dangling. We were both troubled by details that didn't quite fit, questions that remained unanswered. But we really had no solid proof that his account was untrue. Denial is a powerful thing.

JULIE AND I both needed to get on with our lives. The demands of law school didn't permit breaks in concentration for long, and I was soon back at the books. When not immersed in my studies, I was in New York City with Marie.

While staying at Marie's Upper West Side apartment over the March break, I asked her to marry me. Living in different cities had made us realize how much we missed each other, how much a part of each other's lives we'd become. We went to a jewellery store and picked out a ring—not a big diamond, but a pretty aquamarine ring with little diamonds on the side—which I put on my credit card since I didn't have the cash.

In early May, after writing my exams, I returned in my yellow Volkswagen Beetle to glorious spring weather in Manhattan. Marie and I decided that we didn't want, and couldn't afford, the expense of a big wedding. We were happy with a quiet civil ceremony at City Hall in New York, away from all the complications of family back home. I certainly didn't want my father taking over and stage-managing our wedding, as he'd done with Julie's.

Meanwhile, Julie was working at a shelter for battered women in Kingston and trying to focus on her marriage, which she feared was starting to slip away from her. She found she was constantly reminded of our mother and assailed by disturbing thoughts of how horribly she'd died.

Grandma needed Julie's help and attention more and more as her mental faculties deteriorated. Grandma went away for a bridge weekend with some old female friends—"I call them 'the girls,'" she'd say, "even though they're my age, of course"—and they were shocked by the extent and rapidity of her decline.

Finally, Julie had no choice but to take on responsibility for Grandma's affairs. She arranged to place her in a special-care facility, which entailed moving her from her beloved Toronto to Kingston.

While visiting Grandma, Julie reread the letters Mom had written to her parents from Ottawa and Argentina. They saddened yet fascinated her; they were so alive with Mom's zest for life, her compassion, her sense of humour. Why would *anyone* have wanted to kill such a beautiful and spirited young woman?

On a visit to our Scottish cousins at the sheep farm where I'd once stayed, Julie asked what they knew about Carol's death. She learned about rumours making the rounds at the Gooderham family reunion in Toronto in summer 1963, a gathering of some three hundred relatives, which we had attended as kids. There was talk among the adults that Carol had died of arsenic poisoning, and that our cook was suspected. In that case, Dad surely had heard it, notwithstanding his later claim of ignorance. And besides, who had floated the story about the cook? It could only have come from one person.

After Marie and I were married, Julie and I continued to talk on the phone from time to time. Our conversations always revolved around what had happened to our mother. Neither of us could get free of our anxieties around it, and we knew they weren't going away.

Meanwhile, Julie's life was starting to come apart. As she later wrote,

> Mostly my mind seemed to alternate between going on with my daily life, watching my marriage fall apart in front of my eyes, and falling in love with my co-worker. . . . I would be in the middle of doing something mundane, such as cutting up vegetables, and I would suddenly "remember" with a slight shock that my mother had been murdered. I couldn't believe it and, at the same time, I felt that I had always known it.

Anyone who has experienced something even remotely similar will understand. Although I didn't grasp it until later, I think the horror I'd felt when Julie first told me the news had come from that same strange place of déjà vu that she described—a sickening awareness deep down that I already knew Dad was responsible.

Within a year, Julie would file for divorce. Shortly after that, a realization came to her: "One day . . . I was going about my business and I realized that somewhere along the way, I had stopped believing Dad."

I too was having doubts. But as troubled as I remained by the knowledge of Mom's death, and by Dad's initial response to it, and though the gaps in his story continued to haunt me, I still hadn't given up on him completely—not as completely as Julie had.

BY FALL 1984, I'd completed my bar exams. Marie and I were back living in Ottawa. She'd returned to an earlier job as a curator of Inuit art at the federal Department of Indian and Northern Affairs. I was looking for full-time work.

From my conversations with Julie, I knew how thoroughly she'd changed her mind about Dad. She felt quite alone in her renewed conviction that he'd been lying to us. Doug, disturbed as he'd been after we told him about the autopsy results, admitted he didn't know what to think. Of the three of us, he most wanted and needed our father's approval.

I wasn't entirely sure what I believed, but before long I came to the same conclusion as Julie had. "The more I think about it, the more I'm convinced you were right and I was wrong," I told her.

Ultimately, Dad's claim that he'd known nothing about the arsenic didn't make any sense to me either. As Julie put it, "It was an explanation that required no explanation."

She and I were now in agreement: there were so many signs pointing to Dad's culpability that we simply had to take action. We decided to take time out of our lives to investigate for ourselves.

THE OBVIOUS PLACE to start was the Montreal Neurological Institute. I telephoned the MNI to request information about my mother's death twenty-five years earlier. After being transferred from one official to another, I wound up speaking to Dr. Graham, the institute's registrar and one of the physicians who had treated Mom. He understood immediately who I was and agreed to a meeting with Julie and me whenever we would like.

A week later, we made the three-hour drive from Kingston to Montreal. Located near the base of Mount Royal, on the McGill University campus, the Montreal Neurological Institute looked like a drab Soviet politburo building. The office where we met Dr. Graham provided the same impression: grey walls, a government-issue wooden table, and four nondescript chairs. Dr. Graham himself was grey and unremarkable—a balding middle-aged man carrying a slim file.

Yet there was no mistaking the doctor's sharp intellect. He was guarded and forthcoming at the same time. He knew he was dealing with a very tricky situation. Though he'd offered to help us, he was no doubt conflicted by the need to protect the MNI's reputation—and his own.

"Thank you for seeing us, Dr. Graham," Julie said pleasantly.

"I'm happy to help, if I can. What may I do for you?"

"After discovering the autopsy report on our mother's death," I said, "we'd like to follow up with some questions." In my hand I held a pen and our list of questions, typewritten on a sheet of paper.

Dr. Graham thought about this for a few seconds. "I'd like to take a look at all the questions first," he replied.

Julie and I were in no position to say, "No thank you. We'd prefer just to ask our questions, if you don't mind." Dr. Graham could shut down the interview at any time and slam the door on any further access to information at the MNI. I handed him the paper.

Dr. Graham read the list without expression and handed it back to me, saying nothing.

"All right," I began. "Could our mother's poisoning have been the result of suicide?"

"No," Dr. Graham replied flatly. "That's not the way people commit suicide. Even if she'd tried, she'd have been highly unlikely to succeed. A massive dose was found in her digestive tract. The arsenic would have been administered by someone who had access to her food."

On that issue, he was quite unequivocal. The possibility of suicide would have provided a very convenient way out for Dr. Graham, I thought. It would have left the door open to clear everyone of blame: the hospital, the police, the Department of Trade and Commerce, George Blackstock. But even Dad had never suggested suicide as a possibility.

"What led you to look for arsenic?" Julie asked.

"To tell you the truth, we didn't know what it was at first. So we put a team together and talked around a table. This is a teaching hospital, and we do that sort of thing. After a while, someone said, 'You know, this is the kind of thing that happens with heavy-metal poisoning.' There was a physical autopsy of the body. [During the autopsy, tissue samples were taken for microscopic examination, and for toxicological testing afterwards.] A new technology had recently been introduced, gas spectrometry, and it was used to test for the presence of heavy metals in the toxicology work. Arsenic was found throughout her body, including a very large amount in the intestine and smaller quantities in the hair. This indicated that it was not only substantial but had been ingested over an extended period of time."

Dr. Graham sounded more in his element now. What he didn't mention , however, was this statement from the toxicological report: "The spectrograph has been used to determine that we were dealing with arsenic and nothing else." The toxicologists knew what they were looking for. They'd been directed by the doctors who had conducted the physical autopsy, and who believed, on the basis of microscopic and other examinations they had made, that they were dealing with arsenic.

I asked if the Montreal police had been involved.

"Yes, they were notified. They had only one suspect, and they wanted to observe what that person would do."

Now the doctor was being very careful. But we didn't have to ask him who that one suspect was. It was perfectly obvious.

"What did they find?"

"We don't know. Once a case is in the hands of the police, we leave them to do their work."

I asked how long it had taken for the toxicology work to be completed.

"The autopsy was done right away. The toxicology would have taken more time, but I couldn't say exactly how long. I wasn't involved with that end of things."

"Do you know whether anyone ever communicated the cause of death to our father?" Julie asked.

"I don't know about that. Your grandfather inquired some time later and was informed."

"May we look at that file you have with you?" Julie asked him. I admired her boldness.

Dr. Graham paused. "Since it's not a hospital file, I suppose you could." He paused again before finishing his thought. "I'll just step out for a few minutes."

Not a hospital file? So evidently Dr. Graham had been holding on to his own personal file on Carol Blackstock for the past twenty-five years. That's a long time—and I doubted the doctor normally opened private files on his patients.

Initially, I'd been surprised that he'd agreed so readily to see us. Now I understood that, since he'd kept his file for so long, refusing to meet with us might have made saving it pointless.

He'd been careful to check all our questions before answering the first one—yet now he was willing to have us look through his file unsupervised. Why all the cloak-and-dagger? I wondered.

Left alone in the room, Julie and I pored over the file. Our eyes were drawn at once to one letter in particular. It was from Assistant Deputy Minister Leslie Brown of the Department of Trade and Commerce. Brown was writing in reply to a communication sent by hospital authorities immediately after Carol's death, telling them he'd be arriving right away to deal personally with the matter.

So Dr. Graham's purpose in showing us the file—and presumably the purpose of the MNI, since it was unlikely he was acting alone— was to let us know about the involvement of Dad's employer, the Government of Canada. The Department of Trade and Commerce had been informed of Mom's death immediately. Brown had responded not merely with a conventional note of acknowledgment expressing official sympathy for the family, but with a message of unmistakable urgency. The department had considered Carol Blackstock's death serious enough—from the government's own point of view—to dispatch a senior bureaucrat to the scene.

The file contained nothing else of equal importance. From Dr. Graham's earlier remark that the police had taken control of the case, Julie and I were left to conclude that the MNI had let the matter remain entirely in the hands of the police and the Department of Trade and Commerce.

After ten minutes, Dr. Graham re-entered the room and sat down.

"I'm not sure there's anything more I can tell you," he said, taking his file back. Then he sighed and remarked, in a resigned tone, "I hope this isn't going to turn into a Hatfields and McCoys family feud."

It was a peculiar and tasteless remark, seeming to trivialize a death that the doctor had once considered important. It angered Julie and me, but we said nothing. It revealed that Dr. Graham was well aware the object of our suspicions could be none other than our father.

If I can paraphrase the good doctor's advice, he was saying, "Let bygones be bygones." But if so, he was being unrealistic. How could he expect that, once this was out of the bag, Julie and I would let it go? This was no ordinary bygone.

Was Dr. Graham trying to help us? Or was he an instrument of a self-serving institution? I think probably both.

"THAT WHOLE PLACE gave me the creeps," I told Julie, as we pulled out of the parking lot.

"Me too," she said. "To think Mom died in that cold, barren mausoleum, knowing nobody. She couldn't have found much comfort there."

"I certainly didn't."

"And I didn't hear an ounce of sympathy from Dr. Graham. Not even one of the old clichés: 'We did everything we could,' 'I'm sorry for your loss,' etcetera. Or, 'At least she didn't suffer—much.'"

"He didn't want to go anywhere near the most damning question: Why couldn't they diagnose arsenic poisoning before she died? Perhaps they could have saved her," I said.

"And what was all that hocus-pocus about letting us view the file while he stepped out?" Julie said.

"It was weird, all right. Maybe he was trying to help but felt constrained about how much he could actually say."

"Or maybe it really wasn't his file at all, just something the MNI put together. They obviously wanted us to see that letter from Leslie Brown."

"What did you think of his 'family feud' comment?" I asked.

"Like we should just forget about it? That was presumptuous. It wasn't *his* mother who was poisoned. Maybe he's under pressure to get us to drop it."

"Then why rule out the possibility of suicide?"

"They obviously had no basis for calling it a suicide. So if they promoted that idea, it would look like they had something to hide."

Julie had a point. I paused for a minute, running the meeting through my head. There was one particular revelation of Dr. Graham's that struck me. "He didn't have to tell us about the police having only one suspect—and wanting to wait and see what that person would do," I said.

"So maybe he *was* being helpful. But as far as waiting to see what their suspect would do, maybe that explains why they never made an arrest. I don't know. I feel more disgusted than anything."

Julie was bitter. I could hardly blame her. So was I.

WE PAID ANOTHER call before leaving Montreal, and ultimately it would prove even more revealing than our meeting with Dr. Graham. We went to the office of Dr. J.P. Valcourt, the pathologist who had performed the autopsy on Carol for the coroner's office.

At first, we were told by the receptionist that Dr. Valcourt wasn't available. It was only after I made a loud fuss about how far we had come, and how serious this case was, that the doctor himself emerged from his office. He seemed ready to throw us, or at least me, out of the building. But when he heard who we were, his attitude changed completely. He apologized, explaining he couldn't see us right then, but if we made an appointment he'd meet with us at the earliest opportunity.

A week later, Julie returned to Montreal by herself. After my first encounter with Dr. Valcourt, I thought it best if she met with him on her own.

It turned out to be the right decision. Julie was able to spend two hours with him, and she handled the interview magnificently. Dr. Valcourt even agreed to let her tape their conversation, and his words below are from that recording.

Dr. Valcourt told Julie that ever since our mother had died, he had been waiting for *someone* from our family to contact him.

"Would you say, looking at the amount of arsenic, that it was murder?" she asked.

He began by responding, "Oh, yes," but, perhaps remembering the limits of his professional competence and authority, abruptly changed this to, "Ah, no, I can't say *murder*. . . . Our job is to say *medically*. Medically, it's an acute intoxication. That is all we can say. . . . With probably previous chronical intoxication.

"The last amount could have been more substantive, in our opinion," he continued. "That is all we can say. The last amount taken of arsenic was more in quantity than the previous one. That is all we know. Who, how, when it was taken, we don't know." But, he concluded, "In our opinion, there was no, no doubt as to the cause of death."

"Have you ever come across a case where someone committed suicide that way?" Julie asked.

"No," Dr. Valcourt replied, "because it is not a good way to suicide. . . . It takes too much time. And it is too painful. . . . I wouldn't say it is impossible, but I wouldn't say it is probable. . . . [People who attempt suicide] take usually a more rapid and quick method."

Dr. Valcourt had heard that Dad and his cousin Mary's husband, Dr. Sam (as we called him in the family), felt "quite hard done by" because of the delay caused by the autopsy. They were pressing for the earliest possible release of the body.

After the autopsy, Dr. Valcourt recalled, he and his colleagues in the coroner's office began preparing their medical findings, including the final autopsy and toxicology results, as evidence for a *criminal* trial. It was to be a "big show," as he put it, involving expert witnesses.

But then, all of a sudden, it "fell down"—dropped from sight, vanished.

In the end, of course, there was no trial, indeed no public inquiry of any kind. But it was such an unusual case that Dr. Valcourt and his colleagues decided some four years later to present it at the September 1963 annual meeting of the Canadian Society of Forensic Science, in Quebec City.

They identified the subject only as "Mrs. C.B.," "looking some 25 years of age," who had died of acute arsenic intoxication. They provided the date of the autopsy (July 27, 1959) from which the date of death could be approximated (July 25, 1959). The following year, the society published the presentation in the proceedings of its annual meeting. According to Dr. Valcourt, "Dr. Camp" (probably Dr. Francis Edward Camps), one of the world's most renowned forensic pathologists, came all the way from England to attend the meeting.

Julie asked Dr. Valcourt about the risk that Canadian foreign service officials had taken in allowing a potential murderer to stay in our house, even after they knew the cause of Carol's death was arsenic poisoning. Dad had stayed in Canada for almost two months after Mom died. During that time, although surely suspecting she'd been murdered, the Canadian authorities did nothing to ensure the safety of her three children back in Buenos Aires. From the timing of Carol's death, only fifty-five hours after her arrival in Montreal, they'd have presumed she'd almost certainly been poisoned in Argentina. In fact, Dr. J.B.R. Cosgrove, the head of her MNI medical team, wrote an undated letter "To Whom It May Concern," stating that, "from a clinical point of view, it seems highly probable that this illness was related to her domicile in Argentina."

Julie underlined for Dr. Valcourt that the domicile, where Carol spent her last days in Buenos Aires, was our home.

JULIE : Someone decided that, even though someone had been murdered, possibly by someone living in the home, there was no danger to us children, because no one was fired from our house after this, and the same person cooked for us, and . . . the same people were looking after us. And yet someone had been murdered. . . .

DR. VALCOURT : I understand your point of view.

JULIE : . . . And the foreign service knew this and they took a huge risk by doing nothing. They must have known something in order to take that kind of risk.

DR. VALCOURT : If you take it as an accidental case, it would have been very dangerous for you. . . . But if it's an *intentional* . . . murdering of some people, there was no danger to you.

JULIE : No, but you have a murderer on the loose.

DR. VALCOURT : If you are [unintelligible] *some* [his emphasis] people in particularly | sic], you don't want to kill all the family?

Despite Dr. Valcourt's imperfect English and heavy French-Canadian accent, what he was saying was clear enough: the authorities reckoned that Carol's poisoning was intentional and that she was the only intended victim. Thus, there was no danger to us children, and no reason to believe the murderer would want to kill the whole family. Conceivably, however, a deranged maid or cook might have killed the woman of the house and still be present in the home. Who was to say that person might not want to wipe out the family?

But instead of entertaining such a scenario, the Canadian author-ities must have concluded there was no danger to us from the house-hold staff in Buenos Aires while my father was in Canada. We don't see any other way of reading Dr. Valcourt's words. As if to reinforce that point, the doctor added, "We were always suspecting someone in the family."

Dr. Valcourt expressed surprise at Dad's evident lack of interest in learning his wife's cause of death.

"Has he tried to enquire?" he asked Julie.

"No. He said he never tried to get the autopsy report."

"He never tried it? . . . He was not interested at all?"

On the recording, the incredulity in the doctor's voice is unmistakable.

Julie asked Dr. Valcourt if our father had ever approached *him* about the results of the autopsy.

No, he replied. And yet, in these kinds of cases, he said pointedly, someone from the family would usually pressure him for the results.

JULIE ALSO HAD a session at the Montreal Neurological Institute with Dr. Cosgrove. The physician who had headed Carol's medical team was cold and guarded, saying he was constrained in speaking about the case by doctor–patient confidentiality. Julie was taken aback. Hadn't Carol been the patient, not George? Wouldn't she have wanted her adult children to know what had happened to her?

Julie asked Dr. Cosgrove point-blank if Dad had been told the cause of death. Dr. Cosgrove wouldn't answer the question. But he did show her an index card recording the fact that George Blackstock had visited Montreal's Royal Victoria Hospital (the MNI was a part of that same medical complex) back in 1970, requesting information about his late wife's cause of death.

When Julie visited Marcel Monastesse, the official at the Coroner's Court of Montreal with whom Grandpa had corresponded in 1964, he couldn't find her file at all. Monastesse showed her the coroner's journal entries for July 1959, written in longhand and listing deceased persons who had been examined. In one journal, the deceased were listed by date, and in the other alphabetically by name. Carol Blackstock's name didn't appear in either journal. Monastesse acknowledged that she had definitely been there, since her body had been transferred to the coroner's office from the MNI for autopsy. Since we already had the autopsy report, this told us nothing new— except that there was something very wrong with the coroner's record-keeping.

Monastesse was nonetheless familiar with the case. He told Julie that Dad was suspected from the start—and remembered four-hour interrogations of him. Julie asked him outright if Dad was told the cause of death. Monastesse would only say that it was normal prac- tice to inform a suspect of the cause of death when murder was indicated, and it was inconceivable he'd have failed to realize he was being questioned as a murder suspect. Monastesse wouldn't answer Julie's question directly, however. He remembered Dad being instructed to remain available pending further investigation.

Julie and I simply wanted someone in authority to tell us defini- tively whether Dad had been informed of our mother's cause of death. But we realized we weren't going to get a straight answer from the medical authorities in Montreal. They would dance around the question and tell us things that pointed in one direction only— to our father—but they weren't going to tell us that he had been informed of the cause of death, perhaps fearing legal consequences. Dr. Valcourt was the most honest and forthcoming of a sorry lot, and we will be forever grateful to him.

I DECIDED TO try another angle by phoning Mary, Dad's cousin in Montreal with whom he was staying when Carol died. I was a little reluctant to call her; because she was family, she'd likely be guarded in response to my questions. And I didn't want to go too far in alert- ing others in the family about what Julie and I were doing, because the walls would go up. But Mary was in a position to know things we needed to know. It was too good a chance to pass up.

I'd met Mary only a handful of times in my life. I remembered her from the Gooderham family reunion in Toronto. We'd also visited her on trips to Montreal with Dad in the 1960s. She was tall, with dark hair tied back in a no-nonsense bun, Virginia Woolf–style. Most Blackstock women seemed to be married to men in the professions—doctors, lawyers, architects—and had a preference for large Victorian houses with English gardens. Mary was no exception.

"Hi, Mary. It's Jeff Blackstock. You remember me?"

"Of course, Jeff. How could I forget? How are you? It's been a few years since we've seen each other. How is your father and the family?"

"I'm fine, and so are they. How are you?"

"Fine, thank you."

With the niceties out of the way, I dove into dangerous territory. "My sister, Julie, and I have been looking into the cause of our mother's death. You were with my dad in Montreal when she died."

"Yes, your dad stayed with us."

"Could I talk to you about what happened?"

"It was a long time ago. But I'm happy to tell you what I can, if that will help."

"Well, we've discovered that Mom died of arsenic poisoning. I don't know if you were aware of that."

"Yes, I have heard that."

"We also understand the police were involved. Can you tell me anything further?"

"Why, yes. I was with your father when he was questioned."

"What did they want to know?"

"They wanted to know whether he had killed her!"

"So was this just . . . routine questioning?"

"Oh, no. The police were quite aggressive."

"What came of it?"

"I don't know. I guess they didn't come up with anything."

"What did my dad say about it?"

There was a long pause.

"Mary?" I said.

Her voice came back changed—the tone deeper, suddenly hostile. "Listen to me, Jeffrey. This is your *father* we're talking about. How do you dare ask about something like this? Your mother's death was a tragedy, of course. But it occurred a *very* long time ago. The whole matter has been closed for many, many years."

She was becoming increasingly heated, but I pushed ahead regardless. "Did you know that Dad's department sent someone to Montreal to deal with the hospital and the police?"

"No, I didn't know that."

"I'm sure you can understand why Julie and I are concerned about this. We want—"

"No, I can't. Jeffrey, your mother is dead, and life is meant for the *living*. You need to put this whole thing behind you."

"Thanks for talking to me, Mary. May I call you if I have any more questions?"

"No, you may certainly not. I do not wish to discuss this anymore, and neither should you. Goodbye, Jeffrey." And she hung up.

MY CONVERSATION WITH cousin Mary was a disaster from the family relations viewpoint, but far more importantly, it yielded vital information we hadn't known previously. It was now undeniable that George had known the cause of Carol's death, even though Mary wouldn't say so explicitly.

I called Julie to report on what I'd learned. Characteristically, she went straight to the heart of the matter.

"So we have further confirmation that Dad's meeting with the police wasn't just routine, as he told us. They grilled him *hard*. They wanted to know if he'd killed his wife. Of course they did! Mary's version is much more reliable. It makes perfect sense when a man's wife has just died of arsenic poisoning."

"No kidding."

"Her story isn't self-serving like Dad's, either. And her hostility proves she wishes she hadn't shared it with you—especially once she realized she was contradicting him. Did I get everything?"

"I think you got it."

"Oh yeah," Julie added, "I forgot about the life-is-for-the-living bit. We hadn't thought of that, had we? I guess we should be grateful for the sermon." We agreed at once: we needed to see Dad right away, before he got wind that I'd talked to Mary.

16

CONFRONTATION

GEORGE AND INGRID were now living in Ottawa between postings, in a large house in upscale Rockcliffe Park. This was a piece of
luck: Julie and I would be able to talk to him in person.

I suggested we ask Doug if he wanted to be there, so he too could
hear first-hand what Dad had to say. Julie thought that was a good
idea. "Making any progress is going to depend on Dad," she said. "He
has to talk to the three of us." She was more determined than ever
to get the truth out of him. Now that we had greater certainty about
how Mom had died, we were resolved that her murder wouldn't be
consigned to the garbage can of history.

Julie and I knew we had to be thoroughly prepared. Dad was
canny, and more than adroit at twisting the truth completely out of
shape, leaving it unrecognizable—and leaving us with more questions than before, but no answers.

First, we had to satisfy ourselves about one remaining question,
which could turn out to be crucial: Had Dad ever told anyone else
about the cause of Carol's death? We had in mind someone who
wasn't a relative or a friend in Canada, who might alert him to what

we were doing, but rather a person he couldn't have avoided telling *something*.

We decided to call María.

We had María's full name, her old telephone number, and the district where she and Martín had lived. With those pieces of information, the Argentine operator was able to find María's current number and put us through to her.

When she answered, we spoke in Spanish. "María, it's Jeffrey and Julia. Do you remember us?" I hoped she could hear me over the crackling on the line.

"Oh, Jeffrey! How could I ever forget you and Julia? I hear you still speaking in perfect Spanish!"

"And we've never forgotten you, María. Now we're finally able to speak to you again. How are you?"

"I have had some health problems, so I am not working much anymore. But I am happy to be at home in the house we built when you were here."

"And Martín and Cristina?" I asked.

"Martín is still working, but he is ready to retire as well. Cristina is still not married and lives with us."

"We wanted to let you know our grandfather died—Carol's father."

"Oh, I am so sorry. Your grandfather and grandmother were very kind," María said. She remembered the letter they'd written to her after Carol had died. They'd enclosed a watch that had been intended for Carol as a gift with an engraving for María to remember her by.

"María, we want to thank you again on their behalf and ours for everything you did for our mother. And for us."

"There is no reason to thank me, Jeffrey. I loved your mother very much, and I loved you children too."

Cristina would tell me later that when María learned my mother had died, she said it was the worst day of her life.

"We also wanted to ask you something, María."

"Yes?"

"We went through our grandfather's papers after he died. We found out what caused our mother's death."

"I thought it was cancer of the cervix, like your father told me."

This was a shocker. I cupped my hand over the mouthpiece. "Dad told her it was cervical cancer," I whispered to Julie. We looked at each other wordlessly, shaking our heads.

"No, María, it wasn't cancer. Our mother was poisoned. It was arsenic."

"*Ay, por eso!*" ["Aha, so that's why!"]

"Did you ever know anything about arsenic being in our house?" I asked. "Or hear anything about it?"

"No, no."

"Can you tell us anything else about that time, anything that would help us?"

"Your mother was very, very sick. All I know is what your father told me," María said over the increasingly fuzzy line.

"Was anyone else feeding her?" I asked.

"No. Señora Krapf was very helpful when your mother was sick, but there was no one else feeding her that I can remember."

"I'm sorry, María, the line is becoming very bad. We'll have to go."

"I hope you will keep in touch with me. *Abrazos fuertes* [big hugs]."

"We will. *Abrazos fuertes de nosotros,*" I replied.

So Dad had fed María a brazen lie, on a par with telling our grandfather that Carol had died of a tropical disease—yet another to add to the list. Julie and I weren't completely surprised. But we were disappointed to learn that Dad had told her nothing about arsenic poisoning. It removed whatever vestige remained of our hope that he might prove innocent after all.

In time, we came to understand why Dad would have chosen to tell María that particular lie. Our mother's death had come as a shock to people who knew her in Buenos Aires. When someone as young, beautiful, full of life, and popular as she was died suddenly, they wanted to know—needed to know—the reason why. If there was no explanation, they'd start looking for one. Nature abhors a vacuum, as Dad liked to say. The expatriate rumour mill would have gone into high gear, and maids were always one of the main conduits for gossip.

Dad also knew from his government training that in managing situations like this, the objective is to put an end to speculation as swiftly as possible. An explanation like cervical cancer would have done just that. Most people didn't understand cancer as well as we do today, apart from the fact that it was often fatal, and there were few effective treatments. This particular cancer was considered "a woman's problem," to be kept private—not a proper subject for polite conversation in the conservative 1950s. Since we'd be leaving Argentina soon, Dad wouldn't have to answer any further questions there. And what were the chances that anyone in Buenos Aires would check up on his story years later from thousands of miles away?

María's honesty and directness in telling us about the fairy tale Dad had spun only confirmed our belief in her. Sadly, when Julie and I would call her a few years later, Martín would tell us that María had died.

JULIE AND I discussed our next moves. Some part of myself was amazed that the man we were talking about was our father. I saw him now in a very different light from the godlike figure of my past. For that transformation I had Julie to thank in part—but mostly Dad himself.

How, exactly, do you deal with a character like George Blackstock? He was extremely intelligent, slippery, unconstrained by moral conscience. Judging from the way he'd dealt with our grandparents, he could be ruthless in getting what he wanted. If we gave him too much information, he'd concoct a new story that would leave just enough doubt to be possible. If we pushed too hard, we'd give him an excuse to walk away from his crazy, cruel, ungrateful kids. If we didn't push hard enough, he'd walk all over us. We couldn't trust him for a second.

"How long before we talk to him?" Julie asked.

"I think we're there," I said. "The only thing that might open him up is some kind of shock treatment."

"If he won't tell us the truth, I don't want anything more to do with him. I don't want to hear one more phony alibi."

"Once he knows we want to meet, he'll figure we've found something out."

"But for me to believe him," she said, "he'll have to admit knowing all along why Mom died. I don't see how he can talk his way out of it, but he'll try. You know Dad: Mr. Smooth."

"He can't just say he knew nothing and did nothing for twenty-five years."

"It's getting to be a hall of mirrors," Julie said. "He knows that we know that he's circulated completely different explanations to different people."

"Slippery" didn't even begin to describe our father.

I PHONED DAD at home in Ottawa and told him Julie and I wanted to get together with him.

"Of course, Jeff," he said. "What about?"

"She and I have some concerns about our mother's death. We've got to meet with you as soon as possible."

"*Got* to meet? That sounds rather dramatic. What's the urgency, if I may ask?"

"It's important to us."

"Can you give me some idea what you're looking for?"

"We have some questions about what happened. We're hoping you can help us."

"Okay, but I don't know how much I'll be able to add. As you're aware, I've told you everything I know."

"We can talk more about it when we meet, Dad."

"Can you at least give me some specifics, Jeff? It would help me to provide more considered responses."

"Well, we're interested in knowing about our cook in Buenos Aires."

I'd been hoping to avoid getting into a discussion with him before meeting. But I also knew he'd try to pry information out of me, and, if possible, I wanted to allay his fears of an ambush.

"I see," he said. "Interesting you should mention Alejandra. She was a strange person. Anything else?"

"Various things. We'd like to know more about what happened in Montreal."

"What about Montreal? I've told you everything I can."

"We'd just like to be sure we have all the information possible, Dad. We'd like to include Doug as well. We've never all sat down together as a family to talk about this. We think it would be useful. Valuable." I was appealing to his paternalistic side.

"All right, then. If sitting down together would help, I'll join in, of course."

I PHONED DOUG, now living at Canadian Forces Base Petawawa, a couple of hours' drive from Ottawa, and filled him in. He agreed to come to the meeting. I knew he wouldn't want to be left out.

We'd meet Dad after dinner at the apartment where Marie and I lived in a downtown Ottawa neighbourhood called Sandy Hill. Though we were no longer students, it was student-style accommodation—an old house near the University of Ottawa campus, with creaky floors, cracked walls, exposed pipes going to the apartment upstairs. We would have been far more comfortable at Dad's house, but he'd probably be more at ease in the privacy of our place. We knew he wouldn't want to include Ingrid in the discussion. Neither did we. This was strictly between us and our father. Marie went out for the evening.

It was chilly late-October weather. Doug and Julie arrived a couple of hours before Dad, so we could talk things over and get settled. We had pizza at the simple oak dining table given to me by my grandparents, sitting on uncomfortable Victorian chairs from Dad's mother. Somehow, I'd wound up with them after Granny's death five years earlier.

After going over the events around the time of Mom's death and afterwards, I asked Doug if he saw why we needed answers from Dad.

"Of course, Jeff. But I don't know what you and Julie expect to gain. It all happened a long time ago."

"Some of it not so long ago," Julie said.

Maybe it was my legal education taking over, but I felt we all had to be clear on the main issues. "We need to ask Dad the tough questions," I told Doug. "How can he deny ever knowing the cause of death when everyone else seemed to know? Why didn't he try to find out? We want to know why his version of the police interview in Montreal is so radically different from Mary's. Among other things."

"Yes, Jeff," Doug said. "I know that."

"But you don't seem terribly concerned about it," Julie said.

"I've never heard *his* explanation before."

I SHOWED DAD in through the kitchen, and the four of us sat down around the dining table. He hung his fall windbreaker over the back of his chair. He didn't look nervous, just vigilant, wearing his usual air of calm control. We were his children—what could he fear from us?

I led off. "As you must realize, Dad, it was a horrible shock to learn our mother died of arsenic poisoning. And then learn nothing was ever done about it. The three of us need this opportunity to hear how you see it."

"Well, as I've already said, it's really very simple: nobody ever informed me what had happened." He spoke very matter-of-factly.

"Julie and I have been looking into it some more, because—"

"What exactly do you mean, 'looking into it'?" he demanded, staring indignantly at me.

"We visited the Montreal Neurological Institute. We spoke to one of the doctors who treated Mom. He told us the arsenic was discovered shortly after she died, even though the full autopsy report wasn't released until later. He confirmed she was poisoned through her food. Our grandfather found the autopsy report, and it showed she'd been poisoned over a period of months. Apparently, she received the final, massive dose just before leaving Argentina."

This seemed to be more than Dad wanted to hear. He started to intervene, but I held up my hand to stop him. I wanted to review for him and Doug the full picture of what we knew before he hijacked the conversation. I was all too familiar with Dad's diversionary tactics: he'd steer us into a time-wasting exercise, going back and forth over the same old alibis, fragmenting the story into bits and pieces until there was nothing left of it.

"Dad, the doctor at the MNI was clear with us: it wasn't a case of suicide or accidental death. Mom was *deliberately* poisoned. The police were called in as soon as the cause was suspected. And by the way, we've also spoken to Mary." For once, Dad's rigid expression changed, betraying surprise. "She told us the police questioned you aggressively. As she remembered it, they were trying to determine if you'd *killed* Mom."

"Well, I really—"

"So you can see how troubling this is for us."

"I really can't, Jeff. I had no idea what your mother died of until you told me five years ago. I had no idea the police were investigating anything. There was a routine questionnaire, a police functionary asked me questions. I assumed it was standard procedure. Maybe Mary understood it differently, but she didn't say so at the time."

"You know," I said, fed up with his recitation of the same old lies, "that's a huge discrepancy in interpretation. Wouldn't you say Mary is a reliable person?"

"Wait a minute, now. As you can imagine, I was pretty distracted right then. I may have missed a lot of what was happening. My wife had just died. I was trying to deal with that emotionally. I was thinking of you kids and what I was going to tell you. I was thinking of your grandparents and what I was going to tell them. There were funeral arrangements to make, transportation arrangements. There were forms to fill out. I needed to get in touch with the department. There was a lot going on in my mind, and I probably wasn't all there, as they say."

By this time, Dad was crouched forward, his hands in his lap, speaking to the table. "May I have a glass of water, please? My throat is a little dry. I think I may be coming down with something."

I got a glass of water, and Dad took a long drink.

"Now, where were we?" he continued.

"The police in Montreal," Julie interjected.

"Right." He paused to take another drink of water, leaned back in his chair for a few seconds, and stared at the ceiling before continuing.

"I don't remember them being particularly aggressive. I suppose they had to ask some difficult questions. That's their job. They were asking what they would ask anyone in those circumstances. It wasn't to be taken personally, and I didn't. But I really don't remember the questions or what I said at the time. I was in a daze, as anyone would be. If the police had anything to pursue, I assumed they'd be back in touch with me. The same with the hospital. When I didn't hear from either of them, I naturally concluded they had nothing to tell or ask me."

He was back in his crouch, speaking to the table again. We waited in silence.

"But you know," he resumed, straightening up and crossing his legs to make himself comfortable, "I've thought about why I didn't follow up with the hospital. I believed it was their responsibility to get back in touch with me. But also, I wanted to avoid reopening old wounds. It would have brought back a whole lot of pain," he said with a grimace. "And I asked myself, 'What good would it do? Would it bring her back?' No. She was gone forever."

He continued his soliloquy while we watched him intently, alert to every nuance.

"I guess I also felt a bit guilty. My wife had just died, and I'd been unable to save her. We had a friend in Buenos Aires who'd urged me to change doctors. But I'd been advised her doctors were the best for treating her condition, so I didn't. It seemed counterproductive to run the risk of starting all over from scratch.

"After she died, maybe I felt responsible in some way. So maybe I was unconsciously avoiding revisiting everything. It's a question I've never resolved. But I knew I'd never resolve it and I wanted to get on with life. There were you kids to think about."

He turned to us wearing a wan, desolate expression, like a man who had just relived terrible memories.

Julie had been right: his performance was very smooth indeed, even in front of a critical audience. He'd covered a lot of ground so seamlessly and quickly, it was hard to put your finger on any serious missteps. He'd handled Mary and the police problem especially well. Amid all the practical issues, he'd thrown in some psychology ("unconsciously avoiding revisiting everything"), even an appeal to our emotions, our sympathies, by saying how guilty he'd felt. An added touch was *our* role in the story: we needed his attention, so he really didn't have time to focus on Carol's death, which in any case would have been an exercise in futility.

I knew there was no point getting mired in debating the gaps, inaccuracies, exaggerations, and self-serving distortions in his story. We needed to move forward.

"We've heard rumours that Alejandra might have been involved in Mom's death," I said. "Did you ever suspect her of anything?"

"I don't know if I ever really *suspected* her. We never felt comfortable with her as our cook, but I had no particular reason to think she'd done something criminal. It was just a feeling. I remember searching her room at one point after your mother died, with that same family friend—just to see what we might find. Of course, we didn't find anything."

This was a new twist. We'd never heard him say he'd searched Alejandra's room. It opened the door to new questions, and Julie picked up on it immediately.

"So you *did* suspect she'd been involved?" she asked.

"We were grasping at straws," he replied. Dad had a cliché for evading every question.

"One thing I don't understand," I said. "Your wife dies very young of mysterious causes, with a lot of physical suffering. You ask yourself if the cook might have been responsible. You have an uncomfortable feeling about her. But despite your suspicion, you keep her on to cook for us the whole time, and for several more months after you return. Why?"

"As they say, Jeff, hindsight is twenty-twenty. At the time, there was no reason to suspect anyone of anything. You know, there are some things medical science can't explain. Some deaths remain unexplained no matter what. Your mother's death was one of those. It could have been caused by anything."

"Oh, come on!" Julie said.

"If you let your imagination run wild, you could spend your entire life looking under every rock. There were times I was tempted to do that. Looking around Alejandra's room must have been one of them. But then I had to ask myself, 'Where would it all end? How many people would I have to question? The doctors? The other people in our household? Our friends? Where would you stop?' I didn't have a clue what I'd be looking for—or even if there *was* anything to look for.

"And again," he concluded, "would it bring her back? Of course not. It made more sense to let the professionals do what they do best. When I didn't hear from them, I had to assume they'd come to the same conclusion I had: there *was* no answer."

He ended with a look of satisfaction on his face, as though he'd just worked through a particularly complex syllogism.

"Weren't you even curious, Dad, about what she died of?" Doug asked. (It would take Doug a long time to accept that Dad could no longer deny knowing the cause of death once the police questioned him.)

"Well, *of course* I was, Doug," he said, as if correcting an errant schoolboy.

"Does our stepmother know about all this?" Julie asked.

Dad paused for a moment, as if for reflection. "I don't know whether she really does."

"Give us a break!" Julie fired back. "Either she knows or she doesn't."

"I guess she does," he said placidly, turning toward her.

"And what does she think of it?"

"She probably feels these things happened before her time, of which she has no personal knowledge. She feels it's none of her business."

"So, it *really* didn't occur to you to check back with the hospital in Montreal?" Julie said.

"No, Julie. As I've told you already, it did *occur* to me," Dad said, with just a hint of annoyance.

"And after all these years you still swear the first you heard of Mom's cause of death was when Jeff called you in Minneapolis?"

"That was the first I'd heard of it."

Julie fell silent, shaking her head in disbelief.

There seemed nothing more to say. Dad, sensing it was time to go, gave each of us a rare, exaggerated hug and vanished into the night. Neither Julie nor I felt comfortable being hugged by him.

Much later, we heard from Ingrid that Dad arrived home that night in an angry mood, slamming the front door behind him, scowling at her, throwing his coat on the hallway chair, and walking directly to his study.

"Did it not go well with the kids?" she asked. "Do you want to talk about it, George?"

"No. Just leave me alone, please."

From then on, Ingrid referred to that night as "Black Tuesday."

JULIE AND DOUG stayed behind with me.

"He's got an answer for everything," Julie said, almost admiringly.

I nodded. "I nearly believed him too. He just cruised through the minefield around Mom's murder. He never faltered."

"He even finessed the inconsistency between Mary's version of the police interview and his," Julie said.

"Oh, sure. He was too dazed to realize it was an interrogation. He thought it was a bureaucratic exercise!"

"He handled Alejandra pretty well. Did you like 'grasping at straws'?"

"That was excellent," I said, "but I wasn't expecting the bit about searching her room."

"I wonder why he said that. He could have left it out. It only raises more questions. Maybe he needs to cover it in advance, so as not to be caught in a lie later. Maybe he wants to say he did *something* to look into Mom's death."

Julie was reading this exactly as I was.

"What do you think, Doug?" she asked. "You were listening carefully the whole time."

"I don't know," he said. "I just can't believe Dad would do what you guys think he did. It would have been such a huge risk. What if he got caught? He would have lost everything! It doesn't make sense."

"Then why does he lie?" Julie asked. "Look at it logically: if no one ever told him, one way or the other, why Mom died, how could he credibly claim no one ever found out? *That's* what doesn't make sense. The fact is, a multitude of people did find out—the coroner, the MNI, the police, that forensic medical journal and its readers, Grandpa and Grandma, Mary, us—and God knows who else."

I asked Doug, "Do you really believe Dad didn't know until I told him?"

"No. That can't be true."

"Then why would he lie about it?" Julie repeated.

"I don't know, I don't *know*. I just can't believe Dad would do something so risky. And so terrible." It was obvious how disheartened he felt.

"Doug," I reasoned, "what if he was experimenting on Mom with arsenic, a little at a time? What if he was waiting to see what would happen? And he got trapped in a situation where he either had to finish her off or get caught? What choice would he have?"

"It's too crazy. If he wanted to hide what he was doing, why would he have brought her back to Canada?" Doug said.

"Perhaps," I continued, "it reached a point where she was so sick that he didn't have any choice. She'd been in and out of the hospital two or three times, and they still couldn't figure out what was wrong. She'd get better, go home, and wind up sicker than before. The department, the hospital in Buenos Aires, and probably Mom herself were telling him to take her back to Canada—but if he did, the doctors might discover the arsenic before she died. Then they'd question her about who'd been feeding her, and Dad would have been exposed. Under those circumstances, he'd calculate it was better for him to finish her off in Argentina than risk taking her back to Canada alive—and that's apparently what he tried to do."

"That sounds so horrible, I just can't believe he'd do it," Doug said.

"Can't believe it? Or won't believe it, Doug? What about *our mother*?"

"Jeff, she's been dead for twenty-five years! Do you really think we're going to solve the mystery at this late date?"

And so the conversation went. I knew Doug wasn't going to change his mind—at least not then. Julie and I, though, were more convinced of Dad's guilt than ever. He'd given us little choice but to cut him out of our lives.

I TOLD JULIE that I would meet with Dad to deliver the message. With her working in Kingston, it would take too long to arrange a meeting among the three of us, and we didn't want our resolution to lose momentum and peter out. If there were any remaining hope of jarring the truth out of him, this was the only way.

"I've got to meet with you, Dad," I told him on the phone. "Just the two of us. I've got something to say to you about our mother's death."

"Again? Really? My God, Jeff, I thought we'd exhausted this subject. You know I've told you everything I possibly can. Wouldn't it be better to let the dust settle first? We could meet later, if you still want to."

"No. I need to meet without delay."

"*Without delay!*" he said scornfully. "All right then, if we must, why don't we meet here at our house?"

"I'd rather go somewhere else. Somewhere private, away from interruptions."

We agreed to go for a drive that afternoon in my second-hand Russian Lada.

I picked him up at the appointed time, and we drove to a quiet park. When we got there, I put the stick in neutral, turned off the ignition, and pulled the handbrake.

"Julie and I don't believe you."

"What do you mean, you don't believe me?" His voice sounded quizzical, as though he'd just heard something about quantum physics that he didn't understand.

"I mean we don't believe your story—about how you never found out how our mother died until I told you."

"Don't say *that*. My God! How can you say you don't believe me? What part don't you believe?"

"None of it. None of it makes any sense. Everyone seems to have known about the arsenic but you: the doctors, the police, our grandparents, the department, Mary, now us. How in the world could *you* not know?"

"I told you. I relied on the hospital to inform me if there was anything to report. When they didn't, I gathered they never found anything."

"Yes, yes, we've heard you say that over and over. But no one with any common sense would believe it. No reasonable person could accept that you'd take so little interest in your wife's shocking death that you wouldn't even bother to check with the hospital or the coroner or any of the others who knew the truth. It's absurd."

Dad sat silently with pursed lips, staring through the passenger window into the distance.

"And how could you tell me so categorically that time in Toronto that no one had discovered her cause of death? How could you state that as a *fact*, if no one ever contacted you about it? That was an out-and-out lie."

"I'm not sure if I put it quite that way."

"Of course not. So you have no basis for contradicting me when I tell you that I remember your exact words very clearly."

More silence.

"We think we know why you came up with this story," I said, finally.

"What do you mean, *came up with this story?*"

"Your claim of total ignorance eliminates the need for you to explain anything further."

"All I can say is that it's the truth, Jeff."

"It eliminates the need to explain, for example, why you didn't press for an investigation into Mom's death."

"I believed the police would have contacted me if there was anything to investigate."

"Really? We noticed your story about your police interview in Montreal evolved somewhat from the first version we heard. At first it was a clerk ticking off boxes on a form. But when we met with you last time, you allowed as how it may have been somewhat more aggressive. We expected that."

"You *expected* that? Don't say such a thing. It sounds like you're scrutinizing me."

"We are."

"*My God!*"

"We also figured you'd elaborate on the cook's role—though we weren't expecting the part about searching her room."

"You *figured!* . . . You *figured!*"

"Yes. We figured you'd realize how strange and unseemly it would appear not to have shown at least some interest in your wife's death. But we weren't satisfied that in searching Alejandra's room, you were just 'grasping at straws.'"

"I don't know what else to tell you, Jeff."

"Why would you search her room if you didn't suspect her of murder? And if you did suspect her, how could you not know how our mother died?"

"I wish I could tell you more, but—"

"If you suspected Alejandra of using arsenic, why did you keep her in the house with us kids?" After a pause, I concluded, "Unless you already knew she didn't do it."

A long silence ensued.

(Much later, Cristina told me that Dad did, in fact, enter Alejandra's room on one occasion. But his purpose was to confront her about a stolen radio. He fired her on the spot when he saw the missing radio right there in the room, and her boyfriend came around the next day to pick up her things. This would have been in February 1960, some seven months after Carol died. Thus, it appears likely that Dad inserted details from that episode, which did occur, into his story about searching Alejandra's room, which did not occur.)

Finally, I broke the silence between us. "Another problem we have is your reaction to all this," I said. "When Julie phoned to tell me about the autopsy report, I was shocked and horrified. When I called to tell you, your first response was silence. Then you became matter-of-fact. Not a scintilla of surprise, let alone shock. You were too busy waiting to hear what I knew to express any emotion. You showed no feelings for your wife and the terrible way she died. No sorrow or pity. And what about us and our feelings for our mother? No compassion. None at all. Even now, I'm getting no such feelings from you."

"I guess it was all so incredible," Dad muttered.

"Yes, I guess it was. Julie and I now realize the horrible ordeal you put our grandparents through, threatening to cut them off from us if they did anything to expose you."

"You already know my views on your grandparents. However well-intentioned they may have been, and I'm not at all certain about that, they were a pernicious influence on our family. We're sorry their only daughter died so young. But that didn't justify their interference with you kids. Perhaps I have *them* to blame for all this—"

I cut him off. I didn't want to get sidetracked into an argument about my grandparents.

"You have no one to blame but yourself, Dad, for your conduct and your lying, lying about the death, the *murder*, of our mother—by *arsenic poisoning*, for God's sake. Lying about it for a reason, which can only be a pretty terrible one."

I felt like calling him the bastard he was. But I didn't want to give him an excuse to get out and slam the car door, armed with a "hysterical" quote from me which he could trot out later.

After another long silence, I said, "Listen, Dad. I've done some things in my life that I'm ashamed of. But this is extreme. Julie and I don't want to live like that. We won't be seeing you anymore—at least she and I won't. Doug needs to make up his own mind. The door is always open if you want to tell us what really happened. But you'd better be prepared to answer some tough questions, because we won't buy any more of your stories."

"I just can't accept not having my children around," he said quietly, and for once he sounded genuine.

"That's what's happening."

"Maybe I could take you two to Argentina and we could investigate down there."

"You could. But only if we have a credible accounting from you first. We're not going down there on some useless fishing expedition."

"But then, what good would it do?" he said, backtracking. "Would it bring her back? No. So what would be the point?"

"Exactly."

After a short pause, he asked, "When am I going to see these documents you keep talking about?" He said this with a sense of entitlement.

"Here they are. Feast your eyes. They're photocopies."

He opened the manila envelope I'd brought and quickly perused the papers inside, which included only the autopsy and toxicology reports. I wasn't going to show him the rest of our evidence.

"It's horrible," he said, returning them to me at once. He sounded as if he were reciting a line from a script. If he wasn't interested in reading the reports, he must have already known their contents.

"Meanwhile, Julie and I will continue our investigations."

"Will that involve the police?"

"It might."

We drove in silence back to Rockcliffe Park.

As we approached his house, he offered, "If you and Julie ever want to talk about this some more, we can do that."

"Sure."

"I love you, Jeff."

Where the hell did that come from? It was the first time I could remember hearing those words from my father. How I had longed to hear him say that during my childhood. Now it only sounded hollow.

"Goodbye, Dad."

I felt a sudden flush of sorrow as he walked away from the car and up the front steps to his house. It was the last time I would feel that sorrow, which would soon turn to contempt.

17

MIND GAMES

DAD RESPONDED TO rejection by Julie and me in the only way he knew how: he counterattacked.

Several weeks passed after our tough one-to-one conversation in my car. There had been no further contact between us. Ingrid called me attempting to make plans for a family Christmas; I put her off. Dad phoned Julie proposing to meet separately with her, without me; she turned him down.

In mid-December, Dad phoned me. He wanted me to go over to his house and discuss what had happened. I told him I wouldn't, unless he had something new to tell me. He assured me he did, so I felt I had to hear him out.

It was cold as hell in Ottawa. When I arrived at the house in Rockcliffe Park, I peeled off my heavy parka, winter boots, gloves, and toque, and left them in the front hall. Dad showed me into the kitchen.

We sat down at the kitchen table, he and Ingrid on one side, me on the other, Inquisition style.

Ingrid seemed to be there mainly for show. Perhaps Dad felt better having an ally at his side. He did all the talking, leaning toward me over the table, hands clasped firmly together like a school principal.

"We called you here tonight, Jeff, because we want to get to the bottom of this business about your mother once and for all. We need to put this behind us so we can spend Christmas together like a normal family."

"Fine. Tell us the truth about what happened."

"As we've already discussed, I've told you everything I know about—"

I cut him off. "Not from our point of view."

"We all have our points of view in life. That doesn't mean we don't have to live with the facts. Now tell me this: What proof do you have that I haven't been completely honest with you? That I haven't told you everything I can? None. I think we have to agree on that."

"No, we don't. You're omitting the autopsy report I showed you. You're forgetting you lied about the police interview, and how they grilled you. You lied about the cook, trying to deflect suspicion from yourself. And you lied about how no one ever found the cause of our mother's death. Among other things." The summary was for Ingrid's benefit.

"Well, we may disagree on your interpretation of those things. And we can talk about that. Nevertheless, I think you'd have to agree you have no *proof* of anything. Until you can provide proof, we need to put all this aside and get on with life as a family."

The old shifting-the-burden-of-proof tactic.

"There's plenty of proof as far as we're concerned," I told him.

"Really? Where? When do I get to see it?"

"The proof is in what you've already said and done, Dad. And in the documents we have. Let's not go through all that again."

"So when do I get to see those documents? I ought to be entitled to see them, don't you think?"

"I've already shown you the autopsy and toxicology reports. You looked at them in the car and returned them. The rest stays with us until we hear the truth from you. Why all this new-found interest?"

"How can I meet your demands if I don't know what's in those documents? How can I be expected to prove a negative?"

Prove a negative. Slick.

Ingrid, who had been watching Dad intently while we spoke, looked off into the distance. Some of this was way over her head, but her instincts were telling her the conversation wasn't going well.

"Tell you what, Dad," I offered. "You write down everything that happened, and we'll look at it."

"*'We'll look at it?'* Be reasonable. How in the world can I be expected to write down *everything*? How can I know what would be relevant if I don't know what you consider proof, and if I don't know what's in those documents?"

"If you have doubts about the relevance of something, just include it. Julie and I can ask you follow-up questions if we need to know more."

"You're being completely unreasonable and grossly unfair. What you're proposing would lead to a wild goose chase. If we just looked at those documents together, we could narrow down what's bothering you and sort it all out."

And if we give you a chance to study the documents, you'll figure out how to whitewash everything and absolve yourself of responsibility.

"You say you want to continue seeing Julie and me," I told him. "Yet when we ask you to write down what happened, you refuse. You also said you had something new to tell us. I'm listening, but all I'm hearing is the same old line."

"Well, of course I want to see you and Julie. That's why I'd like to work with you."

"The trouble is, we think you were implicated in our mother's death. So the best way to prove us wrong would be to write everything down."

"*Implicated*? You can't mean that," he said, as though referring to some wild-eyed, fantastic theory.

"We do."

"So you're not going to give me a chance to know the basis of your thinking."

"I think we've made ourselves clear. I'll see myself out."

A MONTH LATER, in January 1985, Ingrid asked me to come and see her at their house while Dad was away. She said it was important.

I was mildly intrigued. I was ready for anything, including some surprise planted by Dad, so I went prepared.

We sat down in the TV room. Ingrid quickly got to the point: "You are not coming around to see us anymore, and it bothers me. I know you have problems with your father about your mother's death. I just want to tell you it has *nothing* to do with me."

This was quite a statement. I decided to venture a little farther. "I'm sure you can understand why we have problems with Dad's version of events," I said. "Just to show you our concerns are genuine, I brought along our file with the documents. We don't want anyone to ever tell you we made this up. Here's a copy of the autopsy report."

As I opened the file, Ingrid recoiled. "Oh, no! I don't want to see that!" She turned aside, raising her hand to shield her face as if protecting herself from a blow.

I closed the file, and she was visibly relieved.

"I just don't want you to push me away because of your problems with your father," she said softly.

I got out of the chair and gave her a hug.

In hindsight, my impulse to show her some compassion was a measure of how badly I wanted to believe *someone* was innocent in this whole awful business. Naively, perhaps, I was willing to take Ingrid at her word. I believed her because I wanted to believe her.

Later, after more detached analysis, I wondered if I should have tried harder to engage her in a conversation about what she really knew. I might have received answers to questions that still trouble me.

How, for instance, does a woman feel when she learns that her husband's first wife died of arsenic poisoning? How does she respond when offered evidence that it was murder, suggesting her husband was implicated?

In Ingrid's case, she betrayed no shock, no fear, not even curiosity. She made no attempt at denial. Significantly, she didn't even try to defend George.

Nor did she betray the slightest hint of horror over the possibility that the man she'd married, whose children she'd borne, and with whom she'd lived for the past twenty-five years, might be a murderer. She showed no fear that she herself could be his next victim. She expressed no confusion about the contradiction he presented to the world: a respected professional man, a well-bred diplomat representing his country abroad, whose eldest son and daughter were convinced he had poisoned his late wife.

Ingrid didn't try to dismiss our narrative by saying it was far-fetched, or insisting there must be some logical, innocent explanation. All she was concerned about, to take her words at face value, was that her ties with us, her stepchildren, shouldn't suffer the same fate as her husband's relationship with us. Perhaps most importantly to her, she wanted us to believe that our accusation against our father had nothing to do with her.

Yet when I had the opportunity, I didn't press Ingrid on any of these questions. Somehow, I knew there was a limit to how far I could risk foraging into the past with her about my mother's death.

ABOUT A MONTH later, I received a phone call completely out
of the blue from the Krapfs, our parents' old friends from Buenos
Aires. I remembered them only vaguely. But Carol had mentioned
Louise and Rolf Krapf frequently in her correspondence with her
parents, which Grandma had shared with us, so I knew them by
name right away.

The timing, and the subject they wanted to discuss, suggested
strongly that Dad had orchestrated the call.

Louise Krapf, sounding very cordial, explained that she and
her husband, Rolf, had retired to the Gatineau Hills, in Quebec, just
across the river from Ottawa, her hometown. Yes, I did remember
them from Buenos Aires, I told Louise, and she invited me for a drink
at their home.

When I arrived at their front door, it was evident the Krapfs were
comfortably well off. They lived in a big, newish bungalow on a large
lot a short drive from the Gatineau River, now frozen solid and covered with snow. Very nice, I thought—and completely unlike the
boulevards of Buenos Aires. But as beautiful as the place was, it might
as well have been on the moon.

"It's so nice to see you after all these years," Louise said warmly
across the antique pine coffee table. She was an attractive woman of
about sixty, smartly dressed and wearing silver earrings—slightly
more formal than you'd expect in that rustic setting. "We heard you
were living in Ottawa and wanted to find out how you were."

Rolf, grey and balding, smiled amiably from his easy chair under
a lamp in the corner.

"It's nice to see you too," I said. "Thank you for calling. What a
surprise after all this time."

"You may not remember us very well," Louise said, "but we loved
your mother. We were very sorry when she passed away."

This confirmed the agenda for the meeting and gave me my cue.

"What a coincidence that you'd mention our mother. My sister, Julie, and I have discovered she died of arsenic poisoning. We have a copy of the autopsy report from Montreal. We've been trying ever since to find out what happened. Perhaps you can help us?"

The conversation was unfolding as though we were all reading from a script.

"Have you spoken to your dad about it?" Louise asked. She looked sympathetic and concerned, but not surprised. Clearly, she'd known about the arsenic.

"Yes, we've spoken with him a great deal. We naturally thought he'd be able to explain it to us."

"It doesn't necessarily have anything to do with him," Louise ventured.

I let this pass. "It was a shocking discovery. We wanted to know if he could shed light on it."

"Of course."

From the other side of the room, Rolf piped up. "There was a serious problem with the cook, I understand."

I turned toward him. "We've considered that story. There are too many things about it that just don't add up. She remained in the house cooking for us for months after our mother died. Dad's department knew Mom had died of arsenic poisoning. If they suspected the cook, why would they take the risk of leaving her in the house?"

"Maybe your father was trying to catch her in the act," Louise suggested.

"Actually, my dad said he never discovered why Carol died until we found the autopsy report twenty years later."

"Is that so?" Rolf said.

"How is that possible?" I asked them, looking from one to the other. "Do *you* think it's possible?"

There was a long pause.

"No. No, I don't think that's possible," Louise replied quietly.

We chatted about other subjects, and after finishing my drink I thanked them and made my way home.

Julie's turn came a while later, when she too was invited to visit the Krapfs at the house in Gatineau. They may have been reflecting on what I'd told them; Julie learned some surprising new things.

Again, Louise said she'd been very fond of Carol, describing her as a delightful young woman, the life of the party, while George was a bit of a cold fish. On his return to Buenos Aires after Carol died, George had shocked Louise and Rolf by regaling them with stories of his outings in New York and the marvels of Mexico City, displaying no sorrow at all over Carol's death.

Not long after that, Louise had offered to adopt Julie. George declined. Louise told Julie she'd always suspected Carol had been poisoned. She spent several months after Carol's death mustering the nerve to do something about it. Finally, she went to Ambassador Richard Bower and shared her suspicions with him. He listened to her politely and sent her on her way.

Wow—that was quite a revelation. Not only our grandparents but the Krapfs had offered to adopt Julie after Carol's death. What did Louise know that motivated her to make such an extraordinary offer? And her suspicion of poison: Was it based on anything more than a hunch? She must have had a reason to take the bold step of sharing this with Ambassador Bower.

I wondered how Bower had really taken her allegation. Louise didn't say he'd been surprised. As Carol had written in one of her letters, the ambassador was no fool. It's likely Bower would have been troubled, despite his dismissive response. In Louise's eyes, George was a murder suspect, and he may have been suspect in the eyes of the expat community. Bower had once supported George's appeal for the completion of his posting; now he probably felt the sooner George was gone, the better.

Julie and I were sure Dad had engineered these encounters with the Krapfs. What we didn't understand at the time was why they had agreed to approach me. It was clear from what they'd told Julie that they didn't like or trust George. Perhaps they'd hoped to learn more from us about what really happened to Carol. If so, they learned more than they'd bargained for. We concluded that they now realized George's story about the cook was a sham, and he had been trying to use them to influence us in his favour.

Once the Krapfs learned that we believed the criminal had been George himself, they disappeared from our lives. Although Louise had spoken of getting together with us once more, they didn't return phone calls from Julie and me, and we never heard from them again. In that respect, they were like so many other bystanders in this story: they preferred not to get involved any further.

Still, Julie and I remain grateful for Louise's attempt to pursue the truth about our mother's death, and for the enlightenment she provided.

GEORGE AND INGRID'S marriage had been rocky for the past several years. They'd already been experiencing problems when I visited them in England. The rather long-awaited birth of their son had apparently offered a welcome hope of renewal, at least in Ingrid's mind. But it was followed by trouble over allegations of unwanted advances to a locally-engaged staffer at the embassy in Stockholm. Nothing was ever concluded legally, but their posting to Sweden was significantly foreshortened, followed by an early departure to New York.

Manhattan was exactly the kind of huge, congested metropolis that made Ingrid uncomfortable. She and George and their three children lived in a five-bedroom, six-bathroom, two-storey penthouse on East 86th Street. The apartment would have seemed like luxury to most people, but she considered it cavernous and cold. Her customary quiet afternoon naps were disrupted by the doorman hailing cabs with a whistle on the sidewalk below. When she was out walking the dog, she disliked having to dodge the constant flow of delivery trucks, yellow Marathon cabs, joggers, strollers, and street people in Carl Schurz Park. The whine of sirens was a frequent reminder of the city's serious crime problem in the late 1970s.

After two years in New York came the move in 1979 to Minneapolis, where I visited them in their suburban home on Cedar Lake. This wasn't Ingrid's cup of tea either. In 1984, they returned to Ottawa between postings—a city she hardly knew, having lived there for only two years in the mid-1970s. Returning to Ottawa after years on posting abroad is a shock to the system of any foreign service family member, as I can attest. All of a sudden, you're a nobody again. No perks and privileges, just frigid winters, slushy streets, and, in Ingrid's case, practically no friends.

After living around the world with George for twenty-five years, often in places she didn't particularly like, only to wind up in Ottawa, Ingrid felt entitled to live somewhere that suited her. She'd always wanted a posting in Germany—a homecoming dream for her—and she reminded him about this. After a couple of years at headquarters, he'd be on track for another overseas assignment. It would probably be his last, in light of which he'd normally be shown some consideration regarding the choice of country.

For years, George had been holding out for an ambassadorship. This probably would have eliminated Germany as a posting, since the top position in Bonn would have been too senior for him. When once again he failed to make the list of ambassadorial assignments, he was crushed about being passed over.

"He was like a hurt animal," Bob Borden told Ingrid. Nevertheless, another post in Germany became a possibility. When an opening as consul general in Munich was offered, she told George this was exactly what she wanted, and he really couldn't refuse.

After this stroke of good fortune, imagine Ingrid's despair when she began suspecting George had another woman in his life. She recognized the telltale signs: late nights at the office when he was supposed to be working but her phone messages went unanswered; a mysterious trip to Montreal on which George failed to show up at his overnight destination, cousin Mary's home, where, it turned out, he wasn't even expected. Ingrid put these clues together with other developments: twin beds on the occasional road trips they took together, a husband who didn't want to talk about anything, unidentified callers on the home phone.

She became increasingly upset, and finally anger took over. After finding the keys to his desk at home, she rummaged through the drawers. There she discovered some correspondence between George and a woman I'll call Helen, an English fashion designer he'd met on a trip to London. The letters confirmed that they were more than just friends. Apart from the betrayal, Ingrid was particularly stung by George's avowal to Helen that he felt proud of her, something that Ingrid had been longing to hear from her husband for years but never had.

In a rage, Ingrid confronted George with the evidence of his affair. She made it clear he was to get rid of this tramp at once, but he brushed off her allegations and insisted there was nothing serious going on.

Temporarily mollified, Ingrid began making arrangements for their move to Munich. But she was still suspicious, and she monitored his behaviour for more signs. When he declined to participate in the moving preparations, then refused to discuss plans for travelling together to Germany, despite her entreaties, she pushed him: "How can I make all the arrangements for Munich if I don't know when I will be going?"

George allowed that he needed to proceed to Munich on his own initially—something about overseeing repairs to the official residence. She could follow once he had settled in. Ingrid thought this story had a hollow ring to it and was likely a ruse. She called me to enlist my help.

At first, I provided mainly a sympathetic ear. I was at their house just after Dad moved out on a trial separation basis. Ingrid was in tears, curled up on the sofa in the study under an afghan and protected by her beloved golden retriever. A more hard-nosed observer might have told her, "Good riddance." But when she whimpered, "I still love the guy," it didn't seem the right thing to say. I felt sorry for her.

Although Doug and Julie had kept their distance from Ingrid for the last several years, they too were drawn in as sympathetic listeners. Doug found himself unable to refuse and for a while was getting calls from her every other day. Julie was disinclined to hear from Ingrid, but an acknowledgment and apology from her about the childhood abuse brought Julie around as well.

I too heard a litany of complaints. Listening to Ingrid spill out her grievances against my father, and hearing similar reports from my siblings, I realized they went far beyond his obsessive tightness with money and even his philandering. Ingrid recalled that, on more than one occasion, he'd struck her, one time so hard he knocked her down. Apparently, George's violent outbursts were triggered when Ingrid talked back to him.

I began to see a pattern forming. Julie had suffered violence at his hands under similar circumstances. She'd told me that during a skiing holiday in Switzerland, when she was nineteen, she'd talked back to Dad in a sarcastic tone and he'd struck her with a backhand to the head. He hit her so hard, she could have fallen down the stairs where she was standing. Later, he apologized, seeming to realize he'd crossed the line. But the apology didn't stop Julie from feeling afraid of what he might do.

As it became clear that the separation was looking more and more like it might end in divorce, I introduced Ingrid to a lawyer friend, whom I'll call Janet, to represent her interests. Ingrid had resisted the idea of getting a lawyer, unwilling to accept that it was necessary or desirable. Perhaps she still hoped she could coax George into a reconciliation. I offered her another viewpoint: once he received the cold shower of hearing from a lawyer how much a separation and divorce would cost him, he'd be back.

It turned out I was right. Ingrid persuaded George, who was anxious not to antagonize her, to meet her lawyer. She hoped Janet would sweet-talk him into coming back to her. Instead, the meeting was all business.

"Mr. Blackstock," Janet asked, "is Mrs. Blackstock free to accompany you to Germany?"

"No," George replied.

"Then the situation we have between you and Mrs. Blackstock is what we call a separation, and it needs to have a legal basis to ensure that her rights are protected."

With Ingrid's permission, I talked to Janet about the meeting afterwards.

"How did my father seem during the discussion?"

"On stage, Jeff. Very controlling."

"What do you think he'll do?"

Janet replied that we might not be able to stop George from leaving, but he was certainly going to realize the cost involved.

George's reaction to Janet was to complain about her. "Keep that lawyer out of this," he told Ingrid, completely missing the point of why she'd engaged a lawyer in the first place.

Janet set Ingrid up with a family psychologist. To my amazement, Ingrid actually convinced Dad to attend a session with him. If there was anyone who doubted the value of psychologists, it was my father.

As far as he was concerned, psychologists and psychiatrists were crutches for the weak and the sick.

Part of the psychologist's approach was to see other family members too, so that he could "get the full picture"—which, of course, was impossible with our fractured family. I had a session with him and received a report on his meeting with George and Ingrid. The psychologist viewed my father as a challenge, but felt he was up to it. I got the impression he regarded their interaction as a competition of wills.

The psychologist had told Dad, "You know, yours is not the first foreign service matrimonial case I've had."

"Really?" he replied, apparently surprised. This seemed to make an impression on Dad, if nothing else did.

"None of your kids are taking your side on this," the psychologist told him.

"I don't know about *that*," he said.

"But they're supporting your wife."

"I think they would probably prefer to stay out of it. I didn't want to drag them into this."

The psychologist shared with me some observations of my father, who seemed to intrigue him.

"He uses money to control people around him, to the point where it has become an obsession," the psychologist told me. This wasn't exactly news. "He has no *true* sense of humour," he added. I hadn't thought of that before, but it struck me as spot-on.

To the psychologist, George was living in a fantasy world in which he could walk out on his wife and move to Germany without any obligations to her and live happily ever after with his girlfriend.

To buy time, George let Ingrid keep her hope of a reconciliation alive. It was a cynical move, since he appeared to have no desire to remain in the marriage. What followed was the oddest resolution, if it could be called that, of the situation.

George left for Munich alone, and Ingrid was to follow shortly afterwards. As I would discover, Helen was all set to move to Germany, where George would be waiting for her. Years later, I would speak with Helen, and she'd tell me George had invited her to live with him in Munich, and she'd agreed. As he knew, this would require her not only to quit her job but to pack up and move to a new country where she didn't speak the language. How did he think he was going to get away with this fantasy?

Naturally, Ingrid had different ideas. She'd intercepted messages between Helen and George. She'd poked through his agenda books, credit card receipts, and Swiss bank account statements. When she arrived in Munich, she had a pretty good idea of what was going on. And by the time Ingrid set her feet on the ground of the consul general's residence, she had made up her mind that she wasn't leaving.

The next time Helen tried to secretly phone George, she got a shock: it was Ingrid who answered. Ingrid knew exactly who was calling. She told Helen that she was never, *ever* to call again.

A conversation then ensued between Ingrid and George. Exactly what Ingrid said, I don't know. But it must have been very convincing, because George called Helen back within a few minutes.

"Hello, Helen."

"George! What's going on?" she said, alarmed.

"Helen, darling, it's over," he replied, and hung up.

According to Helen, those were the last words he ever spoke to her. She attempted to call him several times afterwards and never got through.

Later, Helen would tell me that she was left emotionally shattered, her life in a mess. Eventually, she found happiness back in London, restarting her career, marrying, and having kids. She never did learn whatever it was Ingrid told George that brought their relationship to such an abrupt and crushing end.

WHILE GEORGE'S MID-LIFE melodrama was playing itself out, Julie and I were arriving at a difficult decision: we agreed to explore the possibility of a criminal prosecution, charging Dad with our mother's murder.

We knew the chances of a prosecutor agreeing to take on the case were slim. But if there was even the slightest chance of obtaining a measure of justice for Carol through the courts, some public recognition of what had happened to her, and some degree of retribution— even though it would be against our own father—we needed to try. This may seem like an extreme step. If so, perhaps only someone who has lived through a situation comparable to ours can fully understand how much finding justice for our mother meant to us.

After doing some legal research on my own, I spoke with an experienced Crown attorney in Ottawa who was introduced to me by a lawyer friend. The Crown attorney confirmed that any attempt to prosecute such a difficult case some twenty-five years after the fact would run up against serious obstacles.

From the outset, we faced a major jurisdictional barrier. The crime had apparently been committed, according to Carol's doctors at the Montreal Neurological Institute, in Argentina, not Canada. The medical evidence pointed to the arsenic having been administered in Buenos Aires. That meant an Argentine court would have had to try our father.

This was not possible. As a Canadian diplomat serving his country in Argentina, George enjoyed immunity from prosecution there, and even from full investigation by local police authorities. The time-honoured conventions of diplomatic immunity protected him, unless the Government of Canada waived that immunity—something that most governments, including Canada's, never do; it would expose their diplomatic personnel to threats abroad, especially in unfriendly countries with dubious judicial systems. A Canadian diplomat might be arrested by a hostile or corrupt government on trumped-up charges, convicted in a kangaroo court, and thrown in jail as part of a shakedown designed to extort secrets, payoffs, or political conces sions. As the Crown prosecutor pointed out, the diplomatic immu- nity issue meant we might not even be able to get to court.

In my view, it *was* possible that back in 1959 a Canadian court could have asserted jurisdiction over an alleged crime committed in another country, provided it was reasonably soon after the crime took place. Certain conditions would have been required: strong ties to Canada on the part of the main protagonists, for example, as well as compelling reasons to prosecute. This would explain why Dr. Valcourt was preparing evidence for a criminal case following the autopsy.

In this case, both victim and accused were Canadian citizens on Canadian government service. Moreover, the victim died in Canada, where medical and oral evidence of a possible crime had been gath- ered. No permission from Argentine authorities would have been required for Canadian police to search and investigate our diplomatic residence, since it was considered Canadian territory. Permission from the Argentine authorities might have been obtained for Canadian police officers to investigate in Buenos Aires, and witnesses from Argentina might have been summoned or interviewed for pur- poses of a prosecution in Canada. A tall order, but not impossible, if the interests of justice were to be served—and if the Canadian authorities had been sufficiently interested in justice.

But for a Canadian court to assert jurisdiction twenty-five years after a crime was committed in Argentina, the prosecutor acknowl- edged, it would be necessary to have very strong evidence and very compelling reasons indeed.

On the one hand, there was the testimony of Julie and me. This might have supported a guilty verdict by establishing that our father had lied to us about our mother's death in a most material way. Sometimes, his lies had been claims of ignorance about matters he knew perfectly well; at other times, he simply provided non-answers to our questions. You had to have been there to appreciate how cold and expressionless his silences could be.

On the other hand, in the mid-1980s we didn't have the powerful documentary evidence that would come into our possession after our father's death in 2007. Moreover, key witnesses, such as our maternal grandparents, were dead, incapacitated, or unavailable, and material evidence in Argentina had long since disappeared.

I was quite aware of the legal challenges. I was also aware that we weren't dealing with a high-profile Nazi war criminal and thousands of victims; we were talking about Carol Blackstock, a little-known wife and mother from North Toronto, as the victim, and her well-connected husband and the Government of Canada, who would have to answer regarding her death.

Our father might have *looked* as guilty as hell, but I doubted very much we had enough evidence for the technical requirements of a conviction. Unfortunately, the Crown attorney shared that assessment.

For Julie and me, it might still have been worthwhile to take Dad to court anyway, if only to expose the truth about our mother's death and his role in it. But if we did so, we weren't going to get the support of the criminal justice system. Bringing a civil suit against our father might have had a better chance of success, except that the statute of limitations on a wrongful-death action had expired long before 1979, the year when we'd learned how Mom died.

We also realized it could be counterproductive for us to go to court. If we didn't win, Dad would claim he'd been proven innocent. That wouldn't be true; just because someone isn't convicted on a criminal charge doesn't necessarily mean they're innocent or might not be convicted later on the basis of new evidence. But if our efforts had resulted in an acquittal, *that* would have been the legacy of Dad's crime against our mother—an impossibly bitter pill for us to swallow.

No doubt Dad himself had already figured all this out. And we felt sure that as soon as we took legal action against him, he'd destroy any incriminating documents in his possession.

We had to settle for exerting whatever pressure we could by leaving open our threat of involving the police, and by treating our father as an outcast, in the hope he might feel compelled to give up *something*. Our shunning him was also in retribution for what he'd done, considering that he placed such a high value on family appearances—perhaps the only retribution he was ever going to suffer. The niceties of the justice system would be of no help to us in this savage business.

Still, I will forever feel guilt for not having had our father prosecuted. I know this isn't rational, and he, not I, was the guilty one. I can't explain it, but there it is.

18

DETERIORATION

JULIE AND I had tried everything we could to obtain justice for our mother. We felt bad that we hadn't succeeded, but for the time being we would get on with our lives, knowing that was what she'd have wanted us to do.

Mom had been a very young woman when she died, just twenty-four. Julie and I had long since grown beyond that age. Still, she remained timeless for us. No matter how long we lived, we would always feel younger than her.

And yet her story was far from over. Life had more surprises in store.

IN 1990, GEORGE AND INGRID returned to Ottawa when their Munich posting ended. By then, Marie and I had a two-year-old daughter, Jill, whom they didn't know. I was working at the Department of Foreign Affairs and International Trade, which, having absorbed the foreign branch of my father's old department, was also where Dad worked. An opportunity had come up through a connection of Marie's in the department who was looking for lawyers, and, with her encouragement, I grabbed it.

The posting in Germany had turned out differently from the happy homecoming Ingrid had expected. Her childhood friends were now middle-aged professionals with busy lives and little time for someone they'd known long ago. The old-world charm of the Europe she remembered was gone. The return to Canada didn't offer much consolation either.

Now that there was no longer an ocean separating them, Julie brought her relationship with Ingrid, such as it had been, to a close, writing her a letter saying she wished to have no more to do with her. With Dad cut out of her life for the past ten years, Julie had very little contact with our stepmother anyway. At this point, Julie and her new husband had a son, born around the time of Dad and Ingrid's return from Munich, and Julie made it clear she didn't want them to be a part of her son's life. Ingrid wrote her a note in response.

> *Dear Julia.*
>
> *I'm very sorry to hear how you feel about me. We can not do anything about our pasts, but we can hope and pray for the future.*
>
> *My door is always open.*
>
> *With love,*
>
> *Ingrid*

Doug had more or less banished Ingrid from his life years ago. He'd never forgiven her for the way she'd treated him. It was a different story between him and Dad; Doug received extra attention from our father now that Julie and I were out of Dad's life.

About a year after his return from Munich, Dad retired and started working on contract for the department, handling access-to-information letters from the public. His duties gave him access to files kept in the basement of departmental headquarters, the Lester

B. Pearson Building, on Ottawa's Sussex Drive. When we found out about this, Julie, in particular, worried that he'd remove files containing information about our mother. She sent letters and made phone calls to the department expressing her concerns.

According to the department, there were no such files in its possession. Julie also made access-to-information requests about Carol to various other departments, all to no avail. The government that had sent Carol Blackstock with her husband and family to Argentina, where she was lethally poisoned, now knew nothing about her.

Officially speaking, she had become a non-person.

IN EARLY DECEMBER 1992, I got a call from Dad asking to see me. I declined, telling him nothing had changed. He offered to discuss the matter of our mother's death, but I told him there was no point unless he provided some new disclosure about the questions we'd left on the table.

I called Julie to let her know he had been in touch. She hadn't spoken to him in years, but we anticipated he'd be phoning her as well.

She took his call on December 16. Suspecting that he would want to revisit the issue of Carol's death after thirteen years, she recorded the conversation, just in case he revealed anything we didn't already know.

He wondered if he could stop by to see her and her son.

Julie replied, "This business about Carol has to get resolved before we can have a normal relationship." He should write down everything he remembered happening, she told him, and they could start from there.

"It's not going to do me any good to write the whole thing down . . . unless I can find out things that I don't already know," Dad said.

After a long silence, he sighed, and said, "One thing you could do is let me see my grandson."

"When he becomes an adult, if he wants a relationship with you, that's fine. In the meantime . . . I am not prepared to [allow that]," Julie replied.

Another silence. "You know, I think grandparents have rights . . . to see their grandchildren."

"Under normal circumstances. These aren't normal circumstances."

Silence. "I think you are being cruel," he said finally.

"I think I had better go," Julie said.

Dad's assertion of grandparents' rights was worse than cynical, given the way he'd treated our grandparents.

Although the conversation ended with the same old impasse, it was a very difficult one for Julie to have. She was still scared of George and what he might do, she told me. But she stood up to him and challenged him with courage and resolve. It was more obvious than ever that he wasn't going to comply with her repeated requests for his written account of what had happened to our mother. After all, it wasn't going to "do him any good."

NOT LONG AFTER Julie's conversation with Dad, Ingrid decided she'd had enough of him and moved out of their home. She left him a note saying that he'd been telling her she could leave if she didn't like it in their marriage, so she was taking him up on his offer.

This time, Ingrid didn't require my help. She had plenty of family money from Germany, and her interests in Canada were being looked after by Janet, the lawyer I'd found for her earlier. Her financial future was secure. I could hardly avoid getting involved, however, when Janet called me to say she was having trouble collecting her fee; I had to remind Ingrid she should pay her lawyer.

I also responded to Ingrid's call for help getting Dad to pay their now-teenage son's boarding school fees. George was in arrears, and the school was pestering her after failing to get any response from him. His neglect of his son's needs, all because he didn't like to part with money, made me furious. I confronted him in the basement of the Pearson Building, where he was working. "Just pay the goddamn fees!" I yelled.

After selling the Rockcliffe Park property, Dad moved into a very comfortable townhouse in Ottawa. He was on his own—but not for long. "I've discovered his new girlfriend's name is Ruth, and she's no girl," Ingrid reported.

George appeared to have landed on his feet with Ruth. Soon, he would move in with her.

Ingrid and I had a falling out when I refused to do her bidding and talk Doug and Julie into reconciling with her.

"I can't do that," I explained over the phone. "I may be their older brother, but they're adults and they make their own decisions. I'm not going to lean on them."

When she realized I wasn't going to budge, Ingrid turned hostile. "There is a big difference between my *younger* children and my *older* children," she pronounced in a royally aggrieved tone.

IN 1992, MARIE and I had a son, Scott. His sister, Jill, was now four, old enough to understand she had grandparents and to ask about them. Dad, as usual, was pressing to see his grandchildren, and we had to decide what to do.

Julie had chosen to sever contact with him altogether. Marie and I took a different course. We decided not to complicate our kids' lives by depriving them entirely of a relationship with their paternal grandparents, but we kept the contact to a minimum. After Dad moved in with Ruth, I would take Jill and Scott over to her place once in a while, so he could read them stories while I went shopping.

As soon as Ingrid became aware of Dad's visits with our kids, it led to a competition for time with them. Again, the most important things for Marie and me were our children's needs and their natural desire to see their grandparents. And so, despite some misgivings, I took Jill and Scott over to see Ingrid from time to time as well.

For similar reasons, we wanted our kids to have a relationship with their extended family on my side—all those Blackstock aunts, uncles, and cousins, who gathered once a year at Bass Island, my father's summer retreat in Muskoka, three hours north of Toronto. Bass Island was a ten-acre property with three cottages, enough space to accommodate eighteen people—a wonderful place for swimming, sailing, and running around in the woods. The annual family retreat provided an occasion for Jill and Scott to stay in touch with relatives without our having too much to do with Dad.

IN 1996, MARIE AND I went on our first overseas posting—to San José, Costa Rica. We made the trip with our children, our cat, and a pair of guinea pigs. You don't go on posting with kids and leave their pets behind, unless you want family misery.

While in Costa Rica, I got a call from Julie saying that Grandma wasn't expected to live much longer. She had been bedridden in a long-term care facility in Kingston, where Julie had moved her a few years earlier. She was now ninety-four, and she'd been unconscious for a long time. It was nearly twenty years since Grandpa's death.

I flew back to Kingston in time to see Grandma before she died. I remember her taking her last breath, and the stillness afterwards. It was as though some great power had quietly pulled a plug. Our grandmother had been a happy person, despite the gross injustices she'd been forced to endure in silence. I was determined that silence would be broken.

Doug, Julie, and I attended Grandma's funeral service along with some friends of Julie's. We made a very small gathering in the funeral home chapel, but the attendants said they had never heard "Amazing Grace" sung so loudly.

AFTER WE RETURNED to Ottawa from Costa Rica in 1999, Ingrid reached out for my help, and again I found myself unable to refuse. I set her up with a new financial advisor to manage her Canadian investments, sitting in on sessions with the advisor to help Ingrid understand what was happening with her Canadian money. Most of her wealth remained invested in Germany.

When Ingrid's mother died, I accompanied Ingrid to the funeral in Germany along with her own three kids. This was at her request. One of my half-sisters told me, "Mum would appreciate it if you came along as part of the Canadian side of the family."

"But to her relatives in Germany, I'm not family," I pointed out to her.

Still, it seemed the right thing to do. Symbolically, I suppose, I was a stand-in for Dad.

OUR NEXT OVERSEAS posting was to Sydney, Australia. We lived in a house with a beautiful garden and small pool in the Eastern Suburbs. It wasn't a huge place, or particularly fancy, but in the red-hot Sydney real estate market, it was what we could afford on our foreign service rent subsidy.

From Doug back home, I began hearing more and more about Dad. He was suffering from dementia. He'd spoken at a lunch organized by Bob Borden, which Doug had also attended, and had made a total botch of his speech, misplacing his notes and forgetting what he was supposed to be saying. Doug was spending increasing amounts of time helping Dad with chores and errands. Some were mundane, like repair work around Ruth's house, others more difficult.

Doug decided, with my support, that it was necessary to take away Dad's driver's license and beloved Saab after a number of traffic incidents clearly indicated he was a danger to himself and others.

Bob Borden called me in Sydney. "Why is Doug having your father's driver's license revoked?" he asked indignantly. Removal of driving rights is a very sensitive issue for senior citizens.

"Because he doesn't want his father to hurt somebody," I replied.

"Quit interfering from the other side of the planet," Bob said.

Doug would later suffer the consequences of looking after Dad. In the meantime, he'd become a regular visitor at Ruth's house. When she told Dad that he'd have to move out, Dad asked Doug to intervene on his behalf. "Can you talk to her, Doug?" he said plaintively.

Doug asked Ruth why she was sending him away.

"Because he's driving me crazy," she replied. "At first it was okay with the sex. But with the way he is now, I can't take it anymore." She couldn't deal with him not remembering things from one minute to the next.

Doug helped Dad move out of Ruth's place and into a deluxe seniors' apartment building in Toronto, rented by Bob Borden on Dad's behalf. Doug also had to dispose of the Saab. It was quite an ordeal for him, contending by turns with a man who couldn't remember what had happened five minutes ago and with the more familiar side of his father, who was used to wheedling and pushing Doug to get what he wanted.

"There are times when Dad is completely lucid," Doug told me. These would soon become fewer and fewer.

WE WERE ON summer home leave from Australia when I saw Dad for the second-last time. It was at his Muskoka retreat on Bass Island. Like the rest of the family, we were there for a last visit before the island was sold. Marie and I wanted Jill and Scott to have one more weekend with their cousins at the summer place where they'd played together and got to know each other. Even Julie came to see everyone.

Dad was fond of saying this was where he'd spent the happiest times of his life—probably the only place where he'd experienced something akin to a normal family existence. It was where his grandchildren would splash in the water, water-ski, sail the Laser, and play in the boathouse. He loved the place so much that he had Bob Borden promise to sprinkle his ashes there.

Dad had bought the island, with Bob's guidance, when the real estate market was very low. Some twenty years later, the maintenance costs had become prohibitive, but the market was at an all-time high, and Bob sold it on Dad's behalf at a very handsome profit—almost half the value of his estate. Bob had done very well for Dad.

On the day we visited, Dad was in pretty bad shape, emaciated and looking much older than his seventy years. His younger children were helping him off the powerboat and onto the dock.

"One more step, George," his son-in-law said, lifting him under one arm.

Dad looked very shaky and disoriented. After stepping onto the dock, he noticed me standing nearby.

"Who are *you*?" he asked.

"It's Jeff," his youngest daughter said.

"Oh," Dad said.

Julie and I had a talk with Bob about Dad's deteriorating condition. The conversation turned to a painting of a scene with golden retrievers, which Dad had given Bob to thank him for all his help over the years. Bob had raised golden retrievers and had given Ingrid her first golden retriever pup. Bob appreciated the painting—until Dad asked to have it back.

Julie asked Bob, "How can you stay friends with a guy who treats you like that?"

I was expecting Bob to reply with something like, "Your Dad is one of my oldest friends. He's obviously not himself right now, so

I'm not going to hold it against him if he takes back the painting." I would have understood that. What I couldn't understand was what Bob actually did say: "It's because of your mother. Carol was such a wonderful person." He said this with apparently complete sincerity.

To this day, I don't know where that statement came from. If Bob had cared so much about Carol, why would he remain friends with Dad at all—especially if he knew, or even suspected, what had happened to her?

"She died in a horrible way," I told Bob. "If you ever want to know what happened, I'll be happy to tell you."

Bob expressed no surprise or alarm at this, but he would never take me up on my offer. I was left to presume he already knew the basics of what had happened. Dad had shared his closest confidences with Bob, including tales of his love affairs.

"Your father was a great guy, but he did screw around a lot," Bob told me later.

"Sometime in the not-too-distant future, I'd like to talk with you about our mother's death," I replied.

"Sure, Jeff. I'll be glad to sit down and talk with you about that summer of '59."

After Dad died, Julie and I tried on different occasions to meet with Bob. But somehow, between illnesses and cancellations, and later the onset of Bob's own health problems, it kept getting postponed. When Julie did meet with him, he was recovering from a heart attack, and she accepted his assertions that he knew nothing of substance. I was quite sure we wouldn't have got much new information out of him in any event.

After dinner that day at Bass Island, a group of us took the twenty-minute walk around the island for the last time. Dad wasn't up to it and stayed behind at the main cottage. In the meantime, he must have remembered who I was, as well as the status of our relationship.

"This is *my* house," Dad said to me in a pleading yet accusatory tone after I returned to the cottage. To me this meant, "You have no right to be here."

"Dad, I'm here so that my kids, your grandchildren, can see their cousins and stay on the island one last time. Somebody needed to drive them. And I'm not leaving them here without me."

"But this is *my* house," he repeated doggedly.

"I thought it was meant to be for the whole family. Anyway, I'm not welcome here because of the problems you and I have about my mother's death, remember? Now, if there's anything you'd like to tell me about that, this would be a great opportunity."

Dad retreated into himself to contemplate what I meant.

It was the last time he ever spoke to me. But not the last time I heard from him. Soon afterwards, I received a letter beginning, "I know I probably haven't been a very good father." It went on to express his regrets about that, followed by his hopes for some kind of reconciliation between us. No mention whatever of Mom.

I showed the letter to Marie. Her eyes welled up when she read it. It was certainly eloquently written, especially for a man who couldn't deliver a speech coherently and had forgotten who I was. I couldn't help but see the hand of Bob Borden, who now had Dad's power of attorney and was executor of his will.

I chucked the letter into the wastebasket.

THE LAST TIME Julie and I saw Dad was at the care facility in Toronto where he was living. It was early in 2007, shortly before he died. He was in a wheelchair, crippled, non-verbal, and far past being able to recognize us. Bob said he had "aphasia." It looked like Alzheimer's, dementia, and multiple sclerosis all put together. "There's a scary-looking human being," Ingrid remarked to me later, after she had paid him a final visit.

There would be no further words out of Dad's mouth. Julie and I stayed for a couple of minutes and left. There was nothing for us there.

"I wonder what's going on inside his head," I said to Julie.

"That's just a broken-down old man," she replied.

19

DEATH AND REVELATION

OUR FATHER DIED in his sleep of natural causes, nearly half a century after the unnatural death of our mother. He was seventy-three.

The funeral took place on an April morning in 2007, at St. John's York Mills Anglican Church, Toronto. It was attended by George's relatives and former classmates from Upper Canada College. Of those who came to remember him, the only one close to Dad was Bob Borden. Bob stage-managed the proceedings, composed *The Globe and Mail* obituary, and rounded up enough family and friends to fill one-quarter of the church. Julie, Doug and his wife, Maureen, and Marie and I were all there with our teenaged kids. So were Ingrid, her children, and her grandchildren.

I almost stayed away. A few days earlier, I'd argued heatedly with Bob about a crucial detail in his draft of Dad's obituary. He'd wanted to include a reference to our mother having been Dad's first wife. Bob ought to know better, I told him. He protested vigorously. He wanted to leave a "normal" memory of Carol as George's first wife, remembered in his obituary as though nothing out of the ordinary had happened, and that would be that.

"If her name goes in there, Julie and I will not attend. She would turn in her grave after what he did to her," I shot back.

It was unthinkable to us that she should be mentioned as though her murder had never occurred. The glaring omission might make people take notice, ask uncomfortable questions, and reflect on what had happened to Carol—which was exactly what we wanted.

Bob backed off but didn't give up. Soon afterwards, I got a call from one of Ingrid's daughters asking why Carol couldn't be included in Dad's obituary.

"Because we're not going to whitewash what happened," I replied. It was really none of her business—Carol had died well before she was born—but I could understand how the optics would look terrible to some. Tough.

I checked the newspaper obituary columns before the funeral just to make sure. Indeed, Bob had removed any reference to Carol.

His final version of Dad's obituary was an odd piece of work in any case. It began conventionally enough: "George died in his sleep on April 16, 2007, just short of his 74th birthday." But the order of precedence in naming Dad's family was pure Bob. First were George's parents and sister, all deceased. Then came the main women in his life—at least the ones who could be named—Ingrid and Ruth, both relationships long since moribund. Then came Bob himself, his life-long friend, in the middle of things as usual, directing traffic in the mausoleum. Next came Dad's nephews, who were very fond of him. Only then, at the very end, came his children, all six of us, and his grandchildren. Julie and I couldn't have cared less, but I felt a bit sorry for Doug, and for Dad's other kids and his grandchildren, who could now see in black and white just where they stood in the pecking order of George's life.

Bob, stationed at the church entrance to greet everyone as we arrived, was in no position to complain about our spat over the obituary. But just as I thought we'd make our way to our seats without incident, Jenny Borden appeared. She glared at me full in the face.

"Disgracing your own *mother*!" she hissed, making no effort to soften her voice.

"Hello, Jenny," I replied.

Poor Jenny. She appeared to have missed the point entirely. Perhaps Bob had never told her the whole story. Or maybe she just wanted Carol to be remembered, the shameful circumstances be damned. I wasn't going to argue with her right then, and she knew it.

As we continued to our places, I took in the scene. Front and centre was a portrait photograph of George in his prime. He was wearing a blue suit, his face bathed in light and framed by gladioli. Since he'd elected cremation, there was no casket. Later, Bob would arrange for his ashes to be scattered on his beloved Bass Island as he had wanted. Thankfully, his remains wouldn't be placed in the Blackstock family burial plot, where Mom was buried.

Ingrid, sitting with her children, nodded to us, as Marie, Jill, Scott, and I slid into the pew behind her. I heard Ingrid say to one of her daughters in a stage whisper, "Poor Jeffrey. He's an orphan now." At fifty-six, I found this an amusing concept. And I realized what Doug and Julie had already known for some time: Ingrid didn't really consider herself our mother.

"But I thought we were *all* your kids," I had said naively during her visit to Australia a year earlier.

"I suppose I could have adopted you," she'd replied offhandedly.

I wasn't surprised by her comment as we took our seats behind her. But I wasn't the only one to hear her. Jill was crushed. She was nineteen and immediately understood the implications of Ingrid's careless remark. But she still had a child's heart when it came to her "Nana," as she called Ingrid.

"I didn't know Nana doesn't see herself as our real Nana," Jill told Marie later, almost in tears. Our hearts went out to our daughter.

Across the aisle, I noticed Ted Rogers, the telecommunications and media baron, who was Doug's godfather and once "Uncle Ted" to us. I recognized one or two other old chums from Dad's Upper Canada College days, now captains of industry. Collectively, they probably hadn't seen him for more than a month in all the years since they'd left the school.

Behind me I could hear Uncle Grant speaking to his son, my cousin, and his family. Aunt Katherine had died five years earlier, when Marie and I were in Australia, so we hadn't been able to attend her funeral. Now, her widower and their kids were here for Dad's. "Uncle George" had been a model for some of the younger members of the extended family, who had looked up to him. They'd admired his colourful career, his stories about living in exotic places, his impressive properties and other trappings of success.

"Good morning, everyone," said the Anglican minister presiding over the service. She was a fortyish woman dressed in church vestments, and a bit of an anomaly in this context, since George had probably never known a female minister in his life. She had certainly never met *him*. But she did add a modern touch to the proceedings.

"Welcome," she continued, "and thank you all for coming. We are here to celebrate the life of George Blackstock, and we are going to begin with one of his favourite hymns, 'O Worship the King.'"

It was indeed one of Dad's favourite hymns, and one of mine too—he had introduced it to me. After some shuffling of hymn books, the organ piped up, and the congregation joined in.

The minister read Psalm 23, "The Lord Is My Shepherd," followed by a few well-chosen words suggested, no doubt, by Bob. I pricked up my ears when I heard her say, "We are here to send George in peace, not to judge him."

"That was quite a mouthful," Julie whispered to me. "Bravo, Bob."

Funerals are supposed to bring "closure" of some kind. But Dad's certainly didn't, at least not for me. I wish it had. I was approaching the end of my own foreign service career and wanted to look forward, not backward. But with Dad's death, too many questions from the past remained unanswered. There would be no deathbed confession now, however faint that possibility had been. Confession is good for the soul, they say—but for some, taking one's secrets to the grave is a better idea.

Forgiveness is also supposedly therapeutic, but I had no appetite for that. Since Dad hadn't admitted to anything, or asked for our forgiveness, we were in no position to provide it. Even if he had asked for forgiveness, I don't think I could have given it.

Did I feel grief over his passing? Even less likely.

Guilt? Yes, I still felt guilty for all I hadn't done to give our mother the justice she deserved. Instead, I was a silent participant at his funeral, a "celebration" of his life.

At the tea after the service, an elderly lady and long-time friend of the family asked indignantly, "But why was Carol not even *mentioned*?" She spoke loudly enough that people around her looked up, startled, from their teacups. Perhaps a few of them, the older ones who had known Carol, felt a nagging discomfort over the omission. It was an unwelcome reminder of someone who hadn't been seen or discussed for years, and now couldn't even be mentioned in George's obituary.

But for me, Mom's voice was all the louder for the silence.

SURELY, WE THOUGHT, that was the last we'd hear from Dad. But he wasn't quite finished trying to direct the narrative.

He had always been a pack rat. He'd accumulated piles of paper over the years, which he stored in boxes and shipped around the globe from posting to posting without ever reopening them. In the boxes were mementoes from his schooldays, newspaper ads for once-new automobiles all the way back to the 1950s, airplane ticket stubs, travel expense receipts, letters, photos, you name it. Bob Borden disposed of whatever he thought belonged in the trash. What remained eventually came to Julie, Doug, and me some six years after Dad died in a plastic box about a cubic foot in size, full of items of our father's. Some of it, Bob said, related to our mother.

Julie and I opened the box. The first thing we saw was Carol's red diplomatic passport, the one she'd been carrying when she returned, fatally poisoned, to Canada. There it was, fifty-five years old but looking brand new. And there she was in her photo inside, the mother we loved, looking strong, confident, beautiful. We were there too, her three children, listed with our names and dates of birth. There were just four stamps from border crossings she had made.

Dad had kept her passport through eight postings in six countries, a second marriage, the births of three more children, and a common-law relationship, until the day he died—as though some day it might be needed again. Why had he kept it for so long, after telling us that memories of Carol's death brought back too much pain, and after disposing of her other possessions without leaving a single thing for us? Now we inherited this small booklet with a tiny photo, a few vital statistics, and some official stamps.

Digging deeper, we found a group of black-and-white photos that struck us as strange. They portrayed several teenaged young men sitting or standing on the rocky shore of a lake on a hot summer's day. They were all well tanned, and all in the nude. One of them was Dad, at perhaps sixteen or seventeen. Some were smoking cigarettes, others diving into the water. We could only wonder what significance these photos had held for him.

Other contents of the box were more predictable: a photo of Dad as a small boy, posing stiffly with his father; his father's citations from the First World War; souvenirs of our 1958 voyage on the

SS *Argentina*; a group portrait taken during Dad and Ingrid's wedding celebrations in Germany.

Then there were the big surprises.

First among these was a series of yellow foolscap sheets covered with notes scribbled in ink in Dad's familiar handwriting. They appeared to be notes to himself, written in the heat of the moment with a sense of urgency, an agitation verging at times on panic. They resembled spontaneous journal entries, although to my knowledge he had never been in the habit of keeping a journal. The earliest dated from 1984, the year when Julie, Doug, and I confronted Dad in Ottawa with our questions and accusations about Mom's death. They ended in 1993, after he pleaded with Julie to let him see her son and to give him copies of our documents.

The jottings jumped from thought to disconnected thought. They showed that he was obsessed by our belief that he was responsible for Carol's death.

> *How could they think I could have believed that I could do such a thing successfully – the trouble is they think I <u>did</u> do it successfully?*
> *Why don't they do something about it?*

The way we read these words, it didn't worry Dad so much that we believed he'd killed Mom, as that we believed he could have done it *successfully*. Perhaps he'd been counting on our thinking him incapable of murder since he'd fear being caught, and therefore it was too high a risk for him to take. This was certainly Doug's belief.

When, in the third line, he questioned our inaction, he seemed to be asking, "Why don't they get it over with instead of torturing me with suspense?"

That question led to another: Why didn't Dad himself do something about it? Why didn't he take proactive steps to convince us that our suspicions were wrong, that someone else was responsible for Mom's death? Instead, he seemed paralyzed, unable to take action while waiting for the next shoe to drop.

Although the logic and sequence of the notes are sometimes hard to follow, their overall purpose seems clear: to protest his innocence and clear himself in our eyes.

In his mental quest to find the true culprit, he provided himself with an ambitious to-do list: speaking to the police; going to Buenos Aires, where he might contact a lawyer; hiring a private investigator; and examining medical records at the Montreal Neurological Institute, including "the coroner's reports." We have no evidence that he followed through on any of these things.

In one note, he made a very telling reference to the renowned Harvard lawyer Alan Dershowitz.

Get v.B. book + film Dershowitz hung on his having 1 nite spends

I think "v.B." was the wealthy socialite Claus von Bülow, whose 1982 murder trial in Newport, Rhode Island, was infamous. Von Bülow was convicted of attempting to murder his even wealthier wife by injecting her with an overdose of insulin, allegedly to put himself in a position to marry his girlfriend and inherit his wife's fortune. His wife survived but remained in a coma for the rest of her life. Von Bülow appealed his conviction, hiring Dershowitz to lead his defence team, and was finally acquitted on all charges. The case was the subject of Dershowitz's 1986 book *Reversal of Fortune* and of the 1990 film of the same name, starring Jeremy Irons as von Bülow and Glenn Close as his wife.

I believe "1 nite spends" was intended to mean one-night *stands*, but I'm not sure exactly what Dad's point was. In any event, the von Bülow case would seem a highly dubious basis for arguing his own innocence. To us, it would only point more convincingly toward his guilt.

What, then, had he hoped to learn from the von Bülow book and film? Lessons from Dershowitz's skillful use of legal arguments to acquit someone convicted of wife-murder? To George, the method allegedly employed by von Bülow, a form of poisoning, would have been reminiscent of Carol's case. As I understand it, however, and as the film version suggests, big question marks remain about von Bülow's innocence, despite his acquittal. After all, the acquittal did not determine that he was innocent and wrongly accused, only that it was not proven beyond a reasonable doubt that he was guilty.

Elsewhere in his notes, George speculated about deflecting blame onto the doctors.

> *Can any fault be attached to the doctor in charge for not discovering what the problem was in time?*

In an equally remarkable attempt to scapegoat others, he cast aspersions on the Royal Canadian Mounted Police (RCMP).

> *RCMP – Im [sic] very leery. They must know that they left me in a terrible position*
> *They might open case up + stage a hearing just to protect themselves.*

This was the first written indication Julie and I had seen of Canada's national police service investigating George as possibly responsible for Carol's death. It is logical that the RCMP would have been involved, along with the Montreal police, given the international dimensions of the case. Julie and I had access-to-information searches conducted, but they turned up no references to Carol Blackstock in RCMP files. If any such references had ever existed, the files may have been dumped.

Apart from the reference in our father's notes, we do impute knowledge of Carol's case to the RCMP. As Julie astutely observed, the president of the Canadian Society of Forensic Science in 1963, as recorded in the proceedings of the society's annual meeting for that year, when Carol's case was presented, was none other than Dr. B.B. Coldwell of the Crime Detection Laboratory, Royal Canadian Mounted Police, Ottawa. Not only that: the proceedings were printed courtesy of that same Crime Detection Laboratory. How many copies of the journal, I wonder, did our fabled federal police force have to run off before it noticed that the case of "Mrs. C.B." strongly suggested a murder had been committed and the RCMP needed to investigate?

Dad's notes indicate that's exactly what he feared might happen. His comment that "They must know that they left me in a terrible position," and his anxiety that they might still open the case up "just to protect themselves," suggest that the RCMP knew he was a murder suspect, yet took no further action.

The notes then addressed the issue of motive.

J + J: only motive they can think of is that I knew [I] before. Several people know this is not true but no proof positive

"J +J" are Jeff and Julie, and "I" is Ingrid. It's telling that he raised this concern, since Julie and I never once discussed motive with our father—and we certainly never suggested Ingrid was a motive for him to kill Carol. This was entirely his own supposition.

He went on to argue that he couldn't have had such a motive, since he didn't even know Ingrid in July 1959, when Carol died.

– Fishers [sic] know that [I] and I met only in Feb 1960.

He was citing Bibi and Peter Fischer as potential supporting "witnesses" who could attest to the month when he'd met Ingrid. Since Carol had died more than six months earlier, it would have been impossible that being with Ingrid could have been a motive for him to kill Carol.

Dad also referred in his notes to unidentified documents and to a letter on which he could rely to argue his case.

> – *by Sept 12/59 they had not discovered the c.o.d. (see letter)*
> – *Its [sic] bothered me   I've got docus I'll show   1 forte'ls   2 opened won [illegible]*

It's not clear from the notes which documents he was talking about, or who had written the letter in question and to whom. And why was it so important to him that the letter showed that "they" had not discovered Carol's cause of death ("c.o.d.") by September 12, 1959? Who were "they"?

These documents were obviously highly significant to Dad. Yet in the next line of his notes, he scrawled,

> *bury them! Remove crutch of having somebody something to blame*

By this point, his notes have all the coherence of a man howling at the moon. He wrote that he feared any action on his part might "do harm" by opening a "Pandora's Box" or unleashing "a whirl-wind" where he might "lose control"—a state that was anathema to George.

Nevertheless, he did note some possible courses of action he might take, including family counselling. So we were going to straighten all this out through therapy! He professed a faint hope that making a sincere effort to uncover what had happened to Carol might help convince us of his innocence.

> *I can't see that I can prove anything, but perhaps if they see that I am doing all I can to throw light on the matter, and that it is almost impossible to prove I had nothing to do with it . . . perhaps they will be disposed to . . . change their minds about me.*

It's very strange that, even if you give him the benefit of the doubt and assume he didn't kill Carol, George nowhere expressed any personal desire to discover who did. His entire concern was with what *we* thought and how he could persuade us he was innocent. Wouldn't any bereaved husband who was genuinely innocent want to know for himself how his wife, the mother of his children, had come to a horrible death?

He speculated that he might just be fortunate enough to find out what actually did happen to Carol.

> *[What if] I should stumble on the truth of what really did happen –*
> *Lord knows there are fw [sic] enough possibilities – few enough other*
> *people (4) who could have had anything to do with it.*

I can't be absolutely sure who the four other people were, but very likely he was thinking of the live-in household staff in Buenos Aires: Alejandra, the cook; María; María's husband, Martín; and their daughter, Cristina. Neither Dad, Julie, or I, or anyone else for that matter, ever considered any of them a genuine suspect. As far as I know, he didn't do anything with this line of inquiry either. To use one of his favourite phrases, he was "grasping at straws."

As I puzzled over Dad's notes, I asked myself, "Am I reading the thoughts of an innocent man, however emotionally inept? A bewildered man struggling to get at 'the truth of what really did happen'? Did somebody else kill Carol and get away with it, leaving George looking like the guilty party?" I really couldn't say, since his notes didn't follow through to arrive at any conclusions. They were all questions and no answers.

Surprisingly, Dad's notes finally professed anguish over Mom's death:

> *I don't want to die leaving things as they are now.*
> *It was + is a trajedy [sic]*

Loved her – love them
we're all victims.

If Dad was a "victim" of the tragedy of Mom's death, this was the first I'd heard of it. He never expressed any sorrow about her loss to me—not once over the course of a lifetime.

He also bemoaned the loss of Julie and me.

I'd give anything to get my kids back and for them to have peace of
mind. How can I do it.

Apparently bereft of answers to that question, he consoled himself in the end with the wisdom of the ages.

There are some things you can't set straight in life.
Sufficient unto the day is the evil thereof.
The past and the future belong to God.

After hours of reading over Dad's notes, I was left shaken. I felt I'd been reading the thoughts of a man who was losing his mind, a man trapped in a mental maze from which he saw no escape. Julie and I hadn't been the only ones fixated on our mother's death. Dad too had been consumed by it, if only by his inability to disprove our accusations of guilt.

I shared my misgivings with Julie. "I was troubled by Dad's scribblings," I told her. "What if you and I are wrong? What if he didn't do it?"

Julie was far more tough-minded about it. "They're notes for posterity to make himself look good," she replied without hesitation.

So, was this just another of his performances, a post-mortem bill of goods?

There was one key fact I could check to verify whether he was telling the truth: the date when he claimed to have met Ingrid for the first time. He'd always said it was during our holiday at the Fischers' estancia in February 1960. I'd noticed two letters in the box written to him by Ingrid. One in particular had struck me, because it was sent from the Llao Llao, the same hotel in Bariloche where Carol herself had stayed the year before.

I found the letters, written in Ingrid's handwriting. Both were dated December 1959—the first one December 15, the second December 31—some two months before Dad claimed they'd been introduced by the Fischers.

Dad had saved these letters (quoted in full in chapter 9) for the rest of his life. For him, no doubt, they were mementoes of the early stages of one of his most important relationships. It was impossible to deduce from them exactly how long he and Ingrid had known each other before December 15, or how well. But in her first letter, Ingrid had written, "I needed to write to you right away." And in the second, "You can't imagine how happy [your previous letter] made me." From those words, it was not only possible but unavoidable to infer that they'd known each other long enough before then to kindle a warm relationship. That made one thing very clear: Dad had lied to us about the date of their meeting by a significant margin.

Very likely Dad had never expected his notes to wind up in the same box as the letters that contradicted them. The letters weren't invented. But the content of his notes, at least this part of them, was a fabrication.

ANY ILLUSIONS I still entertained about Dad's sincerity were dispelled by what the box revealed next.

This was a letter from Dr. J.B.R. Cosgrove, the head of our mother's medical team at the Montreal Neurological Institute, addressed to Assistant Deputy Minister H. Leslie Brown, George's boss at the Department of Trade and Commerce. Dr. Cosgrove said he'd written the letter on George's behalf, and at his request, to explain to his superior the situation when Carol died. The copy in Dad's papers was evidently a duplicate. It bore Cosgrove's signature in ink, but, as we'll see, its original was definitely received by Brown.

The letter read in its entirety,

September 12th 1959.

Mr. H. Leslie Brown
Assist. Deputy Minister
Dept. of Trade and Commerce
OTTOWA [sic]. ONTARIO. CANADA

Dear Mr. Brown,
    Mr. George Blackstock has asked me to write you about the recent loss of his wife and the circumstances accompanying this tradgedy [sic].
    I am enclosing a formal letter for your information, but George felt if I wrote you personally I would be able to explain more fully some of the recent events.
    As you are aware Carol had not responded to treatment in Buenos Aires. She had been vomiting intermittently for about ten days and I personally believe that George did the right thing to bring his wife to a neurological institute.
    The cause of Carol's illness was obscure, and unfortunately we had so little time to make a definite diagnosis. However, we did think of the possibility of some unknown toxin and consequently both Dr. Graham and myself felt that the coroner should be called.

Of course this has been a nuisance for both George and our-
selves, but we felt we have done the correct thing. At present we know
that the autopsy showed no obvious cause of death. However the
toxicological and histological tests and work will not be complete for
several months.

It was fortunate that George came to Montreal yesterday as the
coroner wanted to obtain further details from him. We were fortu-
nate to be able to arrange a meeting at the Institute.

As soon as we have any further information I will of course let
George know.

Yours sincerely,

JBR Cosgrove

The letter is a very strange document from start to finish. First, it is typewritten on plain stationery, instead of Montreal Neurological Institute letterhead. The letter is signed, but not as "Dr." JBR Cosgrove; nor does it state his official association with the Institute or as the lead physician on the case in question.

It is not at all clear why a "personal" letter was necessary when a "formal" letter on the same subject was enclosed in the same envelope. More fundamentally, it's difficult to see why Dr. Cosgrove was writing to Brown at all. Was he really doing a favour to George, who had requested it?

These questions are only partially answered in the third and fourth paragraphs of the letter. If Dr. Cosgrove knew Brown was aware of the case, why did he write that Carol "had been vomiting intermittently for about ten days"? Anyone familiar with her case knew she'd been sick in Buenos Aires for almost three months before she died. Was this an attempt to suggest that her illness was some kind of surprise, with a sudden onset? It would appear so, since Cosgrove goes on to lament that the cause of Carol's illness was obscure, and there was insufficient time for a proper diagnosis.

The cause may have been "obscure" at the moment when she arrived at the MNI. But if Carol's doctors had thoroughly reviewed Dr. Mercer's clinical record, which accompanied her from Buenos Aires, as well as her condition on arrival in Montreal, they should have set off alarm bells right away—in a teaching hospital, of all places—that her symptoms were consistent with at least one possible cause: poisoning. That cause certainly wasn't obscure by the time Dr. Cosgrove wrote his letter to Brown on September 12. More than six weeks earlier, on July 27, Dr. Valcourt had performed his autopsy, with "findings [that] may be consistent with an arsenical poisoning."

The next sentence in Dr. Cosgrove's "personal" letter showed that the cause couldn't have been as obscure as all that.

> However, we did think of the possibility of some unknown toxin and consequently both Dr. Graham and myself felt that the coroner should be called.

After all Dr. Cosgrove's self-justifying palaver, here is the real reason for his letter: to put on record "some unknown toxin" and the consequent involvement of the coroner. Here at last, among Dad's own papers, is proof positive that he knew, shortly after Mom died, that the MNI doctors thought there was at least a possibility she'd been poisoned.

Dr. Cosgrove's next sentence serves as a huge distraction, but is so outrageous that it demands comment. Calling in the coroner to investigate a potential murder was, he writes, a "nuisance" for "both George and ourselves." The statement is beyond callous. It is so cynical and absurd that I asked myself whether Dr. Cosgrove was being sarcastic. Either that, or he'd forgotten that Carol, not George, was his patient.

His letter went on to make the even more egregious and disturbing statement that "At present we know that the autopsy showed no obvious cause of death." This was simply false. The autopsy, performed more than six weeks earlier by Dr. Valcourt with a team directed by Dr. Cosgrove in attendance, had concluded that the findings indicated arsenic poisoning, although the diagnosis had to be verified by toxicological testing. That's a very far cry from there being no obvious cause of death.

Dr. Cosgrove told Brown that "the toxicological and histological tests and work will not be complete for several months." Just ten days later, however, on September 22, 1959, the "Preliminary Toxicological Report" would conclude that Carol's viscera "contained some large doses of arsenic . . . situated in the limits of those observed in poisoning cases."

Dr. Cosgrove's letter states that only the day before, the coroner had met with George at the MNI "to obtain further details from him." Whether this was any business of Brown's was debatable, but obviously Dr. Cosgrove wanted to make it his business.

From what we know now, Cosgrove's letter to Brown was intentionally misleading—or more accurately put, untruthful. Nevertheless, a letter combining the words "toxin" and "coroner" in the same sentence would have been sufficient cause for alarm on Brown's part.

Why did Dr. Cosgrove write the letter at all? Almost certainly, he had protection of the institute and its medical staff, including himself, foremost in his mind. Carol Blackstock had died of arsenic poisoning under their care. Arsenic poisoning immediately calls to mind suspicious circumstances—murder, for instance. Everybody knows that a coroner, whom Dr. Cosgrove pointedly mentioned in his letter, has a police function that includes investigating homicides. All this added up to a very nasty, messy business from which Dr. Cosgrove wished to distance himself and the MNI immediately.

Sending the letter to Brown shifted responsibility for the case from the institute to the Government of Canada. George Blackstock was *their* man; *they* should deal with the problem. Apparently, the letter wound up serving that purpose very well.

And what was George's perception of Dr. Cosgrove's letter? What did he think about the references to an "unknown toxin" and calling in the coroner? They must have alarmed him at the very least. No doubt he would have preferred Dr. Cosgrove to omit the references, which inevitably would have led anyone reading the letter to ask, What *was* the toxin, and what did the coroner conclude about it?

THE BOX OF Dad's papers we received from Bob Borden also included a one-page document that was, in all likelihood, the "formal" letter Dr. Cosgrove had mentioned in his "personal" letter to Brown.

TO WHOM IT MAY CONCERN: re: MRS. CAROL BLACKSTOCK.

THIS IS TO CERTIFY THAT I WAS THE PHYSICIAN WHO SUPERVISED THE CARE OF MRS. CAROL BLACKSTOCK WHO WAS ADMITTED TO THE MONTREAL NEUROLOGICAL INSTITUTE ON JULY 23RD 1959 ON MY RECOMMENDATION.

SHE WAS A SERIOUSLY ILL PATIENT WHO SUFFERED FROM NAUSEA AND VOMITING AND PERIPHERAL NEURITIS.

IN MY OPINION SHE HAD A THOROUGH INVESTIGATION IN HOSPI-TAL AT BUENOS AIRES BUT NO DEFINITE CAUSE FOR HER ILLNESS COULD BE FOUND WITH THE FACILITIES THEY HAD AVAILABLE THERE.

IN MY VIEW THE TRANSFER TO A NEUROLOGICAL INSTITUTE WHERE SPECIALIZED ATTENTION COULD BE GIVEN WAS JUSTIFIED. THE MONTREAL NEUROLOGICAL INSTITUTE WITH 150 BEDS IS CONSIDERED SUCH AN INSTITUTION BY THE MEDICAL PROFESSION.

UNFORTUNATELY MRS. BLACKSTOCK'S CONDITION WAS SO SERIOUS THAT THERE WAS INSUFFICIENT TIME FOR TREATMENT TO TAKE EFFECT AND SHE DIED ON THE 25TH JULY. 1959.

FROM A CLINICAL POINT OF VIEW, IT SEEMS HIGHLY PROBABLE
THAT THIS ILLNESS WAS RELATED TO HER DOMICILE IN ARGENTINA.
YOURS TRULY,

                                    J.B.R. COSGROVE, M.D.

The document is not dated. But it appears to serve the function of an official statement, signed by Dr. Cosgrove and intended for the eyes of those—especially in the federal government—who might require a medical explanation of Carol Blackstock's "transfer" at public expense from Buenos Aires to the MNI. While perhaps justifying the costs to the government, the statement is conspicuously vague and uninformative about the "illness" itself—except to say that there was a high probability it "was related to her domicile in Argentina." There is no mention here of "an unknown toxin."

BUT MOST IMPORTANT of all was the way in which Assistant Deputy Minister Leslie Brown reacted to the two letters.

Julie and I found, tucked away in the box of George's papers, an extraordinary letter to him from Brown. It looked ordinary enough at first glance. Dated September 12, 1959, the same date as Cosgrove's "personal" letter to Brown, it was addressed "Dear George." Like Cosgrove's letter, it wasn't written on official letterhead. Brown had used his personal stationery, with his home address printed across the top. Not only that, the letter wasn't typed but handwritten by Brown, and signed without identifying his position in the government.

Brown's letter is phrased as a receipt for George, acknowledging, among other things, two letters from Dr. Cosgrove that George had personally delivered to Brown that very day: the "personal" letter quoted above, and a "general" one, which I believe was the formal "To Whom It May Concern" letter. In addition, Brown acknowledged

receipt of various medical bills and documents related to Carol's
death, which George had also delivered to him. But it was clearly all
about the first two items on the list.

Here is Brown's letter in its entirety.

358 Somerset Street East

Ottawa 2

Sept 12/59

Dear George –

*I have today received from you the following documents con-
cerned with Carol's death and related expenses:*

General letter from Dr. Cosgrove (in duplicate)

Personal "   "   "   "   "   "

*Receipt dated Aug/Sept 12 (in duplicate) Dr. Cosgrove's bill for
$100*

*Receipt in duplicate and single copy of statement from Drs.
Dossiter and Beck Sept 12/59 for $85.00*

———————

*Letter of Sept 12, from Dr. Cosgrove (in duplicate) to effect that
nurse must accompany Mrs Blackstock*

———————

*Receipt, in duplicate, & single copy of statement, also receipted,
for $487.85 from Montreal Neurological Institute*

———————

*Original of letter of July 18/59 from Dr. G. Mercer of B.A. giving
his diagnosis of Carol's complaint*

Yours sincerely

Leslie Brown

On the surface, this looked like a routine list of items for reimburse-
ment as part of a bureaucratic medical claim. Several of the items

should ordinarily have been submitted to a clerk in the department's finance section. Why was Brown, George's assistant deputy minister, wasting time itemizing medical bills in his own handwriting? Why was he using his personal stationery? Why was he signing as "Leslie Brown," with no reference to his official title? He might have been George's pal, instead of his much more senior boss way up the line.

And why was it so important that *George* get a receipt for these letters? After delivering them to Brown, he took away not just a copy, but a duplicate, of the "personal" Cosgrove letter, with the doctor's signature in ink—the same letter we found in his papers.

These letters from Dr. Cosgrove and Brown must have been the documents George was referring to in his scribbled notes, which he thought could prove his innocence:

> – *by Sept 12/59 they had not discovered the c.o.d. (see letter)*
> – *Its [sic] bothered me   I've got docus I'll show . . .*

Note that the date mentioned is the date of Dr. Cosgrove's "personal" letter to Brown.

But in the end, George urged himself to "bury" these documents:

> – *bury them! Remove crutch of having somebody something to blame.*

Why *didn't* he bury them?

AFTER SOME REFLECTION on this exchange of letters among Dr. Cosgrove, Leslie Brown, and George, Julie and I came to realize its full significance—a significance that was different for each of the three men.

For Brown, Cosgrove's references in his "personal" letter to an unknown toxin and calling in the coroner must have been disturbing.

We knew from our 1984 visit to the MNI that Brown had gone there shortly after our mother's death to find out for himself what had happened to her. But now he was being informed in writing, by the lead physician on Carol's medical team, about the toxin and the coroner. No doubt Cosgrove's "To Whom It May Concern" letter was no less disturbing to Brown. It indicated that Carol, whom Brown had known personally from his visit to Buenos Aires, had contracted her illness—and both Brown and Dr. Cosgrove knew what that illness was—while on posting there. Brown had to put that together with the fact that the coroner had wanted to talk to George, *his* employee, about it.

Once Dr. Cosgrove had tagged Brown in his official capacity with this knowledge, Brown had no choice but to do something about it. There would be no excuse for claiming ignorance now. Julie and I surmised that for Brown, it would have been even more alarming to know that George was the one and only suspect the police were interested in, as we would learn when we interviewed Dr. Graham at the MNI.

Brown also knew about George's three children living in the house back in Buenos Aires. By September 12, when he delivered Cosgrove's letters to Brown, George was preparing to return to Argentina. If any harm came to his children, or to anyone else in the household there, Brown could not escape responsibility, knowing what he now knew. Even if it was never proved in a court of law that George was Carol's killer, there was considerable risk if he actually was. Something needed to be done to address that risk.

Consequently, Julie and I came to the conclusion that the purpose of Brown's "receipt" letter to George was to serve as a cryptic but stern warning: it put him on notice that not only the police but also the medical authorities and, most importantly, his own superiors in government knew about the poison. They would be keeping a close eye on him, so he had better behave.

From Brown's point of view, George needed to know this, given that he wasn't being charged with murder. And the best way to tell him was through something disguised and innocuous, such as this receipt. It was out of the question to make these communications explicitly, in plain English. That might have implicated the Government of Canada in a crime: aiding and abetting a murder suspect after the fact, and covering up the murder of a woman who had been on diplomatic status abroad and under the government's protection, no less.

Brown wrote to George in a personal capacity on his household stationery, off the official record, with no mention whatsoever of the poison or the police investigation. We can only conclude that Brown wanted no reference to Carol's fatal poisoning showing up in government files. Otherwise, it would have made no sense for him to be so interested, in his personal capacity, in the paperwork for George's medical claims.

Bureaucracy being what it is, it's also inconceivable that Brown would have taken such an extreme risk entirely on his own. He would have needed and obtained the approval of his superiors for his handling of Carol Blackstock's death.

(In this connection, it's worth noting that, eleven years after his retirement from the federal public service, Leslie Brown presented his professional papers to Library and Archives Canada, in Ottawa, in 1979. Yet strangely, the papers for the period from 1959, the year Carol died, to 1963 are missing from the collection. Despite the efforts of a professional researcher, and Library and Archives staff, Brown's papers for those years have not been found, though his papers before and after the gap are there. In 1963, Brown was appointed commissioner general of the Canadian Pavilion at the Montreal world's fair, Expo 67.)

Why did George continue to keep the damning letters from Cosgrove and Brown among his own papers? We thought he'd have disposed of them long ago. Instead, we realized, he must have viewed them initially as his insurance against being turned over to the police by government officials—who would only have been implicated with him after the fact. Many years later, after the onset of his dementia, he forgot all about the letters. In the end, his only escape from the crime he'd committed was to forget who he was.

Far more sadly, Carol too was forgotten, though never by her three children. Multiple access-to-information requests by Julie and me over many years have consistently found no references in Canadian government records to Carol Blackstock or her death. Her murder while on unpaid government service abroad, and any link between it and our father, don't officially exist.

That evidence leads to an unsettling but inescapable conclusion: our mother's killing was covered up—deliberately suppressed—by Canadian government officials, with the tacit collusion of medical and law-enforcement authorities in Montreal.

How is it possible that, even after the coroner's findings of arsenic poisoning, authorities at all three levels of government—federal, provincial, and municipal—failed to conduct an investigation?

How could the wife of a Canadian official abroad be poisoned without consequences for the only suspect, her husband, enabling him to commit, in effect, a perfect crime?

We believe that collusion occurred because it served the interests and convenience of all parties. For the Government of Canada, an investigation of alleged spousal murder by one of its diplomats would have triggered a huge political scandal, both at home and abroad. For the Montreal Neurological Institute, the scandal would also have been damaging, since its doctors failed to recognize Carol's condition in time to save her life. As for law enforcement—whether the local Montreal police, or province of Quebec judicial authorities, or the RCMP—it appears that they all ignored their duty and did as they were told.

Government, medical, and police officials all would have analyzed their options regarding a criminal investigation of George Blackstock. In each case, they would have made careful calculations to ensure damage control for their institutions and themselves. Those calculations did not include justice for Carol Blackstock.

EPILOGUE

REFLECTIONS ON A "PERFECT" CRIME

IN HIS SCRIBBLED notes that surfaced after his death, George asked himself, "Why wouldn't I have just gone the divorce route?"

Although George appeared to be speaking hypothetically, there was something chilling to me in the casual way he mused about the option of "just" taking the divorce "route," as I completed his sentence with the words that were surely implicit: ". . . instead of killing Carol."

It's also a question that many readers may be asking. Today, almost 50 percent of marriages end in divorce. People wanting out of their marriages have a much-travelled and relatively clear legal path to follow. But this was far from true in 1959. George's use of the word "just" grossly understates how problematic and self-defeating that route would have been for him.

Back then, divorce was far more difficult to obtain and carried a heavy social stigma. No-fault divorce didn't exist. In Canada, each divorce decree required passage of an Act of Parliament. To obtain a divorce, the grounds needed to be very serious: adultery, cruelty, criminality, alcoholism, mental illness, and the like.

In George's case, obtaining a divorce from Carol in Canada would have been a very messy business indeed. It would probably have resulted in dire consequences for his career, his fortune, and his hopes for a new life. It would have defeated, I'm sure, any hope of attaining his objective to be with Ingrid, if that was what he wanted. Given Carol's assertive nature, she'd have fought him tooth and nail. The proceedings would have dragged out for a long time, likely beyond the limits of Ingrid's patience.

An Argentine divorce would have been out of the question, barred by local law, given George's civil status as a foreign service officer from another nation. His employer would likely have opposed it too. In the meantime, he would have had no possibility of anything more than a furtive relationship with Ingrid. How long would she have been willing to wait for him to become free to marry her? And how much scandalous gossip would she and her status-conscious parents have been willing to endure?

At best, the storyline emerging from the divorce proceedings in court would have been that George got his fifteen-year-old girlfriend pregnant, had three kids with her, and then dumped her. But it might have been much worse. Unless Carol had some mental illness or had committed adultery, he would have been considered the "guilty" party and become something of a social pariah.

Perhaps worst of all from George's point of view, he would have been saddled with onerous alimony and support payments for a long, long time. Carol had no immediate means of support for herself and her three children, and no good employment prospects with less than a tenth-grade education. He'd have been expected to shoulder the full cost of supporting his family, leaving him to subsist on much-reduced means. Without doubt, his family relationships and career would have suffered, probably with further financial consequences. Ingrid would likely have disappeared from his life. He would have found himself much worse off in every way than if he'd simply stayed married to Carol.

Clearly, divorce was not an option for George. Despite his musing in his notes about "the divorce route," he may have seen killing his wife as the only way out of his dilemma. I'm sure it would have taken him less than a minute to understand all this.

Not surprisingly, George's notes didn't pursue the divorce idea, leaving it as a hollow rhetorical question. As with other questions he left unanswered—unwilling, or unable, to give his side of the story—at some point his accusers have the right to draw their own conclusions.

A MORE FUNDAMENTAL question is why George would have entertained the idea of murder at all. Elsewhere in his notes to himself, he suggested Julie and I might attribute to him a motive of wanting to be free to be with Ingrid. This was purely supposition on his part; Julie and I had never raised it with him.

Even if true, of course, that motive wouldn't necessarily mean Ingrid knew anything about his murderous intent at the time. Nor would it necessarily preclude other motives—probably broader but related ones arising from discontent over his life situation.

George felt trapped in a marriage that, at age seventeen, he hadn't wanted. Carol had been little more than a child when they'd met. Now she was a mature woman with whom, for whatever reasons of his own, he felt he could no longer live.

At that point in the posting to Buenos Aires, Carol was beginning to spread her wings in many ways. She was becoming far more socially active, adventurous, and independent than she'd ever been. This may or may not have been part of the equation for George.

We can't read the man's mind, but we have only to look at his life. Added together, several interrelated considerations could have combined to create a powerful inducement for him to end his marriage in whatever way he could.

THE QUESTION OF *how* he did it is a little easier to answer, simply because we know what killed Carol.

Arsenic has been a murder weapon of choice for millennia because its presence is so difficult to detect: it is colourless, odourless, and tasteless. Arsenic trioxide, a white powder used for rat poison, would have been readily available in Buenos Aires. George could have put the arsenic in Carol's food or drink without her noticing it. She was sick in bed—apparently from other causes, her doctors assumed. The symptoms of arsenic poisoning resemble the symptoms of many other ailments, making it difficult to diagnose unless it is suspected.

George would have had some knowledge of all this from his reading. Agatha Christie was his favourite mystery writer, and arsenic was often used as a murder weapon in her novels. *Arsenic and Old Lace* was one of his favourite plays. Written by Joseph Kesselring, it was a black comedy made into a successful 1944 Hollywood film starring Cary Grant. The classic method was to administer arsenic slowly, in small amounts over time, to avoid precipitating a sudden death that might look suspicious. Instead, victims would be seen as succumbing to some ailment associated with the symptoms they presented.

We think that George began by experimenting with feeding Carol small doses of arsenic. When he discovered that her doctors in Buenos Aires couldn't diagnose it, even after treating her in hospital, he continued poisoning her in the expectation that she'd gradually succumb in the near future, with no one the wiser. In 1959, the police and medical system in Argentina might have presented relatively few obstacles for someone contemplating such a crime. George may have thought he could literally get away with murder there. What's more, as a foreign service officer of another nation, he enjoyed diplomatic immunity from investigation and, were it ever to come to that, from prosecution.

For a while, it looked as though George was going to get away with it. Carol had been admitted to hospital twice with worsening symptoms and her doctors still hadn't made an accurate diagnosis. Arsenic is a tricky poison, however; its effects can be unpredictable, making it difficult to know how much to administer at a time. Too much, and the victim dies suddenly, raising suspicions. Too little, and the process can take too long. Moreover, the body eventually develops a tolerance, necessitating larger dosages. George just needed a little more time to finish the job.

But things went wrong. George's well-laid plans were thrown into disarray when Carol's parents, alarmed by her condition, contacted his headquarters in Ottawa, setting off alarm bells at his workplace and precipitating her imminent return to Canada. The medical crisis he'd created threatened to blow up in his face. He felt he had no choice but to kill her then and there; otherwise, the doctors in Canada might diagnose the arsenic—which in fact they did, at the Montreal Neurological Institute, though tragically too late to save her life. If Carol had survived, she could have become an unwitting witness against him, perhaps confirming that he'd been bringing her meals. An investigation would have been disastrous for him. In for a penny, in for a pound.

So, as the Montreal coroner's autopsy concluded, Carol ingested a massive dose of arsenic just before she left Argentina to fly home—a trip that, in a cruel irony, was supposed to save her life. Due to a blockage in her viscera, it took more than two days after she arrived in Montreal for the arsenic to become sufficiently absorbed by her system to kill her.

THIS QUESTION OF why George would take such an enormous risk initially posed a quandary for us, and especially for Doug. Why would someone who had as much to lose as he did—privilege, affluence, a promising career in a prestigious profession, a young family, his personal freedom—take such a huge risk by killing his wife?

Perhaps he'd become so disenchanted with his marriage that he felt trapped in a jail cell already. But not every disenchanted husband murders his wife. What was it in George's personality and character that enabled him to commit murder—not on a sudden impulse, with a gun or a knife, but with a deliberate, premeditated, cold-blooded cruelty that was equally violent?

These were questions that Julie and I put to Dr. John Bradford when we met with him. Dr. Bradford is an internationally renowned forensic psychiatrist, a distinguished life fellow of the American Psychiatric Association, a fellow of the Royal College of Psychiatrists, in the United Kingdom, and a distinguished fellow of the Canadian Psychiatric Association. He has worked on some of the most infamous serial homicide investigations in Canadian history, including the Paul Bernardo, Robert Pickton, and Russell Williams cases. He agreed to meet with us at his home to discuss our discoveries about our father.

Before our meeting, Dr. Bradford had read an early draft of the manuscript of this book, which contained virtually the same material facts as presented here. His views on George Blackstock were based on what he had read. After agreeing without hesitation with our conclusion that George killed Carol, Dr. Bradford stated that George did so, in his opinion, to be with Ingrid. In cases of wife-murder, Dr. Bradford pointed out, there is frequently another woman in the wings, representing a powerful incentive to the husband.

Dr. Bradford dismissed our uncertainties about why George would be willing to assume such a dangerously high level of risk. Based on what he had read about our father, George appeared to him to have the characteristic personality of a psychopathic narcissist. For people with such a personality, Dr. Bradford said, the risks entailed in violent criminal behaviour are far outweighed by the desire to obtain what they want. Their motivation is all about fulfilling their own needs, in spite of the risk.

In this case, George didn't lash out blindly, without forethought; he calculated his chances of achieving his desired objective and carefully planned both the execution of his crime and his strategy for concealing it. Dr. Bradford was appalled, however, by the level of assistance George received from government, medical, and police officials to cover up his murderous act.

A related factor, which has astonished me, was George's ability to handle the crushing pressure to which he subjected himself during the time of Carol's sickness, treatment, and death, and in the year or so afterwards. He needed an extremely cool head and strong stomach to do what he did and get away with it successfully and without succumbing to a breakdown. I'm sure very few individuals could have done so. Not that this is anything to admire, needless to say— and no doubt it is also attributable to the risk-tolerance of the particular personality type identified by Dr. Bradford.

I would add my personal observation that individuals like George also feed on the adrenalin rush associated with their dangerous enterprise, and relish the sense of power they feel on its successful completion.

And then there was the sang-froid of the medical and government officials who, on the fly, engineered a long-term solution to a very complex problem which threatened to blow up in their faces. It took us a long time to unravel what they put together in a few hours, apparently with the same bloodless calculation and precision as employed by George himself.

ULTIMATELY, CAROL BLACKSTOCK'S fate was in the hands of men occupying positions of power in the Canadian government and in the law-enforcement and medical fields. Fearful of damage to their own interests and those of their institutions, these men did nothing to bring George to justice and much to obscure what he'd done.

My recent research in Buenos Aires reveals that no referral from the Montreal coroner's office about the autopsy findings was ever received by the coroner of Buenos Aires. Significantly, such a referral would have had to be channelled through the Canadian foreign ministry. My interview with a senior Argentine official also revealed that, following such a referral, an investigation by Argentine authorities would not have been thwarted by claims of diplomatic immunity. That is because an investigation involving a foreign diplomat is not prohibited by the *Vienna Convention on Diplomatic Relations*, so long as it does not include diplomatic premises, persons, or property. I think it's safe to say that the Canadian authorities knew this and thought better of making such a referral. Instead, they decided to let George Blackstock get away with murder.

The government and medical officials wouldn't do anything because it was a police matter. The police in Canada wouldn't do anything because, supposedly, they had no jurisdiction over a crime committed in Argentina. The police in Argentina couldn't do anything because no one bothered to inform them a crime had occurred. And this outcome just happened to serve the interests of all those authorities under the circumstances. A perfect storm for a perfect crime.

I know it's hard to accept that, in a country that believes in the rule of law, our government, law-enforcement, and medical officials could stand by and do virtually nothing about the shocking death of a young mother of three. I had a hard time believing it myself. But there it was. No investigation, let alone prosecution.

Having worked in the federal government and the Canadian foreign service, I believe I have a pretty good idea of why the authorities covered up our mother's killing. The decision was based on a calculation of the low probability of success for an investigation and prosecution, and a fear of the very negative consequences for all concerned resulting from a messy scandal, especially for the Canadian government of the day.

Our mother died in an era when women had very little power in a world run by men. Men dominated government, the professions, the police, and other institutions regulating society, even more than they do today. Although Carol was a very capable person, her life and death, and her memory, were all in the hands of men. In Buenos Aires, her doctors considered her neurotic—totally erroneously, and with pernicious results—because of the biases of the men entrusted with her care. The officials who decided not to investigate my mother's death did so with impunity. My father, the most important man in her life and death, was the chief beneficiary of that.

There was an honourable exception on the part of at least one male official. Dr. J.P. Valcourt did what he could by himself to ensure that Carol's death by arsenic poisoning would be exposed, however faintly, to the light of day.

Our maternal grandparents, Howard and Gladys Gray, are, of course, in a category all their own in this story. Without our grandfather's determined investigation and insistence on learning how our mother died, and our grandmother's disclosures to Julie, we'd never have known the truth, and there would have been no story to tell. What my sister and I managed to find out and relate is a completion of the work our grandparents started.

Others, family members and friends, helped too, in their own way. Aunt Katherine stood up for us at the risk of alienating my father and Ingrid. Louise Krapf helped our mother in Buenos Aires, tried to get the Canadian embassy authorities to do something about her death, and shared information with us years later, which must have been very uncomfortable for her. Other individuals did small things that were helpful.

But there were also many in the Blackstock family, and among our parents' friends, who did nothing. Some avoided helping us, even when confronted with the story and the evidence, not wanting to "get involved."

MY BROTHER, MY sister, and I knew that our mother would have wanted us to get on with our lives, and that is what we have done. I've been able to have a great family, good friends, and a satisfying career. So has Doug, who has done so while making his own determination of the limits of pursuing our mother's story. Julie has also managed to have a very good and full life. Of the three of us, I believe she was the most deeply affected emotionally by what happened, perhaps because, as the youngest, she shared the shortest time with our mother and so her loss was perhaps the greatest.

Many have asked me what the murder of my mother by my father has meant to my life. This has been the most difficult subject for me to put into words, and I'm still not sure I can. I could speak about the anger I have felt over what was done to her, and how terribly she suffered because of it. I could speak about the emptiness I feel when I realize that, after she died, I never had a mother. I could lament about never being able to say goodbye. Or about the horror that, when she died, she was robbed of everything: life, family, friends, all that she had in the world. Or the bitter rancour I feel toward my father, who did this to her. Or my deep, deep resentment of those who denied her the justice she deserved.

My own feelings of loss are not so easy to express: that my mother could never be there to provide her guidance and reassurance during the difficult years after she died, and throughout my adult life; that she was not able to partake of my happiest moments, when I married and had children; that we were not able to share our experiences of raising families living abroad; that she would never know my children and grandchildren; that I would never be able to give back to her and show her how much she has always meant to me.

Ultimately, I find that the deepest meaning of losing my mother is literally inexpressible. I hope only that this book will speak, however belatedly and inadequately, of my love for her, and of the love she inspired in my sister, Julie, and my brother, Doug, and that its publication will fill a decades-old void by bearing witness to the beauty and tragedy of our mother's life.

ACKNOWLEDGMENTS

I WISH TO thank those without whom this story could not have been written: my sister, Julia, who believed before I could allow myself to do so, and who has really been as responsible for its telling as I have; my wife, Marie, who has heard the details for decades and has endured countless days of my absence, so that I could sit in front of a computer screen, talk on the telephone, or travel to run down leads; the many friends who read early drafts, gave me helpful advice, or provided valuable information, including Carolina Luna, Cristina Quevedo, Ev Jackson, Bob Brown, Diane Brown, Ric Kokotovich, Alison Wattie, Cherry Muhanji, Regina Kolbe, Allan Stratton, Peter Wallace, Dr. John Doucet, Dr. John Bradford, Dr. Betty Chan, Dr. Robyn Gordon, Dr. J.P. Valcourt, Suzette MacSkimming, Gary Sandblom, Susana van Buren, Margaret McDonald, and my brother, Doug Blackstock, who provided documents and helpful information and advice; the researchers and investigators who uncovered important material, including Arlen Mighton, in Ottawa, and María Fra Amador, in Buenos Aires; our friends Helga and David Zimmerly, who introduced me to my collaborator on the book; our agent, Dean Cooke, who showed faith in this story and took a chance on presenting it to publishers; Penguin Random House Canada, for seeing the merits of the story and taking on a new author; our editor at Penguin, Diane Turbide, whose quick mind and insights were invaluable; Alex Schultz, copy editor extraordinaire; Patricia Gamliel, my personal legal counsel, and Lilia Benaïssa, who worked on the access-to-information cases in Montreal; and, as they say, last but not least, my collaborator and partner, Roy MacSkimming, who believed in the story and has expended countless hours, great editorial skill, and boundless patience in helping to shape and finish this book. To all of them, my undying gratitude.

J.B.